Conjuror on the Kwai

Conjuror on the Kwai

The Incredible Life of Fergus Anckorn

A Biography by
Peter Fyans

Pen & Sword
MILITARY

First published in Great Britain in 2011 as
Captivity, Slavery and Survival as a Far East POW

Reprinted in this format in 2016 by
PEN & SWORD MILITARY
An imprint of
Pen & Sword Books Ltd
47 Church Street
Barnsley
South Yorkshire
S70 2AS

Copyright © Peter Fyans, 2011, 2016

ISBN 978-1-47389-804-2

The right of Peter Fyans to be identified as the author of this work has
been asserted by him in accordance with the Copyright, Designs and
Patents Act 1988.

Typeset by Concept, Huddersfield HD4 5JL.
Printed in Malta by Gutenberg Press Ltd.

Pen & Sword Books Ltd incorporates the imprints of Pen & Sword
Archaeology, Atlas, Aviation, Battleground, Discovery, Family History,
History, Maritime, Military, Naval, Politics, Railways, Select, Social History,
Transport, True Crime, and Claymore Press, Frontline Books, Leo Cooper,
Praetorian Press, Remember When, Seaforth Publishing and Wharncliffe.

For a complete list of Pen & Sword titles please contact
PEN & SWORD BOOKS LIMITED
47 Church Street, Barnsley, South Yorkshire, S70 2AS, England
E-mail: enquiries@pen-and-sword.co.uk
Website: www.pen-and-sword.co.uk

Contents

Acknowledgements

I can give no greater thanks than to my wife, Kristina, who encouraged me to make a start on this book and who has been my constant companion throughout, punctuating my progress with her reactions to the gathering story. In addition, I have my youngest daughter, Jenny, to thank for her enormous help during the interview stages with Fergus and from which she made laborious transcriptions, which became my vital references. There is also the Anckorn family to thank, especially Deborah, eldest daughter of Fergus, and Simon, his son, for their appreciation of my early drafts and their encouragement to go on to produce the finished article.

But, of course, many others have been involved, too. I thank Patrick Toosey in particular for his foreword to the book, which is very special given the high esteem in which his father, Brigadier Sir Philip Toosey, is held by Fergus. Also, Julie Summers, Toosey's granddaughter, author of the definitive account of her grandfather's life in her book, *The Colonel of Tamarkan*. She has guided me on the pathway to publication, as has another author, Andro Linklater, with whom my wife and I have had occasion to celebrate along the way.

No book of this kind could take its place on bookshelves without in-depth historical research and for much of this I have to thank Rod Sudderby, Keeper of Documents at the Imperial War Museum, who helped me not only with the Fergus Anckorn Collection held at the museum, but also steered me in the right direction to find other relevant collections and informative texts that have provided foundation and perspective to the subject matter. I have also to thank Mark Smith, Curator of 'Firepower', the Museum of the Royal Artillery at Woolwich, and his librarian, Paul Evans. Mark took time out to give me his personal attention to matters military and to give myself and Fergus an after-hours tour of the museum, which brought back memories for Fergus of the whole business of being a gunner and of the experience of being in action with the guns in the battle for Singapore.

Sadly, very few of Fergus's contemporaries remain alive and so this book emerges without the many contributions that might otherwise have been made. However, I do have Charles Peall to thank, who was a fellow POW with Fergus at Ubon, Thailand. He has provided further witness to the events surrounding their liberation in August 1945, as well as his own recollections of many other incidents in prison camps along the Burma-Siam Railway. I have also Jack Chalker to thank for the time he has given me and his permission to illustrate the book in part with his sketches, drawn while also a fellow prisoner with Fergus. Other sketches in the book and on the front cover are the work of another fellow POW, Bill Wilder, for whom I have to thank his son, Anthony, once again for his time but also for showing Fergus and I the complete collection of his father's sketches, amongst which there was one as yet unidentified portrait. Fergus recognised it immediately. Bill had made it of him just after liberation.

Much of the other illustrative material in the book has come from the Anckorn family archives, but I have my son-in-law, photographer Toby Phillips, to thank for his masterly work in creating useable images from these for publication as well as for his excellent portraiture of Fergus as he is today. There is also my friend, Stephen Alport, an artist of increasing renown, whom I must thank not only for the maps and for his sketches that have contributed to the appearance of the book, but also for his sheer enthusiasm in working with me on this subject.

Finally, my acknowledgments go to Jonathan Wright at Pen & Sword for his immediate interest in my original submission for the book, and to Linne Matthews, my editor, who has been most helpful and complimentary in the finishing stages.

Introduction

Heroism comes in many guises. This wonderful book refers in the Epilogue to Fergus Anckorn's 'unique ability to entertain, lift spirits and raise morale in the face of unimaginable suffering.' Performing magic as he did, when his life and the lives of others depended on it, was heroic and his story has been an inspiration to me. This one man with such skill, made such a difference in the most extreme circumstances.

To me, the British Army is unique in the world because it draws its strength from the depth and breadth of its resources and the skills of individuals. It instils the determination and drive as well as the discipline necessary to excel. As well as that, there is camaraderie; it really is one big family. When I joined the army six years ago, I wanted to be part of the drum-beating, morale-raising force within it. At school I loved music and had become proficient at keyboard and trombone, so the idea of being part of a military band appealed to me. After spending a year at the Royal Military School of Music, I was posted to the Band of The Parachute Regiment. Then after three years was fortunate enough to be selected to join the Band of The Household Cavalry.

When deployed on tours, I always try to use downtime to learn new skills and the possibilities of magic came to me. I always enjoyed watching magic as a child but I thought now I could start learning and set myself the target of passing the audition to become a member of The Magic Circle. The night I passed, they said that, as I was army, I should meet Fergus who was there that night. I was the newest member meeting the oldest! We talked army and about the things that happened to him. It was an incredible story I was hearing and when they said his whole life story was in this book, I went out and bought it. That was three years ago and it set me on my course. Since then, army and magic has been my life. It's what I'm all about. Magic, like music, communicates across all cultures and defies barriers. It makes the impossible visibly possible and, like a military band, it can bring thrill and excitement where there is none. I just love it!

Entering the Britain's Got Talent competition was a way of testing myself in front of a bigger audience. Each step of the way was a surprise. I never expected to win but I had said to Fergus, 'if I get to the final, let's do it together.' My idea for the show was to bring military and magic together and I thought I would make the act a tribute to this man who is such an inspiration, perhaps not just to me, but to everyone. On that nerve-racking day I wanted to tell his story, and could think of no better way to do that than to perform with him beside me.

I am proud to follow in the footsteps of a fellow soldier and great magician.

'Always believe in the impossible!'

Lance Corporal Richard Jones
2016

Tribute

I took up magic as a child because I loved to see peoples' faces reacting to my tricks. Later, in the prison camps, I took applause, not knowing the deeper good my tricks were doing for morale. Let this book give my applause to all my fellows, especially the many who did not come home. I made it through and had a life but they had none. In commemoration we say, 'They shall grow not old, as we that are left grow old,' and I feel it the more, each year that passes.

Fergus Anckorn
Westerham
2011

Foreword

I had never met Gus Anckorn until a few years ago when he was well into his eighties. You would never have guessed it from the sheer sparkle and *joie de vie* that Gus exuded. However, my late father knew Gus well as they were fellow guests of the Japanese Emperor on the notorious railroad of death – the Burma-Siam Railway. I knew what my father, Lieutenant-Colonel Philip Toosey – the Colonel of Tamarkan, as he was called – had been through. But Gus's story is so different. Left for dead in a storm drain in Singapore and later the only survivor in his ward in the hospital massacre carried out by the Japanese in Singapore just prior to the surrender, he went on to perform his magic in the POW camps, entertaining fellow prisoners and even the Japanese whilst having only one fully functioning arm. Then his chance encounter post-war in London with the very surgeon who operated on him in Singapore saw his damaged arm more or less restored to normal.

When we finally met, apart from stories about my father and POW life, I was amazed by Gus's sparkle – a true performer! He complains to a waitress that his bread roll squeaks (by magic) and proves it; he performs a magic show for my grandson's birthday and keeps an audience of unruly seven-year-olds enthralled; he takes his advanced motoring test and passes it at the age of eighty-eight after a well-known comedienne jokingly remarked that all eighty-year-olds should have their licences taken away. Finally, he congratulates a surly checkout girl at a supermarket for getting her degree. 'What?' she says. 'Degree from where? Gus replies: 'Charm school!'

What a man! It is a great privilege that both my father and now I have known him. Not only a FEPOW, but also the youngest member of the Magic Circle pre-war and now the oldest practising member. Gus, you are truly a star.

Patrick Toosey
North Alton
July 2011

Preface

My wife and I had booked a night out at Salomons, a historic mansion near Tunbridge Wells in Kent, for an entertainment billed as an 'opera dinner'.

It was an odd affair. It took place in a unique, galleried Victorian theatre with round table seating, six to a table, in a cavernous auditorium. The performances were on stage as well as around the tables. In keeping with the operatic theme, the menu was ambitiously Viennese. However, the ambiance and the dinner never got beyond lukewarm, given the logistics of the place and an audience that simply wasn't big enough to inhabit the space. But no matter for us, because we were to find, opposite us at our table, someone who could more than fill any void. A white-haired, distinguished looking figure of a man, neatly turned out in collar and tie and wearing a blazer that proudly displayed a crest on the breast pocket. This was Fergus Anckorn and he was there with a colleague, similarly dressed but a little younger.

In the intermittent small talk we established they were both ex-army and from the same regiment – an artillery regiment that had fought in Singapore in the Second World War. Fergus told how he had been taken prisoner by the Japanese when Singapore fell and how he had been in Changi Prison Camp. Later, he had been sent up to the infamous Burma-Siam Railway – 'Death Railway', as it became known. Our interest deepened – mine especially. Ever since I had seen the film *The Bridge on the River Kwai* in 1957 as a young boy, I had been fascinated by the whole story and been in awe of those who had endured that jungle captivity at the hands of the Japanese, and now I found myself at an evening dinner concert, sitting at the same table as someone who had survived all that – who had actually been there. What did he think of that film? What was it really like as a prisoner?

Mention of the film touched a still sensitive nerve. The colonel was nothing like the character played by Alec Guinness – he knew because he'd been in that camp where the real colonel, Lieutenant-Colonel

Phillip Toosey, had stood up for his men time and time again and made such a difference in the unspeakable conditions of slavery and starvation that they were all forced to endure until, for many, exhaustion, disease and brutality took their toll. How did he personally survive it? By doing magic was his answer.

'I could get food by doing magic and I kept distracting the guards with my magic to get longer rest breaks. They couldn't resist it. I used to do things with whatever came to hand.' He picked up a spoon from the table as he talked, saying that he would typically just play around with a stone or something like that such that all could see and then it would ... disappear ... and the spoon did, right in front of us! More tricks followed and more of his story emerged as the evening progressed. He told how he had been the youngest member of the Magic Circle before the war and how his reputation as a conjuror had saved his life during the battle for Singapore. He told how he had been a sole survivor of a ruthless massacre and gone on to survive four more near-death experiences before the Japanese surrender three and a half years later. He told how he had used shorthand to convey secretly to his family that he was alive and where he was being held and he told what it was like to be finally liberated and return home, only to find he was just one of a forgotten army, bearing testimony to events that few wanted to hear about.

As one who has always felt indebted to those who had to face the fight of WW2, I have always been eager to read and especially to hear their stories. We are fortunate that some of those who experienced that war are still with us. What happened to many of them during those tragic years haunted them for the rest of their lives – many never finding a way of telling the world what really happened.

In writing this book, I have wanted the reader to get to know the person who is Fergus Anckorn, to share his formative years and then to go with him into war, through the war and onwards to the rebuilding of life after the war, seeing through his eyes and experiencing events and associations with his 'fellow travellers', just as he did. It is therefore written in the first person and I have devised to give context and perspective by way of reflection and insight drawn from information made available in public archives since the war.

This is not a history book or an attempt at a factual retelling of sad and catastrophic events but it is a very individual account and series of recollections of life before, during and after the war, forming a timeline of human emotion and endurance. Its centrepiece is not so much a military saga as a love story and its narrative not only records but also pays tribute to many parallel lives. In WW2, ordinary people were called up and many, without choice, found themselves in the front line of battle – clerks, train drivers, musicians, artists, accountants, bank managers, farmers, shopkeepers, watchmakers, coalminers ... Whilst the forces they joined were inevitably measured by firepower, they were also measured by the quality of their human assets and the contribution that individuals made. The 118th Field Regiment of Royal Artillery had a very special asset in Fergus Anckorn, and this book tells of the contribution he made.

Our meeting with Fergus was by sheer chance and the more he told of his life the more it was apparent that chance had been his friend throughout. This beguiling, upright, still strong figure of a man certainly has remarkable stories to tell. Only by sitting with him, writing this book, did I realise just how many!

Peter Fyans
High Beeches, Danehill
2011

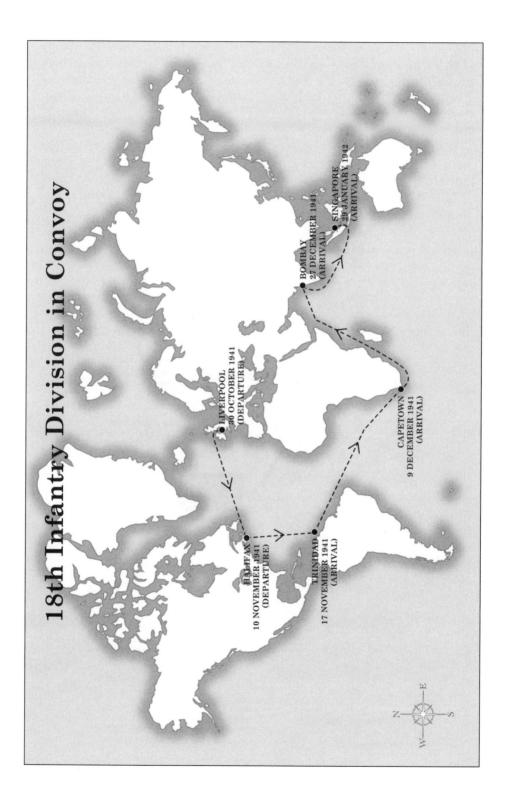

18th Infantry Division in Convoy

LIVERPOOL
30 OCTOBER 1941
(DEPARTURE)

HALIFAX
10 NOVEMBER 1941
(DEPARTURE)

TRINIDAD
17 NOVEMBER 1941
(ARRIVAL)

CAPETOWN
9 DECEMBER 1941
(ARRIVAL)

BOMBAY
27 DECEMBER 1941
(ARRIVAL)

SINGAPORE
29 JANUARY 1942
(ARRIVAL)

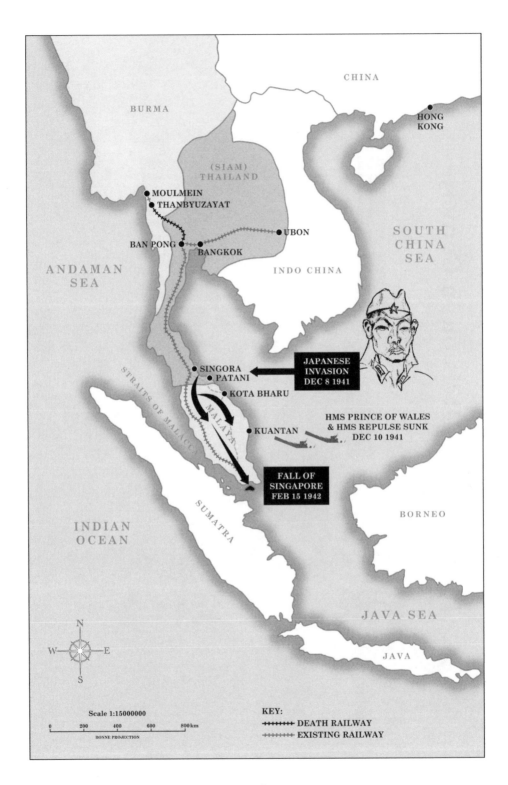

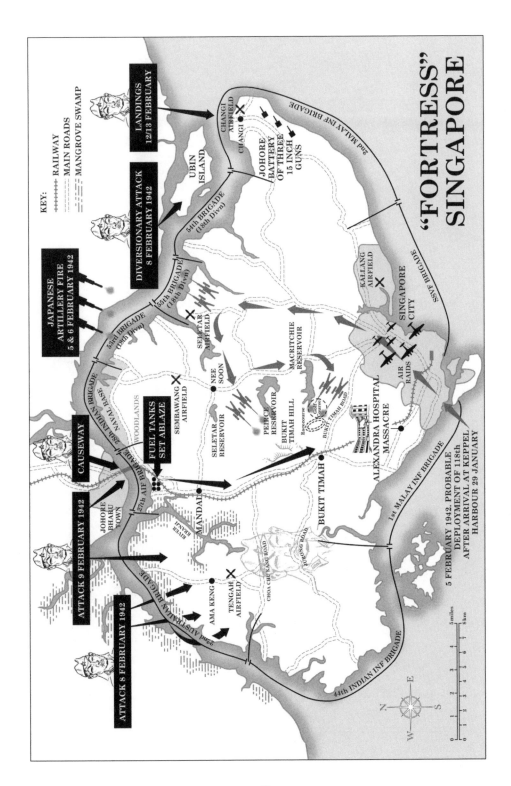

"FORTRESS" SINGAPORE

KEY:
+++++ RAILWAY
------ MAIN ROADS
------ MANGROVE SWAMP

LANDINGS 12/13 FEBRUARY

DIVERSIONARY ATTACK 8 FEBRUARY 1942

JAPANESE ARTILLERY FIRE 5 & 6 FEBRUARY 1942

CAUSEWAY

ATTACK 9 FEBRUARY 1942

ATTACK 8 FEBRUARY 1942

UBIN ISLAND

CHANGI AIRFIELD
CHANGI
JOHORE BATTERY OF THREE 15 INCH GUNS

54th BRIGADE (18th Divn)
55th BRIGADE (18th Divn)
53rd BRIGADE (18th Divn)

2nd MALAY INF BRIGADE

KALLANG AIRFIELD

SINGAPORE CITY

AIR RAIDS

SSVF BRIGADE

SELETAR AIRFIELD

NEE SOON

MACRITCHIE RESERVOIR

SEMBAWANG AIRFIELD

SELETAR RESERVOIR

PEIRCE RESERVOIR

BUKIT TIMAH HILL

Racecourse

Golf Course

BUKIT TIMAH ROAD

ALEXANDRA HOSPITAL MASSACRE

FUEL TANKS SET ABLAZE

27th AIF BRIGADE

MANDAI

RIVER MANDI

BUKIT TIMAH

1st MALAY INF BRIGADE

WOODLANDS

NAVAL BASE

28th INDIAN BRIGADE

JOHORE BHARU TOWN

AMA KENG

TENGAH AIRFIELD

CHOA CHU KANG ROAD

JURONG ROAD

22nd AUSTRALIAN BRIGADE

5 FEBRUARY 1942. PROBABLE DEPLOYMENT OF 118th AFTER ARRIVAL AT KEPPEL HARBOUR 29 JANUARY

44th INDIAN INF BRIGADE

N
W E
S

0 1 2 3 4 5 miles
0 1 2 3 4 5 6 7 8 km

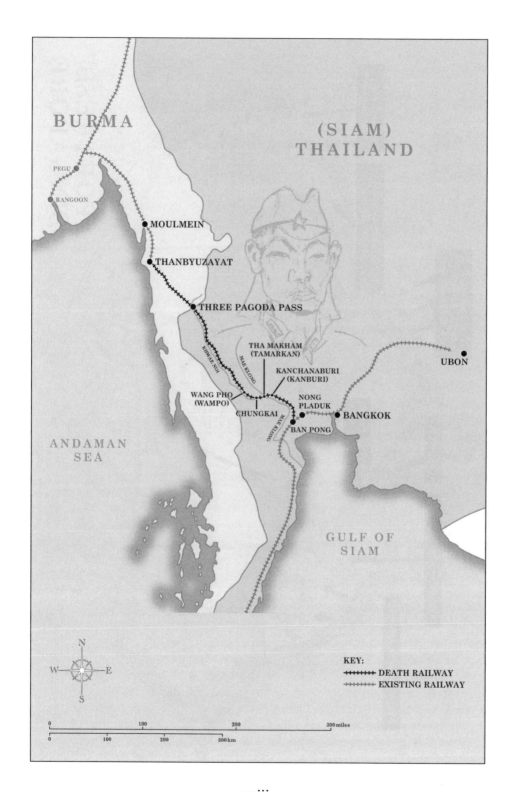

Chapter 1

BEGINNINGS

The *Princess Alice* disaster, 1878

Events, some of them catastrophic, have shaped the Anckorn family history but more often than not, something good has come out of the bad.

On a warm but muggy evening in early September 1878, the pleasure boat *Princess Alice*, pride of the London Steamboat Company with over 900 passengers on board, was returning up the Thames from a day trip to Gravesend. As it passed Woolwich it was struck by a passing ship, the *Bywell Castle*, and within minutes it had sunk with the loss of 670 souls. My great grandparents, John and Helen Anckorn, were among them.

It was reported as one of the worst accidents of the age and news of it reverberated across the land and across the world.

My great grandparents had left eight orphans – one of whom was William John Anckorn, my grandfather. He got himself a job as a photographer's boy in Croydon and was later sent up to Arbroath in Scotland, near to the burgeoning newspaper and publishing industry in Dundee.

There this cockney nonentity married into the Gordon clan and together with his wife, Bella, set up their own photographic business, 'Mr & Mrs W.J. Anckorn – Art Photographers & Publishers'. They became world renowned through winning many exhibition medals for their work in the late 1880s and were bestowed the patronage of Queen Victoria and of other Royals in Europe. My grandfather became a local councillor and JP, and recorded on camera much of local life over those years.

My father, Wilfred Lorraine Anckorn, was brought up in Arbroath, to which his broad Scottish accent gave testimony throughout his life. Strangely, he never thought he had an accent at all. He was a gentle soul and had a passion for the arts and history. He loved poetry and he loved Shakespeare. When he left school, he went to his local library to copy out Shakespeare's plays in longhand because books were not easily available to own at that time. He became a journalist for Thomson & Leng in Dundee, who published *The Scot* magazine and *Sunday Post*, as well as *The Hotspur* story paper. They moved him to London and he stayed with them for sixty-five years, contributing many historical articles as well as crime reportage and, on a lighter theme, stories for *The Hotspur*. During this time he also wrote a great deal of poetry and pursued a private interest in the history surrounding Mary Queen of Scots. By the end of his life he had read practically every book written about her and written his own, which was never published, remaining to this day in our family possession.

Above all, my father had a roving spirit. He said in one of his poems that he saw himself not like a buoy anchored to a harbour seabed but as a sailing ship free on the ocean. He was at ease with tramps and vagrants, often spending time chatting with them and finding their life stories fascinating. He was perhaps a tramp at heart – once taking himself off to wander in Germany for weeks, coming back dishevelled and smelly, much to the disdain of my mother, who by contrast kept a spick and span household with Victorian orderliness. On another occasion he befriended some local vagrants who came to the door and he finished up with seven of them seated around the family kitchen table, where he served them fried eggs – much to my mother's horror this time, when she came home after an afternoon's badminton match.

A character my father often referred to and whom he must have regarded as a kindred spirit was the Norfolk author, poet and linguist George Borrow, whose life in the mid 1800s probably reflected my father's yearnings. As a youngster Borrow liked to wander around Norwich, attending fairs in Tombland and watching bare-knuckle contests or talking to the gypsies on Mousehold Heath. He taught himself Romany, which enabled him to strike up close relationships with them, and he was known amongst them as 'the word master', or *Lavengro*, in Romany. The richness of talent, personal experiences and wisdom within the Romany community that Borrow discovered and recounted must have been a source of inspiration for my father.

When my father was moved to Kent he bought a house in Dunton Green, and later became Chairman of the Parish Council and Governor of the local school there. One of the children at the school, who came from a very poor family, showed natural ability in art to such an extent that my father went to speak to his parents. He suggested that the boy, Tom Robbins, really should be sent to art school but his family needed him to work. In those days we had a local tailor named Frayne who made riding breeches for all the well-known jockeys, and he used to take in poor lads to work for 2s 6d a week. Well, my father offered to pay this amount to the family if they would let him go to art school instead, and he would pay for the schooling, too. We more or less adopted him after that. Before long, this shy little boy gradually got a liking for books and read everything my father had in the house. He came to know history inside out and was interested in everything and loved everything that was going on. He was around our house since I was born and when I was old enough I was always out with him when I had the chance – talking about things. He was a twin soul really.

I was born in Dunton Green in December 1918, right after the end of the First World War – the war that was said to end war because it was so shockingly destructive. I was one of four children. I had a twin sister, whom I called 'Beb' from the moment I could first speak and we had an older sister whom we called 'Bing', but her actual name was Brenda. We also had a brother, Gordon, who was six years older. My twin sister and I were a complete surprise to my parents. They already had a boy and a girl, which was all they really wanted. Then we turned up, two at the same time, so we weren't very popular, I don't think, at the start!

We were a well-knit family under the orderliness of my mother – all eating at the same table – yet we were all separate entities, too. My brother couldn't care less about the family as he was always off somewhere with his pals scallywagging in the woods or breaking the law somehow or other on his own. For instance, in those days lamplighters used to go around lighting the street lamps as soon as it got dark. As they cycled around our area lighting the lamps my brother would follow two lampposts behind, putting them all out again. It was pure devilment, really!

3

My elder sister was musically inclined and always spent her time playing the piano or singing. My twin sister seemed to be always arguing. I never got on with her. We used to fight like hell and the number of times I blacked her eye I couldn't count! She was always getting herself into trouble at home for answering back to my mother and getting a good hiding for it. Like my brother, she would never do as she was told. I remember my mother saying to her, 'Your tongue will be the death of you!'

I think we must have been quite a well-off family, living there in the countryside at Dunton Green, because I don't recall us wanting for anything terribly much. What we did have anyway, I'm sure we made best use of, due to my mother's good management of the household. She would prolong the use of bed sheets by cutting them down the middle and sewing the two parts together again with the outer edges joined. She would always buy food and fuel in bulk when she could and she used all the Victorian techniques for storing food and making jams, lemonade and ginger beer.

In 1925 we were one of only five families in Dunton Green with a car. It was a Morris Cowley and my mother drove it. My father just couldn't get the hang of it and never drove it again after nearly crashing it with us in it. He had held his right foot unknowingly on the accelerator while, at the same time, braking with his left foot. With my mother at the wheel, however, we did many a long journey, travelling to Edinburgh to see the relatives.

My mother was the kind of person that always wanted to be the best at whatever she took on. Apart from running the household, she was a winning badminton and tennis player and Champion Rifle Shot at Bisley from all of Kent, Surrey and Sussex. After leaving school she had gone to Pitman's College to learn shorthand and typing and developed one of the fastest typing speeds in her class. She typed up all my father's stories for him – sixty-eight words a minute!

My mother was really the figurehead of the family – arranging every-thing, while father was the breadwinner. Every Sunday we would have at least ten or twelve people around the dining table and always have a big meal. My twin sister and I would have to help do the work pre-paring, serving the food and washing up. The people who came were writers and musicians, theatre people, business and newspaper people, local officials and educationalists – all people my father knew through his job. Many of those my parents entertained were either well known then or became well known later – the likes of Edgar Wallace and Dorothy L. Sayers. Of course, I had no idea who any of them were at the time – they were just people. I well remember one of those 'persons', Dorothy Sayers, turning up at our house on a motorbike, wearing overalls and with her hair cropped short. That, apparently, was something absolutely unheard of in those days.

Throughout our upbringing, our parents concerned themselves with our education. We were taught tennis and in a very proper manner, were provided with suitable whites. We were taught to swim, to roller-skate and to ice-skate. We were taught to speak and dress properly and I was taught how to tie a bow tie, as a matter of course.

We had a governess, too. She came from a Vicar's family in southern France and she taught my twin sister and I to cook and clean and to sew and knit – all by the age of five! She also taught us French. In fact, French became our second language at home with conversations at family meals being almost completely in French.

One summer, our governess offered to take my twin sister and me to join her parents on a farm they used to stay at in the South of France during school holidays. It was down near Bordeaux – a little place called Soubran. I've always meant to go back there but never have. We were only aged five then and yet I used to take the cows about half a mile down the lane into the pasture and stay with them all day long, so as to keep them off the grapes in the vineyard. I'd be there entirely on my own and to me it was the Garden of Eden. It was wonderful. There would be plums here, peaches there, figs, blackberries, anything – I could just reach out and eat. My inquisitive mind had free rein as I observed the nature around me – the zigzagging of butterflies; the way the clouds formed; the simple blowing of the wind. I wanted for nothing. Then, at about five in the evening, they would sound a cow's horn from the farm – a real cow's horn – and the cattle would immediately rear up and head for the gate, without me doing anything. I would just open the gate and they would take themselves back home to be milked. They all had names, these cows. My favourite was Lunette and I used to ride on her back, but oh – did she have a sharp spine! Each cow had a stall with her name on and when we got back to the farm, they'd each go to their stall by themselves and wait to be milked.

I never thought of it as a responsibility, it was just the way things were done. They also had sheep on the farm and an old boy to look after them. He was a sheep himself, really. He was over eighty and he lived with the sheep. At night-time they were taken into a little room under the house. They would go in through a hole and when they were all in, a shutter was pulled down. The old boy would be in there with them, sleeping all night long. You could hear coughing, and you didn't know whether it was him or the sheep! In the morning, they'd lift the shutter up and steam would come out – sheep steam – then he'd come out on all fours with the sheep. That was his job and no one ever

5

thought anything of it. There we were – an old boy over eighty, and me, aged five. He was sheep, I was cows!

It was a lovely part of my life and my sister and I learned a lot. While I was off in the pastures she was with the girls and they'd be teaching her sewing, knitting and playing tennis. We were both very good tennis players by the age of six. On the farm they had a tennis court marked out in one of the fields with white tape. They would have tin plates with numbers on the back of them placed all over the court. Then they would say, 'Serve, number three,' and you'd have to bounce off the number three plate, and for the person returning they'd say, 'Number eight' and you'd have to return it to plate number eight. I got very accurate at tennis!

We used to go shopping once a week to the local market, which was about 12 miles away, and we went by carthorse and buggy. Nobody spoke any English – they didn't even know the English equivalent of *oui* – so we became completely French.

Another thing was that we had terrible storms some nights, awful storms. I'm still frightened of storms even now. But it wasn't just the storm itself that frightened me. Every farm in the area had cannons on the corners of their fields and when the storm came they would fire these cannons off all night long. They were 'hail cannons'. These special guns would fire off something that created a sort of smoke ring in the sky, which would melt the hail, turning it into rain. Every time there was a storm, off they would go. I thought it must have been like a barrage in the First World War.

They were wonderful, my childhood days. Days of doing nothing much. I was such a happy boy. Nothing nasty ever happened and there was no such thing as nasty men – not to my knowledge, anyway. I used to get out often with my doggy and go for long runs in the countryside around our house and think of nothing much except the enjoyment of it and looking at all the beautiful sights to see. I believed I was seeing things that most people never got to see when going by roads and pathways. They'd never know what was behind *that* hill or in *those* woods ... but I was in all those places and got to know every stick and stone. I'd also listen to all the birdsongs and get to recognise each bird by its trill, and I'd look for their nests and get to know each bird by its eggs, too. Quite often, my mother would give my sister and me some sandwiches and we'd go off together into the woods for the day – you could in those days, quite safely. If a gamekeeper came along, we would talk French and pretend we didn't understand him!

There was another part of my home life that made a big impression on me.

My father often toyed with magic tricks and even had his own little music hall show that he put on from time to time for friends. In his show, he would always have a single candle, lit and standing on a table, throughout the act. At the end of his act he would take the candle and magically eat it – the whole thing – before making a final bow. I was in awe.

I can remember him giving me a box of magic tricks for my birthday when I was four. Every birthday after that I would get another and I would perform the tricks, with my parents pretending they had no idea how they were done. I got a kick out of watching their faces. That was the thing – I loved performing to people because I loved to see their faces when I'd taken them in! I've never lost that.

I got my first paid show when I was seven. Everyone knew about me and my magic because in the village in those days, everybody knew everybody. I went to a private house just up the road from us, where they were having a birthday party. I got paid three guineas for it – more than my father was earning in Fleet Street, I thought – or so he said! They only paid me, of course, because they knew my father, and because they wanted to encourage me, and that was the first real show I did. But from then on I was doing magic for nothing wherever I could – Boy Scouts, Women's Institutes – you name it. Magicians were quite a thing then.

There was a proper one in Sevenoaks at that time – Major Branson. He was a major in the Indian Army, and every three years he would have six months' leave and come home to England, where he'd perform in the music halls under the name of Lionel Cardac. He was always being asked by locals to come and do a show – but often they wouldn't have any money. He'd heard about me and so he sent for me. Of course, the whole object was to see if I was any good because then, whenever anyone would ask him to do a show for free, he could say, 'No, I'm afraid I can't, but I've got someone who I can recommend,' and he would send me along.

When I went to see him he asked me to do one of my favourite tricks. So I put a matchbox on my hand and made it lift itself up, open its drawer and then go down again.

'That's quite good,' he said, 'but what happens if the thread breaks?'

I was wondering how the hell he knew there was a thread there! I was so naïve. Then he said, 'Force a card on me,' which was magicians' talk for 'make me take a card'. So I took the pack and, in my own way at that time, started to shuffle it and sift it carefully, out of his view so he couldn't see. After a moment or two he challenged me.

'What are you doing?'

'I'm shuffling the pack so you can't see it before I force a card on you,' I replied.

He took the pack from me and with the card faces down, he splayed it out with a flourish.

'Now, take the eight of clubs,' he said.

Well I just took any card, with no idea what it was. When I turned it over it was the eight of clubs!

'Look,' he said, 'all these tricks you're doing, they're all very nice but anyone can go and buy those tricks. What you need is these!' And he held up his two hands in front of me like trophies. 'Learn how to use these and *only* these!'

That's what started me on sleight of hand magic and I practised and practised from then on with anything I could lay my 'magic' hands on.

The Major became the vice president of the Magic Circle, and when he did, he proposed me into membership on my 18th birthday – and I was seconded by the president! So at eighteen years old, I became the youngest member of the Magic Circle. Now, I'm the oldest practising member!

I didn't go to school until I was seven or something like that, because we were pretty well educated at home by my parents and by our governess up to that age. My parents saw it as an imperative that we should be sent to good schools when the time came. Yet they placed no expectations on us as to any outcome of such quality education. This was just as well because school did nothing for me or my brother.

Gordon was expelled first from Sevenoaks School and later from Judd. He just wouldn't take authority or 'any old rot', as he saw it, from the masters. He especially hated pomp and ceremony. Sevenoaks expelled him for a prank involving a bottle of ink suspended by a thread over the site of an inaugural ceremony at the school, because of which the visiting luminary, Walter De La Mare I think it was, got covered in ink. He was expelled from Judd because he reacted badly to a teacher taking him by the ear to the blackboard to make a point after finding him reading a magazine under his desk. He punched the teacher in the face. The result was that my brother was more self-taught than anything else – distinguishing himself in photography, just like our grandfather, and becoming immensely practical in all sorts of ways, as well as artistic. He often pulled a motorbike apart and put it back together again in no time, and he sculptured a bust of the Greek mythological character Pan and put it on a pedestal in the garden. He also created a bronze of my father, and painted many a picture of scenes that took his eye. The thing with him though was that once he'd mastered or done something to his satisfaction, that would be that and he'd move on to something else that took his interest.

For myself, schooling was difficult, too – not least because I was following in my brother's footsteps and there must have been some apprehension for a teacher dealing with another Anckorn. I was constantly being told to shut up for asking endless questions and expressing what teachers considered to be fanciful ideas. I learned nothing – often just staring out of the window, looking at the flowers! So I did a lot of self-learning, too. I took great interest in Latin and English and developed a love for language itself, the origin of words and their meanings. Even now I keep a dictionary beside me all the time.

I was shy at school – never approaching anybody – keeping out of the way usually. Nevertheless, I did make some good friends – some of whom became well known. One was Neville Duke, who broke the World Air Speed Record and had other achievements, and another was Terry Lewin, latterly Lord Lewin, Admiral of the Fleet. I sat between the two of them at Judd.

When I left school I had no idea what I was going to do. It bothered me a lot. I thought I was going to end up being a tramp, because I just couldn't see what I could do. The stuff they'd been teaching me at school was quite useless in my mind for getting a job – I mean, I didn't care where the river Ouse started and finished or whether X plus Y all squared is X squared plus Y squared plus 2XY. I couldn't think of a job where that would be useful. Having been such a reluctant learner at school and having performed so badly in tests, they didn't allow me to sit any exams at all, knowing I'd fail. So I was washed up with simply no idea what was going to happen to me.

I don't remember my parents talking to me, or any of us for that matter, about what we might do after school. So it was entirely my own idea to take myself off to the *Daily Express* in London with the notion that I could be a journalist. It seemed to me that it was the only thing I could possibly do. After all, I did write essays well and I enjoyed English and Latin and that sort of stuff and of course, my father was a journalist, and by that time, my brother had also become a journalist on a local newspaper. All I ever saw my brother doing was sitting in a café in Sevenoaks drinking coffee or getting into the cinema free, so I thought 'that's the life for me!' It looked as though you got paid and didn't really have to know anything much. Which was fine, because I didn't!

It was then that I got my first motivation to learn something. The Editor at the *Express* finished the interview saying, 'You learn shorthand and typing and we'll give you a job.'

Well, there was every chance that I might because of my mother's prowess in both those skills, but previously, I had struggled with them. I just couldn't get on with shorthand. It simply meant nothing to me and I ended up one night throwing all my books into the large open fire that we had in our house, right in front of my parents, stating crossly, that was the end of it for me!

Yet now, without a word to my parents, I went straight up to Regent Street in London and enrolled on a commercial course to learn shorthand and typing. With this newfound motivation, it seemed that in no time at all, I had passed the exams and got better marks than anyone else in the blinking place – and what's more, I had loved doing it! Nowadays, I can even read shorthand upside down and I've got novels in shorthand, too – *Sherlock Holmes*, for example. I read it like any book.

So, I had turned a corner in my life and my outlook had completely changed. I felt I could learn anything, absolutely anything, if I put my mind to it. If I decided to do something, I would do it without encouragement from anyone else. The world was now my oyster and I felt I could get any job if I really wanted it.

I didn't go back to the Editor at the *Express*, but took up a job in an art gallery in London at first. Then, when I was passing one of the very impressive buildings in Marylebone on my way to the Magic Circle offices one day, it occurred to me how nice it would be to work in such a fine place. It was the headquarters of the National Cash Register Company and one of the first offices in London with air conditioning. I simply walked in and asked to speak to the Company Secretary. My wish was granted and in a trice I was in front of him.

'What is it you want?' he asked.

'A job,' I replied confidently. 'This is just the sort of place I'd like to work in,' I continued.

'Well,' he said, 'I'm Company Secretary but I started as an office junior. If I can do it, so can you.' He gave me a job there and then!

After some time there, I realised that travelling to London was eating up my wages more than I liked and so I thought I would get myself a position locally. A job came up at Marley, in Sevenoaks, for a clerk. Marley in those days had not long started manufacturing roofing tiles of a special kind and now their business was expanding. The managing director was Owen Aisher – a man who has, of course, since then become very well known – not just for the success of the business, but also for his yacht-racing activities.

The subjects I had studied at the commercial college, along with the fact that it was unusual to find a man who could do shorthand, meant I easily got the clerk job there, and the pay was equivalent to my earnings at the National Cash Register Company. So things really were working out well.

But then war was declared.

Chapter 2

WAR

It was a Sunday. Two days earlier, Germany had invaded Poland and Mr Chamberlain had given Germany an ultimatum to get out or we would be at war. We were to expect a broadcast on Sunday at 11.15 am.

Ever since Mr Chamberlain's 'Peace for our time' statement on his return from the Munich Conference in September the year earlier, preparations for war had been going on. In London I saw that every lunch hour, all the men would come out of their offices and dig trenches in Hyde Park. In fact, whenever there was a spare moment, you'd see people digging in the parks and places like that. Other disfigurements were taking place too, as householders were being required to give up their iron railings and gates, supposedly to turn into ships and tanks and aeroplanes as part of the collective war effort. Stirrup-pumps, to help with putting out fires caused by incendiary bombs, were every-where, and rolls of sticky brown paper were issued to all premises so that windows could be taped up to reduce the effects of bomb blasts. Public Information leaflets were being issued on a regular basis on deadly serious matters such as evacuation, conserving food and gas warfare. All with their ominous directive on the front:

Read this and keep it carefully. You may need it.

So it was pretty obvious war was coming.

I was still hoping it would never happen. My mind was childlike towards it – that if I kept thinking it wouldn't happen it probably wouldn't and to talk about it might upset the applecart and bring it about. I just tried to ignore it all. It was the same at home, actually. My father, even as a journalist, didn't talk about it. The feeling was that 'something would be done about it.'

Many people must have been clutching at straws just as we were because, the day before the broadcast, a newspaper had come out with a headline:

NO WAR. OFFICIAL!

I think it had something to do with the 'Gypsy Petulengro' – the famous gypsy who was often on the radio in those days. He had apparently predicted that there would be no war.

In any event, I didn't want to hear the broadcast. So I left home early that Sunday morning and went for a swim at the open-air swimming pool nearby – the Dunton Green Lido.

The pool was deserted and I took to the cool water with the thrill of being out in the fresh air and thinking how nice it was to have the place to myself in the peace of that Sunday morning. I was absorbed in the rush of the water around me as I took long strokes, propelling myself, rhythmically, length by length up and down the pool. Time meant nothing to me. The freedom of the morning meant everything. I had escaped all thought of war. Then the attendant came out of the office and called out, 'I expect you want to hear this.'

He had brought a big black portable radio out of his office and he came across to place it at the side of the pool I was heading for. So, after truculently splashing my way to a stop by the rail, I got the broadcast whether I liked it or not, six inches from my ear:

> The British Ambassador to Berlin has handed a final note to the German Government this morning saying unless it announced plans to withdraw from Poland by eleven o'clock a state of war would exist between us. I have to tell you now that no such undertaking has been received and consequently this country is at war with Germany.

I got out of the water and no sooner had I got my clothes on than the air raid sirens went off. It was expected. We'd all been led to believe that as soon as war was declared, London would be flattened within hours. It wouldn't be like the first war, they said – five years and all that – this one would be over in a rush. The Germans had shown what they could do with their bombers supporting Franco in the Spanish Civil War and they'd been adding to their armaments all the while since. Evacuation of London had started the day before Poland was invaded.

So when I heard the air raid sirens I thought, 'Well, this is it!' and I headed for home as fast as I could, hoping to get there before it got flattened too.

I met the headmaster of the local school along the road near to my house. His name, oddly enough, was Mr Germaney. I asked him if he knew of anything happening yet and he told me there'd been a small raid on London – two people killed. It turned out, nothing like that had happened at all. It was actually an ordinary light plane coming home from France that hadn't done a flight plan, so he was unidentified – and it created a hell of a fuss, with the result that authority figures, such as the headmaster of our local school, came to be putting about a story like that! It was to be the first of many false alarms in the weeks that followed.

When I got home I found my mother with a houseful of Sunday hikers, one of whom had fainted. She had seen the group passing the house just at the time of the broadcast and, just as the swimming pool attendant had done for me, she had invited them in to hear it. As the fateful last words were delivered, this poor girl had simply collapsed.

On the Monday morning, the newspaper that had baldly stated, 'No War. Official' on Saturday, came out proclaiming:

HITLER DEFIES THE STARS.

The paper reported Petulengro as predicting that Germany would lose the war because war was not written in the stars.

That Monday was a restless day. We had all gone to work as usual but for us at Marley, there was to be more bad news. During the course of the day, the managing director of the company, Owen Aisher, had us all into his office in groups of five. He had to tell us that because of war being declared, we would all have to be sacked. Then he went on to say something very disturbing:

> Whatever you think now, or whatever you're doing now, whatever your life is now, it will change inexorably from what it is now. Your life from this moment is going to be a different life from anything you've ever had or thought of. Some of you will come back colonels. Some will come back majors. Some of you won't come back at all. Whatever happens, if you get back, you'll always have a job here.

We were all a bit shocked and I expect all of us, in the days that followed, felt somewhat bewildered.

For my part, I was already due to go for training at the Royal Artillery Barracks in Bulford, Wiltshire, under the Military Training Bill or 'Militia Act', as it was known, which had come into force in April. This required all fit and able British men, aged twenty and twenty-one, to do six months' military training and afterwards join the Territorial Reserve. I had turned twenty in the previous December. My idea, when the Act came into force, was to do something that involved driving in the army, as I had a driving licence and had been driving the family Morris Cowley a lot by then. Driving was still quite a rare skill, too. Besides, I didn't fancy the job of ever having to kill anybody. So I had applied to the Royal Army Service Corps, but somehow I was to attend the principle camp of the Royal Artillery.

While waiting to go for the training I had time on my hands, and so took my doggy, 'Fag', for many a long walk up on the North Downs as far as Polhill and through the deserted Napoleonic Fort at Halstead, where we often played as children. The woods around those parts were just glorious and there, over time, I had taught myself to recognise every birdsong that could be heard. Now, on each outing, I was intoxicating myself with everything there was about the walk, in case it would be my last. I wanted to take it all in, step by step – the birdsong, the scent of the forest, the wind in the trees, the gemlike views and colours enlivened by the sun, the scampering squirrels, bobbing rabbits, the detail of the undergrowth, multifarious fungi and the carpets of fallen acorn husks – and best of all, Fag running free.

When I wasn't up there I'd be at the Dunton Green Lido, often with my twin sister Beb. During the summer, she and I had befriended a Dutch fellow who'd often been there on his own. His name was Frans Bakker and he was here working for his father's horticultural business as a representative. We had invited him for games of tennis and he had joined the family at weekends quite often, too. It wasn't long before he would be at our house just about every day. He and I became good friends and he and Beb became very close. But then all of a sudden he said he was going to have to go back home and we presumed to Holland, because of the changing situation for us all. We expected that he would keep in touch, but we never heard from him again. I was to find him later, in the Far East.

During that summer and autumn of 1939, life around us had been changing rapidly, with ever-increasing signs of the country being at war. Stringent blackout regulations had been introduced weeks before war was declared, requiring all premises, domestic and commercial, to completely cover their windows at night to prevent even the slightest chink of light giving guidance to bombers. Blackout material was made available at low cost for everybody. My mother had her own ideas on how to use it, though. She wasn't going to have dismal black cloth creating gloom inside the house, so she made blackout boards for all our windows and lined our heavy floral curtains with the cheap blackout material for good measure. The result was total blackout to the outside and no loss of homeliness on the inside. She had her own ideas about air raid shelters, too. She wasn't going to have her garden dug up to install an ugly corrugated iron structure they called an Anderson Shelter, oh no! She had a shelter constructed under the stairs in the house and even then she refused to use it herself, saying she would not give up sleeping in her grand replica Napoleonic bed for anybody!

The bleakness of it all was often relieved, however, by quirks of human behaviour. In Dunton Green, police special constables were called for again, as they had been in the First War. Once a dozen or so volunteers had come forward, the senior amongst them took charge. This was the local barber, who had been a Special in the First War. He would get them to assemble outside his barber's shop once a week for a talk. On one occasion, he wanted to convince the recruits about the merits of the tin hats they had been issued with. So he went inside his shop and up to the flat above it where he lived. His idea was that he would drop a brick on the head of one of the recruits wearing the tin hat and everybody would be suitably impressed with the protection qualities of the tin hats. Well, he opened the window from the first floor and dropped the brick, but it knocked the poor man out cold!

As 1939 progressed it was difficult not to think of what seemed inevitable, even though I harboured the thought it may never happen. While I was in London one day, I passed a travel agency that still had holiday posters displayed. One ironically hailed 'Come to the Black Forest in Germany. Have a wonderful time!' I thought blackly, that was probably where I'd be going, but not for a wonderful time! Another poster beside it displayed exotic Eastern-looking girls, golden temples and sun-drenched beach scenes entreating everybody to 'Come to sunny Siam' – Siam being the country we now call Thailand. I thought, 'If only I could wave a magic wand and go and spend the war there, away from it all.' How true it is that we should always be careful what we wish for!

Shortly after war was declared, arrangements for me to go to Bulford Camp were rescinded and I was told to await further instructions. Those instructions came at the beginning of October. I was called up and required to present myself at Woolwich Barracks on 18 October.

There was a complete cross-section of people in the queue joining up at the same time – one could be a coal miner, the next a newspaper seller, the next one a barrister. Like everything else that was happening in those days, it all seemed so strange. We lined up to go to a table where there were two sergeant-majors with paper and pen and we were given our army number and told never to forget it. Mine was 947556. The man in front of me was, of course, 947555. He is now a name on the war memorial in Westerham. If I'd been one ahead in the queue ... would that have been me on the memorial?

We were joining the 118th Field Regiment Royal Artillery. It was a Territorial regiment so in my mind, I wasn't going into the army 'proper' and none of us were 'real soldiers' – just temporary soldiers – men from all walks of life, there for the duration.

For the first six weeks after joining up, all we were doing was marching up and down, 'square bashing' and being trained in rifle drill and all that sort of stuff on the parade ground, as well as learning how to salute, who to salute and when to salute. It was all about the routine of things.

The crazy thing was – I enjoyed it all, thoroughly. Yet I had always thought that I would die within a week of being in the army, with all that horrible discipline and people swearing at you and all that. But

15

I took to it like a duck to the water. I found I loved being part of a disciplined body of men and I revelled in the exactness required of a couple of hundred of us marching up and down and halting and about-turning, all at the same time. I surprised myself and was amazed that I could be a good soldier – at least as far as that was concerned.

It brought out self-confidence and self-sufficiency in me, too. I had to draw on my innate abilities and what knowledge and skills I had in order to stand up for myself. It surprised me that I could cope with whatever happened without fuss.

There was, of course, the inevitable bully in the barracks. In those first six weeks after joining up, the polishing of shoes and buttons and the blancoeing of this and that, were daily routines. This fellow used to make the rest of the mob do his boots and clean his buttons and things like that. On the day he told me to do it, I just said 'No! I'm not doing it,' and I threw his boots across the barrack room floor back to him. He came at me like a raging bull. He was a big chap. Well, he seemed big.

Fortunately, I'd had the opportunity to learn ju-jitsu in the months before I joined up. There had been a week of sport in Orpington, followed by a national sports day in which every type of sport was demonstrated and you could take part in any of them if you wanted to. There was a fellow there who got up to demonstrate ju-jitsu. His name was Ernst Hamm, from Austria, and he was a Jewish refugee who had fled to England just before Germany annexed Austria in 1938. He had been a doctor in Austria, but now, as a refugee in this country, he and his wife were required by regulations to do only menial jobs. Well, an announcement went out at this sports demonstration event saying: 'Mr Hamm here is an Austrian ju-jitsu champion and he is willing to demonstrate ju-jitsu, if there's anyone that would volunteer to come up here with him ...' So I did – after all, one of the activities I had enjoyed at school and afterwards was acrobatics in the gym and I was quite happy with how to fall properly. Well, after being attired in all the special canvas clothes, I was thrown around all over the shop and when it was over, I asked Mr Hamm if he gave lessons – thinking that if I was going to be in the army, I'd need to be able to look after myself. He said he did and what's more, he would come to my house to teach me. That's exactly what he did and for the next month, I did an hour's ju-jitsu every day. By the time I joined the army, I could do many of the classic moves quite easily.

So this bully came at me across the barrack room in the perfect position for me to chuck him right over my head using a shoulder throw that we called the 'Flying Mare' move. He went over me and landed on his back, sliding across the floor until his head met the coal bunker, which knocked him out. He lay there, out for the count, with everyone flapping around him. When he eventually came round and gasped, 'What happened?' they told him I'd done him over! They didn't know it was pure luck that I'd managed it but from that moment on, Gunner Anckorn earned the nickname 'Tiger Anckorn', and few would take advantage again!

Training on the guns was, of course, a very important part of that first six weeks, too, even though it was really only textbook training. The mood was nevertheless very serious, very studied. The unspoken thought was that this was going to be our 'business' and our lives might well depend upon it. We learned how men and guns would be organised and put into the field of battle, and then how to fire the guns.

Our regiment would consist of a number of gun troops responsible for manning the guns and these would be formed into a number of batteries, depending on the battle situation. The number of batteries was always going to be flexible.

A detachment of five men would be responsible for each gun and in addition, there would be a driver for a special gun lorry that would provide mobility for each gun. The guns might typically be organised such that a troop would have four guns – two in left section and two in right section; two troops would make up a battery of eight guns and there might be three batteries to a regiment – a total fire power of twenty-four guns in a regiment such as ours, the 'one-one-eight'.

We learned how each troop would have its own surveyors who would do the reconnaissance to find the best firing positions before putting marks in the ground for the gun placements.

We learned about the crucial job that's done by a Forward Observation party. This would be to get sight of the enemy and direct the fire of the guns onto specific targets and then to monitor the impact, ordering corrections and changes as necessary during the action. This seemed to me to be the deadliest of jobs to be done, and since every Forward Observation party would consist of one ordinary gunner like me, I tried not to think too much about it. We learned later that the most hazardous job in the field would actually be done by our Signallers, who would have to run communications wire from the Forward Observation posts back to the guns and onwards to a command post that would be set up some way behind the guns. If any damage occurred to the wires, they would have to run out and fix it.

There was a lot to learn about the guns themselves too, and the process of firing them. Our regiment was going to use the latest guns, known as '25-pounders', but we were trained to start with on old First World War pieces, which were their immediate predecessors – '18-pounders' and '18/25s', 4.5-inch Howitzers and 'French 75s'. We were taught who did what in each gun detachment and we practiced the various positions. Each man in the detachment had a number, like players in a team. No. 1 was the gun sergeant. No. 2 was the breech worker. No. 3 was the all-important gun layer, who had to operate the gun sights, responding to the instructions coming from the Forward Observation Officer and the command post. Each time the gun would fire, he might often have to re-check his sights because we were told the whole two tons of the gun would jump on recoil. But, as we never fired the guns during this basic training, it was left to our imagination what that would be like. In my case it would have been a good thing if I *had* imagined it because the very first time we did fire the guns almost a year later, the recoiling gun breech nearly took my head off! No. 4 was the loader and No. 5 had the other most important job – ammunition.

We would be firing high explosive shells with variable fuse options that needed to be set by twisting a cone on the tip of the shell. The fuse would determine when the shell would explode – on contact or in the air above a target, for example. On loading, the shells would be handled separately from their cartridges – shell into the breech first, followed by the appropriate cartridge for the range required to reach the target. Cartridges were the familiar brass casings that you often see littered around a gun after it has been firing for a while. These contained three bags of cordite, coloured red, blue and white, and No. 5 would need to be told which of the bags were required for each round. He might remove one bag or two in order to vary the strength of the charge and therefore the distance the shell would travel. Sometimes a fourth bag might be added when extra distance was needed but the explosive power risked damaging the gun.

The shells and the cartridges would be carried in a trailer called a 'limber' and this would be attached between gun and gun lorry when on the move. The limber would also carry the gun mounting, which was a sort of turntable that had to be taken off and placed under the gun to enable it to swivel. It would take all five men in the detachment to lift it. Each limber had two compartments, side by side, which could hold thirty-two shells in one and thirty-two cartridges in the other. The gun lorry might also carry some ammunition but every troop would have an extra gun lorry that would just pull two more limbers so that each troop could be armed with 128 rounds of ammunition.

We endlessly practised the whole brawny, yet meticulous process of loading the guns until we could do it faultlessly. We worked in strict silence and disciplined postures according to our allocated role. Mine was loader. The firing process started with first hefting the shells between the ammunition man and the loader, who would then place the shell quickly but carefully into the breech before ramming it home with a pole. If he got it wrong, not only might the shell jam in the breech and disable the gun, but he might also lose a finger or two. Once the shell was home in the breech, the cartridge would follow and the breech operator would then slam the breech door shut. On the order 'Fire!'

given by the gun sergeant, the gun layer would pull the firing pin and Boom! Off would go the shell as each man stood away from what would be a violently lurching gun as it recoiled. The breech operator would then open the breech, the spent cartridge would drop out and the whole process would start all over again. We were expected to get up to such a speed of operation that we could fire ten rounds per minute in continuous fire, if necessary. We trained using replicas of shells made of wood but with a lead core to give us a good idea of the weight of the real thing whilst avoiding damage to the gun barrel.

Whilst we each had an allocated position in the gun team, we also had to be able to do any of the other jobs on the guns, if necessary, and that included driving the gun lorry. But we hadn't actually got any gun lorries to train with and we weren't going to get any until a year later, as things turned out. We trained instead on whatever kind of lorry the army could get their hands on, which meant, at first, using an old 'Thornycroft' from the First World War. After that, we used a sand truck and then we used numerous furniture lorries that had been requisitioned. As I was one of the few amongst us with driving experience, I was detailed to train the others using these odd vehicles. On my first outing with the Thorneycoft, the clutch went in half an hour!

When all our daily routines were done and training finished for the day, I used to get myself off for a run on my own whenever I could. Most of the other lads would be off into town to see whatever was on at the cinema or to go to the pubs, but I never seemed to have enough money to do all that. It was just like my childhood – couldn't afford a bus so I used to run instead. When my friends and I were to go to the Sevenoaks swimming pool, they'd catch the bus and I'd set off running and get there at the same time! I ran everywhere and thought nothing of it. The thing was – I just loved running.

In the army, it wasn't long before my running got noticed. As part of getting us fit, our sergeant-major started us on morning runs, assembling at 7.45 am. For some reason, on the first one, I thought assembly was 8.00 am so when I turned up they were all ready to set off. I was told just to get ready and set off with the others but before I did, I asked what the course was, as this was a run around the streets of Woolwich. The sergeant-major dismissed my query and repeated that I should just go along with the others. I protested.

'Sergeant-Major? If I'm running, I usually finish up at the front of the field, so if I don't know where I'm going, it could be difficult.'

Of course, this was an invitation to the sergeant-major for some typical sardonic humour.

'Oh well, everybody, shall we just hold on a minute while we tell Anckorn here what route it is that he's going to lead you all around?'

Continuing with that tone, he gave me the briefing and eventually we all set off. Meanwhile, he went to have his breakfast. Halfway through his breakfast, another lad and I returned – much to his consternation. That did it. The word obviously went out and I was to find myself put up for every regimental athletics competition there would be, from then on.

My athletics at school had been quite good because I simply enjoyed running. But during my time at commercial college in London I discovered that I was actually a damn good runner. One day they had a senior schools' athletics event at the White City in London. Three days before that, there had been a sports day for the commercial college and I ran the mile race. When we came to the last lap, I was last in a field of nine. Then it suddenly came to me that I could beat the lot of them if I wanted to and at that moment, I really did want to! I wasn't going to have people just writing me off as a non-contender. So I put my foot down, accelerated past them all and won the race. After the race, the man in charge of athletics at the college came up to tell me he'd never seen a last lap in a mile race run as fast as that and he was going to enter me for the White City event.

When it came to the White City event, I was up against serious opposition from foreigners, including several Germans as it happened, and God knows what else. There was I, wearing ordinary plimsolls, no spikes, no proper running shorts, just bloomers and in the race itself, such a fool, because I had no idea about tactics! I paced myself as normal until the moment came to make my move. Thinking, 'Right, I'll take the lead now,' I went up in front of the field and trotted along quite happily towards the finishing line. But when we came to the last 100 yards, they all swept past me. 'My God!' I thought, 'if I'd known they were going to do that, I would have run faster!' I really had no idea. Up until that race I was just running because I liked it. But it was then that other people saw me as a good runner and it wasn't long before I did learn all about tactics.

After the army found out I could run, they gave me time off for training because they wanted me to represent the regiment in the Brigade sports. I said I would do the half-mile, which was really 'my race', as I had become one of only four people in Kent by the time I left college who could do the half-mile in under two minutes.

On the day before the big event, the officer was lecturing the battery before we all went off and as they were running a tote he said, 'If you've got any money put it on Anckorn for the half-mile. No one can touch him!' So they all placed bets on me to win and I felt confident – until I got to the start line! There, readying myself for the start, I took off my sweater and this other fellow did the same only to reveal Olympic rings on his chest! He'd run the half-mile in the 1936 Olympics and there was

I up against him. Well, using my newly acquired knowledge of tactics, I let him set the pace, keeping just behind him. We damn nearly lapped the rest of the field and as we came to the last 50 yards, I made my bid to take him. Away I went but lo and behold, he just accelerated past me to take the finishing line. They all lost their money and I wasn't very popular for a while!

Anyway, I got known for my sportiness and when a replacement PT instructor was called for, the job went to me. The acrobatics I'd been doing at school and college came in handy again and I found that I just loved teaching PT. Groups would come in from our battery and others every half-hour, and I was happy if it went on all day long! My own fitness increased to the point where I could lift myself on a bar with one arm a dozen times, without any difficulty.

The fact was that I settled in well to being a gunner and into the camaraderie of the 118th Field Regiment. My confidence grew even to the extent that I felt I could cheek the sergeant-majors when they came at you with their usual caustic clichés. It was always in fun and usually they would go along with my impertinence, seeing the opportunity for a bit of banter that they must have thought was good for morale. A classic was when our gun sergeant was telling us about something unpleasant he wanted us to do, and I pulled a face of disgruntlement.

'Are you giving me a funny look there, Anckorn?!' he bawled.

'No, Sergeant-Major. You've got one, but I didn't give it you,' I replied.

After a while, I got a bit of a reputation for my cheek and some saw me as a bit different from the rest of the lads. In any event, the day came when it was suggested to me that I might apply for a commission and go for officer training. My instincts were against it, however. The thing was that I didn't know if I would be a coward or not in action and I didn't like the thought of being in charge of other men and not being able to handle it. Besides, I really was very happy as a gunner in the 118th. Officer training would take me away and eventually lead to me being moved around to other regiments. The camaraderie would be lost. So, I stayed 'Gunner Anckorn'.

Meanwhile, outside our closed community of military training, the rest of the world was descending more and more into war. Not that the army kept us informed of it in any way. What little we did know came from the Pathé News in the cinemas, or from the wireless, as we called it then. As far as I was concerned, the hope was still within me that it would all be sorted out somehow and that real fighting would never happen for us – after all, the expected bombing had not taken place up to that time and evacuees were returning to London. People even talked of a 'Phoney War'. But the sinking of HMS *Royal Oak* in the big naval base at Scapa Flow in the Orkney Islands by a German submarine had made everyone gloomy, and the despatch of an expeditionary force to France that had built up to over 150,000 British troops suggested that, before too long, we could be out there with them. It had become a daily imperative for everyone to listen to the news and at the time of my birthday in December 1939, while I was home on leave, all ears were glued to the wireless during a broadcast about the *Graf Spee* incident. It was like listening to the Oxford and Cambridge boat race!

The *Graf Spee* was a German battleship that had gone into Montevideo for repairs after having been damaged by our warships in what became known later as the Battle of the River Plate. The *Graf Spee* had been allowed to stay for only twenty-four hours by the Uruguayan authorities. The reason for all the interest was that three of our warships, HMS *Exeter*, HMS *Ajax* and HMS *Achilles*, were lying outside the port, waiting for her to come out so that they could finish her off. As the deadline approached, the radio was reporting thousands of people lining the waterfront expecting to see the showdown between the ships. But then the Germans simply gave up and scuttled the *Graf Spee* without a fight. It gave us all good heart.

As we went into the New Year of 1940, the reality of war going on could no longer be denied. Rationing was introduced as a result of the increasing losses to shipping inflicted by German submarines and the cost of petrol was making it impossible for people who had private cars, my parents included, to run them.

But it was at this time that an event took place for me that would have more of an impact on my life than even the war could make. It was to be one of those 'Anckorn events' where bad things turn out to be for the good!

We were still in Woolwich at the turn of the year and one night I became very ill with pharyngitis. It was the night before our battery was to leave Woolwich for the first time and go to Eastbourne. One of the lads in my mess became concerned about my condition and called for the MO, who then had me immediately sent off to the Herbert Hospital in Woolwich at two in the morning. But I couldn't stay there long as it was full and so the next afternoon, I was put in an ambulance to be taken to Joyce Green Hospital in Dartford.

It was January 1940 – infamous for the Arctic freeze that gripped the country and for what we now know was an ice storm that happened in the south-east of England with freezing rain coming down for two days solid. At that time, it was girls driving those ambulances as part of the war effort and our driver was loaded up with five of us – I being the only stretcher case. We set off for Dartford with ice everywhere and our driver was skidding all over the road, throwing us around as if on a fairground ride. How we ever got there safely I'll never know. On arrival, the patients who could still walk got out and left me there on the stretcher with snow blowing in through the open doors. Eventually someone came and I was carried off into a ward, but they took me to the wrong one. They put me in the skin ward with patients that had all sorts of horrible diseases. Infectious ones, too. Someone in there had scarlet fever, which has an incubation period of three weeks. After the first three weeks, someone else went down with it. In the end I was in that place for two months. Then to top it all, I caught a skin disease myself, which was all over my face and had to be treated with gentian – a substance that turned my face fiercely violet. Worse still, gentian is a stain that takes weeks to remove. So there I was, eventually feeling better and ready to go but stuck in the hospital with this violet face, naïvely going into the sluice room every day, where there were floor brushes, hoping to scrub it off. It made no difference at all of course, and really, there was nothing I could do about it.

By way of conversation, the fellow in the next bed to me on the ward turned to me one day and said woefully, 'Your girl won't like that. You're not engaged, are you?'

'Oh god, no!' I said dismissively, 'I'm an athlete. I haven't time for going out with girls.'

'Aren't you ever going to get married then?' he asked.

'No,' I said, 'I can't see that ever happening.'

But just then, a new nurse, who had come on to the ward that day, came along and passed by our beds.

'If I ever do,' I said, 'I'll marry her.' I'd only seen her for five minutes the whole day long but that's all it needed. I really meant it!

Half my days were spent in the sluice after that, supposedly still trying to get the violet stain off, but only because this nurse, being a probationary nurse, would be in there cleaning out the bedpans.

Eventually I was discharged and I joined the regiment in Eastbourne, very white-faced. I reported to the Major but he told me that I'd been recommended for a fortnight's sick leave, which he thoroughly endorsed. I found out later that half the regiment was away on sick leave with measles. So I was off home that very night feeling on top of the world because I had met the girl whom I knew, one day, would be my wife. Her name was Lucille.

Once home, I made arrangements to meet her up at Dartford whenever she was off duty for an hour or so, and so we had many a cup of tea and a talk together in the town. She was on her own in the world and I had met her at a turning point in her life, as she had just taken up nursing.

What had led up to this made a harrowing tale. She had lost her mother when she was only thirty-two years old and her brother and sister had died young, too, leaving her with only her father. But he became something of a philanderer and matters came to a head one

23

day when she came home to find a strange woman coming into the hallway when she let herself in. Surprised, Lucille had asked, 'Who are you?', to which the woman replied, 'Well, I'll ask you the same question. Who do you think you are, just letting yourself in like that?' The incident made Lucille more or less turn on her heels and leave home for good after grabbing as many of her clothes and personal effects as she could. But she only had one penny on her. Thinking what on earth to do, she remembered that she had an aunt in the West Country and so she went to try and get herself there by train. She simply jumped onto the first train to London and used her wits to get herself onwards to Paddington. Then she used her 1d to buy a platform ticket and proceeded to conceal herself on the appropriate train that would take her all the way to where her aunt lived. It was late at night by the time she arrived there and as she walked up to her aunt's house, she wondered what her aunt would say when she opened the door. She needn't have worried. When her aunt opened the door, she said warmly, 'Come in, I've made a bed up for you.' Her aunt had been called on the telephone by Lucille's father, because he expected she might be going there. Next day, however, her uncle faced her with the fact that he didn't want to get embroiled in a family row and so she must return. He gave her money for the train fares and put her on a train back to London the very next day. By the time she arrived in London, however, she had resolved how she might never have to go back home again. During the journey, she had seen advertisements for nursing, which said that trainee nurses were given uniforms and special accommodation during their long training, and so she applied immediately on arrival back in London. That very night she was allowed to take up accommodation in Dartford, and her new life began. It wasn't long after that, that she had walked onto the ward at the Joyce Green Hospital.

Over the next eighteen months, Lucille would often come down to our house in Dunton Green at weekends when she was off duty and gradually, because she got on so well with my parents, our house became her real home.

But then, of course, the war was to intrude on all our lives in the months and years that were to follow and it would intrude in ways that would be unimaginably awful.

Chapter 3

SOLDIERING

While I'd been ensconced in the Joyce Green Hospital, the world out-side had continued to change and the condition of war had become even more marked.

Everywhere, there were posters of different kinds with dire warnings, telling us, for example, about the danger of 'careless talk' costing lives. Worryingly, there had been regular radio broadcasts from Germany by a certain William Joyce, whom everyone called Lord Haw Haw and who seemed to know a lot about everyday life in wartime Britain. He would comment on the smallest details such as a church clock in some small village having stopped and it gave the impression that Germany had eyes and ears everywhere.

The warnings and advice given by the posters was always carried in clever little slogans such as 'Loose lips can sink ships', and some delivered their message in ways that could also bring a faint smile at the same time.

Be like Dad.
Keep mum!

Wall's have Ices.
Walls have ears!

But the progress of the war presented very little to smile about.

By the time I finally rejoined my regiment in Eastbourne, the army had completely taken over the place, with no trace of civilian life anywhere. You couldn't get down to the seafront as it was blocked off with rows and rows of barbed wire and the hotels had all become officers' messes and things like that. Everybody you saw was in uniform – in the shops, in the pubs – everywhere. The only people not in uniform were women. In the streets there were army lorries, gun carriages and other assorted armoured vehicles clunking about and not a single private car. Everyone was busy going somewhere and doing something. It was army, army, everywhere – a hive of activity, contained within road blocks and barbed wire.

We all just got on with it – but some of it turned out to be not as bad as it could have been for me. Troops were billeted in private houses in the town and the army simply put as many soldiers into a house as they could. In some, where only a husband and wife were living, they'd put in ten of us and the men would sleep on the floor on palliasses. These were a sort of canvas sack, like a sleeping bag, but instead of getting in it you filled it with grass or straw and lay on top of it. That's what I expected when I arrived at my billet, but no! – heaven knows how, I got a bedroom, and what's more, the lady there had two daughters, aged about eighteen, who brought me a cup of tea every morning, each in turn!

Whilst the troops of my battery were assigned to tasks right down at the seafront, I, for my part, was thrown in at the deep end as a gun lorry driver or 'Driver IC', as the army called it.

The 118th were beginning to get some proper equipment at this time and had finally been issued with some proper gun lorries and limbers, although we were still using old 18-pounder guns and 4.5-inch Howitzers rather than the 25-pounders we were later to be issued with.

One of our battery officers, Captain Croft, had been appointing drivers just before I reported back for duty and my friend, Cliff Swann, had put my name forward in my absence, unbeknown to me. This meant that on my arrival, which happened to be just as my troop of four guns were about to leave for exercises up on Beachy Head, I was detailed to drive a brand new, four-wheel drive gun lorry, which they called a 'Quad' – a vehicle I'd never seen in my life before. It was a monster.

Cliff Swann walked me over to where 'mine' stood, attached to a limber and gun, ready for the off. I felt like a midget beside it with its massive tyres holding this solid great lump of heavy engineering off the ground by about 3 feet so that you had to reach up for the door handle. Opening the door and hauling myself up onto the footplate, I peered into a great wide cabin and scrutinised the driving position. It looked more than a handful compared to driving furniture lorries and I said to Cliff quietly, 'I don't think I can drive a thing like this!' He asserted that if he could do it with less than half the experience of driving that I'd had, then surely I could do it too. He had laid down a challenge!

The next thing I heard was the battery sergeant-major ordering us all into our vehicles and so there was I, fresh back from three months' sick leave, suddenly in charge of this beast of a vehicle with its articulated attachments, strung out some 50 feet behind.

Hardly had I got myself into the driving seat, when in climbed the gun detachment, filling the cabin beside and behind me. There was nothing for it but to just look confident as always and set off in convoy behind the others, but inside I was hoping I wouldn't send us all through the nearest plate glass shop window or demolish a house with the damn thing, en route.

Fortunately, the convoy moved slowly and I found that I took to this monster of a Quad straight away – or at least after I had got used to the terrific noise inside the cabin and the fact that the steering was extremely sensitive. By the time we got up to Beachy Head, I was ready to try out the multiple gears on rough terrain and to manoeuvre the gun and limber into any required position. It all went surprisingly well and when we returned to our compound, I learned that it was also the driver's responsibility to do basic maintenance on the vehicle too, along with an appointed mechanic, and it was clear to me that this job of gun lorry driver was going to be a real full-time occupation. Over the next few weeks, driving, cleaning and maintenance became my daily routine and I found myself proud to be 'IC' and knowledgeable about the lorry.

But the pace of the war seemed now to be changing rapidly.

Within those first few weeks of being back with my regiment, Germany invaded both Denmark and Norway, and Russia bombed Helsinki and invaded Finland. Then, shortly after that, the Pathé News in the cinemas was reporting that Germany had more or less walked into Holland and Belgium without a fight, and hardly any time later, reports were that they had stormed into France. Our Expeditionary Force was in action over there and here, Neville Chamberlain resigned as prime minister to be replaced by Winston Churchill, whom we heard sometime later was promising nothing but 'blood, toil, tears and sweat'.

Not long after that, Dunkirk happened – the evacuation of our vanquished Expeditionary Force from a continent that now appeared to be totally in German hands. There was increasing talk of the Germans possibly invading us too.

In the weeks that followed Dunkirk, I was doing sentry duty up on the heights behind Bexhill – a place called Little Common. Through powerful binoculars, I saw people coming over from France in rowing boats, two or three people at a time – not soldiers, just ordinary folk. I could see the poor devils being seasick and in a terrible state after rowing and drifting for days. Some looked injured. It was my job to identify everything coming over and enter what I saw in a log.

As fears grew by the day that we would be the next on the list for a German invasion, I was now to find myself thrust into the front line when I turned up for one of these sentry duties. It was dark and pouring with rain, really driving rain. My greatcoat, which came down to my ankles, was soaked through even before I went on duty. That coat was lovely, but when it was soaked full of water, it was as heavy as lead.

Anyway, I trudged onwards for my stint up on the heights and when I got to our station, there was the sergeant waiting for me.

'Now look here,' he said, 'this is your *telephone exchange.*'

Well, I knew nothing about telephone exchanges or why one was up there, of all places. It was on a stand exposed to the pouring rain.

'Why, Sergeant-Major, what's that for?' I asked.

'The only person between Hitler and Bexhill tonight, Anckorn, is you!' was his startling reply.

'You just keep your eyes on the Channel and if you see two red things go up in the sky, then you have to phone the mayor immediately. All you do is crank this handle here, speak into the phone and you'll get the mayor. Then they can evacuate.'

My first thought was that if I did see those red lights go up, I'd be the *first* to evacuate!

So there he left me, pacing up and down with my rifle and with a belief that at any moment, I might be the first to witness an imminent German invasion. The responsibility of it gradually dawned on me and I felt proud to be up there with everyone's safety entrusted to me while they slept. I would give the alarm that would awaken the sleeping lion and unleash everything we'd got onto that mischievous and rampant enemy! I welled up with the significance of it all, to hell with a bit of rain.

Then it occurred to me that I'd better make certain I could actually work the telephone exchange, so I thought it would be reasonable to ring up the mayor and say 'testing, testing', or something, as a check. So, I picked up the phone, cranked the handle vigorously as instructed and ... landed flat on my back having nearly knocked myself out with an electric shock! It turned out the coil in the exchange generated what felt like a thousand volts at the rate I had cranked it and of course, the whole set was soaking wet!

Nevertheless, from that night onwards, sentry duty, or 'sentry go', as we called it, remained something special for me and something I was always proud to do.

We all took our turns at sentry go, and the worst thing about it for most lads was that, if you'd been on leave and having a lovely weekend, you just knew that when you got back to the regiment, it would be sentry go for you that same night. Our sergeant-majors always knew how to bring you back with a bump. As I actually liked doing sentry, it wasn't too bad for me and I would willingly do sentry go for others.

Our battery was moved to various places across Sussex during the spring and early summer of 1940, and at some of them we had to guard ammunitions stores – huge bunkers full of bombs, bullets and shells, usually hidden in woods. Well that was fine for me. I loved doing sentry in the woods, because in standing still on a moonlit night, you could see all the foxes and other animals wandering around. After a while, some would come right up close, too. On one occasion, a rabbit scampered out of the wood and sat on my boot! Then, out of the wood came a fox. He was after the rabbit but the rabbit must have thought I was good protection and just stayed put. I stared at the fox and breathed 'Clear off!' He looked back at me for a moment, then turned round and slunk away. When he'd gone, the rabbit just hopped off my boot and ran away into the night. How nice to know I was guardian of the rabbits as well as the ammunition stores!

The sentry duties I did for other people were often in the woods because the boys from London couldn't stand the stillness and quiet. They were used to trams and trains going all night – and suddenly they'd be in the middle of nowhere and often in pitch-black. If there was as much as a blackbird landing in some leaves, they'd been known to fire their rifle and turn the guard out! If they heard crashing in the woods, they'd think it was the Germans, but it would be a deer or something. Mind you, I wasn't so bright a couple of times.

There was an event when I was doing sentry go in a lane on the perimeter of a wood that concealed a typical hoard of ammunition. The stillness of the night was broken by a panting noise and it gradually got louder and louder, coming towards me. I quietly prepared my rifle and stood still in the middle of the lane, eyes bulging, ready to challenge the oncoming raider. Then, as well as the panting, there was a padding noise, too. I raised my rifle, finger on trigger, holding my breath. Out of the darkness it emerged ... a dog! He didn't even look at me as he padded straight past. On another occasion, I was convinced there were Germans in a field next to me – on the march. Once again I was on the brink of turning the guard out as I crept across to the hedge between me and this field to get a good view. It was a herd of cows chewing the cud!

In those weeks after Dunkirk, when we were moved from place to place, it never occurred to us that the places we were sent to were tactical deployments in the face of an ever-increasing threat of German invasion. Little did we know that the authorities were anticipating a German invasion force that could infiltrate at points anywhere along the East and South East coasts of Britain between Norfolk and Portsmouth. The facts now known are that they expected up to 15,000 airborne troops and 50,000 seaborne troops north of the Thames, and 20,000 airborne and 50,000 seaborne troops south of the Thames.

Our regimental commander, Lieutenant-Colonel C.E. MacKellar, did eventually make our purpose clear, however, in a directive issued during the early summer in what we would come to know as his typical defiant and warlike tone.

Throughout any emergency which may arise, all groups and parties will act with the maximum speed and boldness and all possible means will be employed to prevent the enemy establishing themselves in any area where the 118th Field Regiment are.

Shortly after that our complete regiment was moved up to Norfolk. It was a long trek at a maximum speed of 20mph to our destination near Thetford on the other side of Newmarket towards Norwich. We encamped just near a wonderful forest, which has since become Thetford Forest Park. I yearned to go running in it but no such luck. There was a lot going on. Our move to Norfolk was because we were leaving 12th Division and becoming part of a new division, the 18th Infantry Division, made up of regiments that were predominantly based in the East Anglia area. A big re-organisation was going on in this, our new area, and we were detailed to relieve gun positions from vacating regiments. So, within a few days we were on the move again, this time closer to Norwich, at Taverham, and there would be more moves to come in what turned out to be a restless, anxious and increasingly hostile year.

But for us ordinary gunners, far removed from worrisome deliberations about the defence of our island, just doing as we were told to, life was more simple and foolish.

There was much movement of senior officers and visits by top brass during that time, sometimes at short notice. On one such visitation, I was still cleaning muck off my lorry after an exercise, when word suddenly went round that the dignitaries were only minutes away. Our battery sergeant-major came up and told me to get my lorry off and out of it – 'Go anywhere, go up the lanes, just disappear,' he cried, in order that my vehicle wouldn't be seen in the state it was. So I and another fellow, Bombardier Christian, did just that.

Well, not knowing how long we should stay away exactly, we started to wander around the lanes and get up to mischief. We came upon an orchard, its trees bursting with fruit. The farmer had wisely trimmed his trees so that lower branches couldn't be reached by thieving hands from the ground. This was a job for the Quad.

We didn't want to leave tyre tracks in the field by driving up to the trees so we thought we'd make use of the heavy towing wire and powered roller that we had on the back of the Quad instead. We wrapped the wire around the trunk of the nearest tree to the road and I got the tree shaking by easing the Quad back and forth, slipping the clutch. Perfect! Apples aplenty! Just then, Christian caught sight of the vehicles of the top brass entourage some distance away across the fields, heading along the very lane that would lead to us. Shouting to me that we should get going, he jumped into the cabin without releasing the wire and we made off. The tree came clean out of the ground and we dragged it along the road behind us, until we could turn onto another lane that luckily went off at a tangent. The top brass whooshed past and mustn't have seen us, camouflaged as we would have been by the tree. Fortunately, nothing came of it.

One of the gun positions we were detailed to relieve at the end of July that year was near Cromer, on the north Norfolk coast – to us an idyllic situation in what had turned out to be a hot summer. We manned fixed French 75s hidden in caves on the seashore, aimed out to sea, ready for enemy ships appearing over the horizon. But the war seemed far away for us down there on the beach – so much so that we found occasion to strip off and enjoy the sunshine – with the permission of our gun sergeants, on the proviso we kept our rifles in hand!

The real threat was not to come from the sea during that summer of 1940, but from the air. We now know, of course, that Germany was preparing for an invasion in September by bombing our airfields and attempting to destroy our fighter planes on the ground. But they had got more of a fight on their hands than they bargained for, in what became known as the Battle of Britain.

In Norfolk, the incursions by German aircraft were relatively few in number but the skies in the south-east of England became more and more infested with aircraft as summer progressed. Each time I came home on leave, I would see our fighters up there, battling it out with the Germans and creating white tangled contrails all over the sky with all the ducking and diving going on. You could actually stand and watch the dogfights taking place.

One day, when I was coming home on leave for a weekend, it all got a bit too close for comfort. I'd got as far as Sidcup by some means or other and then I had to walk the rest of the way to our house in Dunton Green along the main roads. As I was walking, a German fighter plane suddenly came screaming down out of the sky and turned level, flying low over the ground – right towards me, no more than 50 feet up. He was flying like hell and then I saw why. There was a Spitfire after him! Within seconds, they were both coming up the road towards me, with the Spitfire firing his guns. I dived for cover over a bank and into a gully as these two screamed past, flat-out, straight along the road and up and over a hill, disappearing on the other side. I listened for a crash or any other sign of them but there was nothing.

Back in Norfolk, much of our duties became focussed on airfields and in the autumn we were stationed at Worstead, to the north-east of Norwich, not far from an airfield at Scottow, which became known as Coltishall. This was an airfield at which the fighter pilot Douglas Bader was in charge. Our battery was positioned to put the airfield out of action by shelling it, in the event of any attempt by Germans to land there. We had set up a Forward Observation post on the perimeter of the airfield, in an oak tree, and kept watch from there round the clock. We'd managed to hoist a couple of old armchairs up there to make ourselves comfortable and I was on watch duties with my friend Cliff Swann. The watch-keeping had become perilous because German bombers had started a routine of coming in low over the coast just before nightfall hoping to hit our fighters on the ground before they could take off – thinking that they would be unlikely to take to the air as night fell because of the difficulties of landing again in the dark. Cliff and I were on watch together when we saw a single German bomber coming in low and heading in our direction. It was a Junkers 88 and we watched him through our binoculars until we saw that he was lining up for a run with his bomb doors open. Two bombs emerged, one after the other, and their trajectory was in a straight line towards us. After the first landed it was pretty obvious the second was heading for us! Without a word to each other we instinctively jumped for it, landing in a leaf-filled cutting below us just before the second bomb exploded less than 50 yards away. Rising from our bed of leaves, we both stood there, dazed and in amazement, as we realised we'd just jumped a good 30 feet down from the tree without even thinking about it. Thank heavens for the bed of leaves that had softened our fall and the depth of the cutting that had sheltered us from the bomb blast.

This was our first experience of bombing and only a small taste of what was to come. The heavy bombing of London that we'd all expected from the start of the war twelve months earlier, finally started in that autumn and history records it as the Blitz. Being stationed in Norfolk, none of the heavy bombing came our way but I began to dread going home on leave.

However, it was around this time, that army life completely changed for me and my soldiering days ceased – for a while.

When our regiment had become part of the 18th Infantry Division at the start of the summer, there occurred shortly after that a change to the command of that division. The new commanding officer was Major General Beckwith-Smith DSO, MC, who had distinguished himself with the BEF at Dunkirk. He would prove to be the making of the 18th Division, getting it fully armoured and intensively trained so that all its regiments could work together as a single force. Under his command it was to become a real pride of the British Army. He was a commander that understood the men and got them on his side. In taking on the 18th Division he got things done just as he wanted and one of the things he wanted was a divisional concert party.

Chapter 4

CONCERT PARTY

The divisional concert party wasn't just any old concert party that was common in those days. It was an *Army* concert party – the 18th Infantry Division Concert Party, sanctioned and auditioned at the highest level. Once formed, small as it was, the concert party was like a regiment in its own right, with a mission to entertain the troops in the division, whenever and wherever required.

All regiments of the division were invited to send men who had any kind of performing talent for audition. I was the only magician sent up, so I thought there may be a slim chance of being selected.

The auditions were held in Norwich, in front of all the 'red-tabs' – our senior officers. At my audition, there were brigadiers and colonels on either side of the Major-General and all were sitting expectantly as I made an entrance. Well normally, I'd be frightened of a corporal, let alone a general, but once I was doing my magic again, it didn't seem to matter. I treated them all just like any other audience and it was a joy, as always, to see the looks on their faces when I deceived them with my sleight of hand! It seemed that while I was on that stage, I was a different person and no longer Gunner Anckorn.

My audition act finished with a flourish. I complimented them all for being such an appreciative audience and said I would leave them with a trick they could do themselves, adding that I wasn't really supposed to, under the rules of the Magic Circle, 'but as they had been so good . . .'

I took out a silk handkerchief from my top pocket and invited them to do the same. Major-General Beckwith-Smith led the others and pulled out a red polka dot handkerchief from his top pocket, laughing heartily whilst doing so, and this was matched by the rest of them. I let my handkerchief hang from one hand, indicating that they should do the same and then straightened it out nicely with the other, again indicating that they should do the same. When I then waved my handkerchief up and down, they all followed suit and I bowed, thanked them all and continued waving as I walked off the stage backwards, saying goodbye!

I was accepted into the concert party.

From those that came up for audition from the regiments, a troupe emerged. We had two very good pianists, Cyril Wycherley and George Appleton – George being the one who would brilliantly improvise the walk-on music for our introductions at each show and much of the incidental music. Cyril was a first-class accompanist, being able to play any music put in front of him. He could play anything you liked, having picked up just about every popular song by ear. We had a top rate violinist, Denis East, who had played in the London Philharmonic Orchestra, and a really top accordionist, Fred Coles. Then we had two very good singers, an actor fellow who could perform anything we dreamed up and an impersonator, Ollie Thomas. I, of course, was the magician.

We called ourselves 'The Optimists', which was to cheekily associate ourselves with the 'Co-Optimists', who were a well-known and liked troupe that had been around in civilian life for some years. One of their players later became a household name, Stanley Holloway. For my part, I was 'Wizardus'. This was a stage name that my father had come up with when I first started doing magic for money. My idea had been to have an Indian sounding name because in those days, everyone thought of magic as something to do with the mystical East. I had come up with 'Ali Khan' as a name but my father advised that such a name could actually be someone's and might consequently get me into legal trouble. 'What you need is a completely made up name,' he said, and he came up with Wizardus on the spot.

Anyway, now that we were 'Concert Party' we were cut out of everyday soldiering – no parades at all, except pay parade, which we would attend at whatever barracks we happened to be in. We were also allowed to dress as we liked, with open-collar shirts and no webbed anklets, so our trousers were like ordinary slacks. We could even wear brown shoes if we wanted! So we were much envied by those that knew us and I think the rest of the soldiery thought we were civilians, drafted in from ENSA. That was the joint forces' entertainments organisation set up just after war was declared, with the same purpose as us, but aimed at all the armed forces. The letters stood officially for Entertainments National Service Association, which later, of course, became degraded, in good army fashion, to 'Every Night Something Awful'.

We might just as well have not been in the army given our new lifestyle. We lived like lords on occasion. Usually we would be quartered away from any barracks and in Norwich, where we got started, they put us up in the Bishop's Palace, of all places. We were the only people in there and each of us had a bedroom to ourselves with en-suite everything and beds that had quilts and soft pillows. How the clergy lived – lap of luxury! We got kicked out of the Bishop's Palace in the end for nearly setting the kitchen on fire by mistake. We'd stupidly left some oil in a pan on the stove while we went to pay parade at the nearby barracks. We expected to come back to make ourselves fish and chips but instead came back to a notice of eviction.

In the first month or so of being Concert Party, we were left to our own devices but our job was to get round to all the regiments in time, wherever they happened to be stationed. Regimental HQs were often in big stately homes and these would usually have their own entertainment halls, enabling us to put shows on there in plush surroundings. Mostly, however, we would be building our own stage in the middle of nowhere in order to do our entertaining.

We used to travel around in a 10 ton lorry with all our gear, aiming to be at a place by five o'clock or thereabouts and to get the curtain up at seven o'clock. Within that couple of hours, we would put up our own portable stage, which had a full proscenium arch and curtains. We were especially proud of our curtains, which we made to draw nice and smoothly using windscreen wiper motors off another lorry – so very professional! At each location we would also use any spare time before the show to find out who the 'character' sergeant-majors were in the regiment we were visiting. We'd get to know what kind of mannerisms they had and the clichés they used, in order that we could mimic them in the show. All the classics were there:

Don't look at me when I'm talking to you! If you want a picture of me I'll give you one!

Don't look down when you're marching! If there's any money down there I'll 'av it!

Our Ollie Thomas did the impersonations and he brought the house down every time.

The shows were made up of all kinds of sketches, plays and general buffoonery, with all of us contributing ideas and performing them, whilst those of us with speciality skills would also have our own spot. Mine, of course, was conjuring tricks.

My stage presence as Wizardus was established by my being dressed in white tie and tails, no matter where the show was held. The contrast with the rest of the players in the show was always dramatic.

Our opening scene in a show would often be a nightclub setting with George Appleton playing some improvised music on the piano and the rest of the cast sitting around a table, playing cards. Our compère would be front of stage to introduce each player at the table in turn and that player would then give a short rendition of his speciality. Denis East used to get up with his violin and produce the exact sound of an air raid siren and incidentally, at the end of the show, he'd do the 'All clear' as well. When everyone else had done their bit, I would be announced and I would walk on in my white tie and tails, moving to each of the players around the table, producing aces or colour cards from behind their ears and vanishing them again. After these introductions we would clear the stage and the first act would commence.

I would always do two sets in the show. The first would be silent and done completely to the music that George would create. Typically in this set I would walk on producing lit cigarettes out of thin air and then vanish them again, after drawing on each to prove it was real. Then I might do various tricks with a piece of thin rope – cutting it and putting it back together again or making it extend and so on. Then I might do the billiard balls trick, producing first one, then two, then three, then four billiard balls between my upheld fingers and vanishing them again. Various playing card flourishes would also come into the act as well as tricks with coloured silk handkerchiefs. In the second half of the show, my set would involve the audience and I would do predictions and memory challenges.

We found we could do practically anything together and had such fun doing so. We were a good mob! The shows would have graced any stage in London.

Unfortunately, the London stages were by then mostly silent because of the Blitz. We were miles away from it up in Norfolk, but it meant that coming home on leave was a very unnerving experience.

On my first leave during the Blitz, I came through London in daytime and was horrified to see the devastation. When I finally got home it was evening and my twin sister greeted me saying it was fortunate that there were still a couple of hours until 'the raid'.

'What raid?' I said.

'Air raid,' she said, and added in matter-of-fact tone, 'every night, regular as clockwork, about seven o'clock.'

Sure enough, just before seven o'clock, all the sirens went off and the damn bombers arrived shortly afterwards. I was frightened out of my skin. My parents and my sister just got on with their evening as if things were normal! Every night this happened. The bombers would come over and drop their loads on London in wave after wave and when they had finished, they might drop the odd remaining bomb randomly on Sussex or Kent as they headed back to Germany. I couldn't take it all as easily as the rest of the family seemed to.

On another leave, I arrived in London by train and as I left the station, the air raid sirens went off. The drill I'd been taught as a soldier was first of all, to put my tin hat on and pull my gas mask into position. This meant bringing the mask in its holder from where it hung at my waist, up onto my chest, where it could hang just below my chin, ready for use if needed. Then the drill was to take shelter somewhere. So I did all that and started to look around for a shelter – plenty of them in London by this time. But everyone was staring at me as if I was mad. I suddenly realised that I was the only one running and the only one done up with tin hat and gas mask at the ready like that! Everyone else was just walking about normally. So I went up to a policeman who was nearby.

'Isn't there an air raid on?' I asked.

'Yes,' he said, 'there is. Why?'

'Well, aren't we supposed to be getting into shelters?' I said innocently.

'*You* can go into a shelter if you want to!' he replied in derogatory manner, probably unimpressed by the wariness displayed by a man in a soldier's uniform. I learned later that Londoners generally took no notice of the sirens until bombers were actually overhead. A sense of 'carry on regardless' was even more evident in cinemas. They would just flash up a message on the screen:

AIR RAID
BOMBERS OVERHEAD
You may stay if you wish

Many would do just that and the film would continue.

Anyway, there I was – a soldier frightened out of his skin, while civilians just took it all in their stride. Even though I would be coming home to see Lucille, it was always a relief when my leave ended and I could get back to peaceful Norfolk and the concert party.

After our first month or so of performances, we were joined by a civilian producer who'd come from ENSA and we became a little more theatrical. He obtained pierrot outfits in the divisional colours, which we were to wear during performances. These were just like the ones you'd see a troupe wearing down at any seaside pier in those days and of course, just like the Co-Optimists. Ours were black tops with yellow pompoms, white neck furls and yellow silk trousers. He spared us the conical hats!

Dressed in our pierrot outfits, we would come on as a troupe singing cheerily and dancing about.

Hello e-v-e-r-y-b-o-d-y, how do you do
Hello e-v-e-r-y-b-o-d-y, you and you and you and you ...
... etc ... etc.

But our civilian ENSA man didn't stay for long. I think he got exasperated with our tomfoolery and probably didn't appreciate the army parlance jokes and quite possibly some of our acts, too. Ollie Thomas could do a perfect impersonation of Edward VIII, which was immediately recognisable the second he walked on and he would have the audience in stitches when he started saying, 'I'm not this evening with the lady that I l-o-v-e.' But when he mimicked the king's stutter, it became all too much and he was told to drop the whole 'Royals' thing.

There was another act that got us into trouble, too.

We had met an RAF fellow around Norwich, who was based at one of the airfields, and he had been a ventriloquist in civilian life. Unlike most ventriloquists though, his dolls were life-sized, so he could dance with them. Tap dancing was one part of his act. He was doing his act frequently and successfully in the RAF so we asked him to come and have a spot on our show. He turned up and did this show but it created a hell of a row. He'd said, in talking with his dummy, 'I eat meat all day and it makes me as strong as an Ox,' and the dummy replied, 'Well I eat fish all day but I can't swim a bloody stroke!' Well, this was the cathedral city of Norwich we were in and they had a Public Standards Watch committee that would censor bad language wherever it was heard, and especially on the stage. Swearing on stage was generally taboo anyway in those days but in Norwich, you couldn't even say anything like 'damn' or 'blast' or you'd be up for it. Sure enough, the Watch committee were there and they were on their feet demanding that the show close and the audience leave at once!

So after the ENSA man left, exclaiming to us all, 'You make me sick to my stomach!' an army lieutenant was put in charge of us. Lieutenant Mackwood. He seemed to have a lot of show experience from some-where or other and the strange thing was that not only was his wife allowed to join us, but also another girl who was a friend of hers. What's more, Mrs Mackwood brought her little dog with her, too – a dachshund. It was unheard of to have two women in a concert party but we did, and they travelled with us everywhere – Johnny Mackwood's wife trailing her little dog that she called Gina alongside her. No wonder the troops laughed, seeing us walking along altogether with a German sausage dog in tow! The girls had both been in theatre proper as chorus line and yes, heads did turn! Johnny Mackwood's wife was the typical dancing girl, very pretty, tall and slender. She would always be over-made-up with blue eyelids – and those were only ever seen in pantomime in those days. They kept themselves to themselves and there was no impropriety as far as I knew. That sort of thing didn't happen then, everything was very proper. In any event, they were not with us for long and so it became just Johnny Mackwood – first-class producer, compère and ideas man, plus ourselves.

In January 1941, the entire 18th Division decamped from East Anglia and went in a vast convoy of over 1,000 vehicles up to Scotland. It was, I understand, the first movement of its kind over such a distance – a complete mechanised army division in one go. On arrival, the brigades and regiments disposed themselves across the Border areas around a divisional HQ based in Melrose. In the months to follow, it meant that our concert party would be doing shows at all points of the compass around Melrose, such as Earlston to the north, Darnick, Galashiels, Walkerburn, Peebles and Kirkurd to the north-west, Selkirk, Moffat, Dumfries and Castle Douglas a long way to the south-west, then Hawick and Stobs Castle to the south, and up to Ancrum and Kelso in the east. I didn't mind – the further away from London and the Blitz the better it was as far as I was concerned. Indeed, as we toured around, we were relieved to find that life seemed very normal. You could even get cream teas in the cafés. But it wasn't to last. The bombers eventually followed us up there.

We were doing our show at the local corn exchange in Melrose the night bombers were seen for the first time in Scotland. They flew over just before the start of the show, heading for Glasgow, and it took many minutes for them to pass, there being so many. Although none were coming our way, I was still apprehensive going back to our billet after the show, as I knew from living in Kent that bombers would often drop any bombs left over, randomly, as they made their way home. I was doubly apprehensive for another reason.

At the end of the show, we had been met as we went off by a crowd of girls and a couple of them had offered to take our pierrot outfits to get them cleaned. The yellow silk trousers certainly had got very filthy, so it seemed like a good idea if they could get them back to us the following night for the show. Well, I had walked that evening down to the town from our billet, wearing the pierrot outfit under my greatcoat. On the outside I looked like any soldier with the yellow trousers tucked into my army boots and a pair of anklets round. So, on the way back, trouserless, I had only my underpants on under the greatcoat. If anything had happened and they found me dressed like that ...!

Our billet in Melrose was not a place to enjoy returning to after our forays into the border towns. It was an old derelict hotel, which we shared with a crowd of other soldiers. Our mob was allocated a bare attic room with a broken window and the winter of 1940 turned out to be one of the coldest on record. Because of my love of fresh air I had chosen to sleep by the window, which turned out to be not such a good idea when the snow was blowing in at night and temperatures fell to minus 30 degrees.

It was so cold in that old hotel that some of the soldiers in the rest of the building were tearing up floorboards to burn them on the open fireplaces that were still functional. A local lady took pity on the other soldiers while we were away one day – thinking of them putting up with the cold and having no entertainment. So she had an old grand piano brought down to the hotel imagining that they would make good use of it. They did. They smashed it up and used it on their fires.

We were mortified when we came back to find what had gone on. A perfectly good piano!

But the best of our time in Scotland, the event that made it all worthwhile, was a show we put on in Edinburgh. It was put on for the public as well as the troops. Johnny Mackwood had arranged for us to put the show on in the huge Odeon cinema there, called the New Victoria. This was an imposing structure with four Doric columns creating an entrance to a theatre that could seat 2,000 people. Unbelievably, there were queues right around the block when it came to show night and there was not a spare seat in the house. I had an uncle and cousins in the area and it was fortunate that I had made a point of getting seats for them in advance. We did a two-hour show to uproarious applause and left that night feeling that we probably made a bit of a name for ourselves.

It wasn't the only time we made a name for ourselves, however.

In April 1941, as spring made a mooted effort to appear in Scotland, most of the regiments moved back south into the Midlands area of England, and we went with them. It was on the journey that we 'distinguished' ourselves – this time with the authorities. We were on a troop train heading down to Uttoxeter and playing cards amongst ourselves when some Red Caps came into the carriage – Military Police, that is. They were after us because they'd seen us get on the train dressed improperly, as they thought. They didn't know we were Concert Party. When they found us playing cards for money they must have thought they were on to something, judging by the looks on their faces. However, we explained that we were Concert Party and to lighten the situation I said, 'Why don't you join us?' Fortunately, they did. Well, I produced a marked pack and we started a game of pontoon. Each time the dealer asked a Red Cap 'What do you want?' he would also glance at me because I knew what the next card was going to be. We skinned those Red Caps for every penny they'd got and they didn't twig. However, sometime later we were putting on a show at a regimental HQ near Milford, which was also the Red Caps' HQ, and two of the Red Caps we'd fleeced on the train were in the audience. Needless to say, they recognised me and they very definitely twigged then!

It was all just a wonderful experience because we were performing in all sorts of different places. Now that we were in the Midlands area we were going out and about again and got to places like Walsall, Rugely, Penkridge, Wolverhampton, Madeley, Nantwich and Crewe. We were doing a show virtually every night and moving on to places new. Once we had the shows done to a tee, we could arrive at a place by lunchtime and then wander around the local town doing anything we liked until it was show time. It was a rare experience and no one could touch us!

The great thing for me was that I was doing my magic every night. In the end I could do it at the drop of a hat in any situation, drunk or sober – nothing fazed me. The funny thing was that I'd always been a shy person but every time I got on the stage I didn't care how many people there were in the audience or what their status was – I just became extremely confident. What's more, the concert party seemed to be going on for such a long time that we all began to think we'd be doing it for the rest of the war.

But then, later in that spring of 1941, we did a show in which one of the closing scenes included a song called *Gloomy Sunday*. It was an odd song to choose as it really was gloomy and it was supposed to have a jinx on it because some people associated with creating or performing it had actually committed suicide. Our producer, Johnny Mackwood, said we shouldn't do it because it would bring us bad luck but we went ahead and did it anyway, thinking it would make a difference if we did it in our own particular style. He was right. We were called back to our regiments the very next week and the concert party was disbanded.

Chapter 5

SOMETHING OR NOTHING

Putting the concert party days behind me and getting back to soldiering again wasn't easy. The odd thing was that although we had toured around every conceivable regimental location, we had never performed for my own – the 118th Field Regiment. Needless to say, there was much ribbing about my now being 'a spare part' and much talk about all the field practice they'd all had and I, of course, had not, after leaving them when we were in Norfolk. They enjoyed telling me how they had taken delivery of the new 25-pounder guns just before going up to Scotland and how they now reckoned that firing ten rounds a minute was like 'a stroll on the pier', which I took to be jibe at the typical end of pier pierrots that they imagined we had been in the concert party.

As things were, the regiment was still on anti-invasion duties. The Blitz of London had been going on all the time I was in the concert party and Birmingham had been bombed several times while we were up in Scotland. When our regiment had come south, their job was all to do with Birmingham. In fact, the war records show that the purpose of all regiments in that area, and at Stourbridge, where the 118th had first camped before moving to Milford, was to destroy any enemy airborne landings at airfields and any successful enemy seaborne landings in South Wales that could advance on Birmingham.

When, at the beginning of May, Liverpool got their version of the Blitz, it seemed to us that Germany was intent on bombing every city in the country. Everyone was becoming intensely interested in the news as we wondered daily where all this was going to finish up.

It was while I and other drivers were cleaning off and doing routine maintenance on our vehicles that we heard something on the radio that produced stunned silence amongst us.

The Deputy Führer of Germany, Rudolf Hess, landed last night in Scotland and has been taken prisoner.

What's that all about? I thought. Has an invasion finally happened somewhere and failed? What's going on? This was Hitler's Deputy that had landed! Is the war to end?

But there was no more said about it then.

My childish hopes that I might never actually have to fight had suddenly re-surfaced with that item of news but those hopes sank again when no more was said except that this man had parachuted from a plane that he'd been flying solo and the plane had crashed.

We carried on with our routines. The war went on. We were left mystified.

Had I been more in touch with goings on in those days, I might have read in a newspaper, a few days later, the comment about the Duke of Hamilton. It was near his family estate in Scotland and not far, in fact, from where we had been based that Hess had landed. The newspaper believed that Hess was trying to get to the duke in order to negotiate a peace settlement. I might have noticed too, that intense and devastating bombing of London on 10 May occurred the very same night as Hess's landing. The bombing was not only the heaviest so far, killing nearly 1,500 people and making more than 10,000 homeless, but bombers made direct hits on the Houses of Parliament and other important buildings. It proved to be the last big bombing raid on London for the entire war, so something had come to a head at that time and it seems perhaps that I was not the only one harbouring thoughts and hopes that the war might be stopped. But whatever it was, nothing came of it and we certainly heard no more about it then.

More has of course become known, or at least speculated upon since the war. It seems that Hitler had notions of a negotiated peace with us right back at the time of Dunkirk, the year earlier, and it is said that the reason our troops got away from France in such numbers was largely because Hitler had stopped the advance of a huge tank force that might otherwise have annihilated us. The suggestion has been that, encouraged by some influential hierarchy in Britain, Hitler thought that a pact was possible and that our forces might join with Germany in an assault on Communist Russia. He saw no point in destroying us completely at Dunkirk if that could be brought about. Unfortunately for him, Winston Churchill had become Prime Minister in the weeks before Dunkirk and he was to put an end to any notions of appeasement. Instead, he set about invigorating the country to face the long fight that he saw ahead. Nevertheless, there were those who persisted with secret talks follow-ing Dunkirk – talks that went on for a full year, apparently ending only when the flight by Hess failed.

History now tells us that in May 1941, Hitler faced a situation that he hadn't expected. The invasion of Britain had not been possible; the bombing of Britain had not cowed the nation into submission and an 'unauthorised' attempt by Hess at direct negotiation on the back of heavy bombing had also failed. So it seems that within a month he abandoned his notion of an alliance with Britain to attack Russia, and set about attacking Russia alone. Hitler's 'Operation Barbarossa' was unleashed on 22 June.

For our part, exercises started in earnest at that time and the rumour was that the division was to be mobilised for action in a 'tropical climate'. But the place we went to first for practice camp was far from tropical. It was Trawsfynydd, in North Wales, not far from Ffestiniog. A more desolate, cold and eternally wet part of our islands would be difficult to find, I thought. The conditions might have explained why we managed to get our range and direction completely wrong on one firing, with the result that we landed a shell in the centre of Ffestiniog!

No sooner had that exercise finished than we were taking part in another and then another. What turned out to be the last big exercise was around a place called Builth Wells, in South Wales, and after that there was respite.

Within the division as a whole, we were now part of 55th Brigade and they decided to hold a summer sports day in Stourbridge. Of course, my regiment were looking to me again to perform but I hadn't done any specific training this time and hadn't been out running for a long while. Never mind, I didn't see why I shouldn't go, and I was duly entered on behalf of the regiment. I said I would do my usual – the quarter-mile, as well as a sprint event, the 100 yards.

On the day, there was a fellow entrant from another regiment in the quarter-mile who came with many supporters and all the gear – spiked running shoes, the lot. He was a quartermaster sergeant with a typically 'robust' character, confident he was going to win the race. The format of the race was a long straight to begin with followed by a run round the track and then back down the same straight to the finish.

Well, from the start, this man led the field and as we went down the straight he was rhythmically chanting to his supporters along the side 'E-e-e-zy, e-e-zy, all too e-e-zy!' in rhythm with his stride. He didn't realise that at least two of us in that race could run a damn sight faster than him. We let him set the pace although his lead narrowed as we went round the track and by the time we all came back to the long straight, he was visibly panting. I finished convincingly a good 25 yards ahead of him.

After I'd taken the tape, battery Sergeant-Major Wilshire came up to me.

'I got to hand it to you, Anckorn,' he said, 'I thought you was just ponsin' about doing nothing in that concert party, but I see you've kept yourself fit!'

44

I went on to win the 100 yards as well for the regiment and at the prize giving, our divisional commander, Major-General Beckwith-Smith acknowledged me when I came up saying, 'Well done, Anckorn. Another of your magic tricks, eh!' and gave one of his great shoulder bobbing hearty laughs in the process.

That night I was brought down to earth again – literally. We were sleeping on the floor at our billet for the night, and during that night, I got the most horrendous cramp in my legs that caused me to writhe around on the floor, madly. The fellows in the same room thought I was having some kind of terrible nightmare and tried holding me down and bringing me to my senses. I screamed that it was cramp and so they left me to it until it finally passed. So much for supposedly keeping myself fit! It turned out to be more than cramp, too, as I finished up in hospital with pains just about everywhere. As to nightmares, well, little did I know it, but there would be plenty of those to come.

After the sports day and my embarrassing but requisite stay in hospital, I returned to camp near Uttoxeter in the Midlands, and it didn't seem very long after that the 18th Division was called upon to achieve its purpose. The mobilisation was on. The 118th Field Regiment was to be in place for shipment overseas on 22 October 1941 as part of 55th Infantry Brigade and all leave was to be completed by 20 October. We were to get just a week of leave before embarkation.

So there it was, my childish hopes of never actually fighting were finally dashed. We were off, to god knows where, but definitely into action as part of the now very proud, 18th Division.

Chapter 6

CONVOY

Oh God, I give him now into your keeping
Safe in your care I gladly place my all.
My whole life's hopes and joys and fears and longings
are all bound up in him
Oh hear my call!
Oh God, before thee I'm in spirit kneeling
and all my prayers are winging fast to thee
Oh keep my boy safe
Guard him from all dangers and bring him through all travails
back home to us.

Mother's prayer

It was a stupid idea that I had and it was an even more stupid thing to actually do, but I did it. I went to see the colonel with the thought that, because I was born with one foot considerably smaller than the other, it would be impossible to get boots of odd sizes once we were out there. We all presumed 'out there' would be the desert, but nobody really knew.

The colonel ignored my concern, of course, and simply said, 'You're going to be needed, Anckorn. You are all we've got to entertain the troops.' I felt big and small in the same moment.

Another thought at the back of my mind was that, being a PT instructor, if I went on to a course to become a sergeant instructor, I would have to stay in this country. As it happened, there was a sergeant instructor there that I could talk to about this. 'Yes,' he said, 'if you're a bit frightened of lead, you could stay in this country doing PT all day long instead – if you like.' I was beginning to look and feel like a coward.

So that was it, no more to be said. We were all sent on our week's embarkation leave to say our goodbyes.

I spent the time at home and with Lucille. At first we just made the most of the time we now had but, as the day of departure drew nearer, I found myself searching for words that would say how much I wanted

46

her to be there when I got back. 'I don't know what happens now,' I said, 'or where I'm really going. I don't know how long I'll be away or what happens when war is over. Just hang on. I will be back.' Words couldn't say what I felt.

During that week I also made two pendants out of a farthing piece cut in two. Lucille was to have one half and I the other. We would put the two halves together on my return. On the last day of leave we got engaged. Whatever happens, I thought, at least we've committed ourselves, and with Lucille to come home to, I was determined I would get through it.

I hadn't got enough money to buy a ring and so my parents loaned me what I needed. Lucille and I went up to Sevenoaks with my mother and found a promising looking jeweller's shop where the rings were mostly £2 or £3. Lucille spotted the one she wanted. It cost £8! A deep blue sapphire with diamonds all around it.

The week had flown by and now the time had come to say goodbye. It wasn't good. Lucille had said she would come on the train with me and get off at New Cross to go to the hospital where she was then working in London. So we went up together. To begin with, we somehow suspended the reality of the situation and chatted away normally. But the last twenty minutes of the journey were just awful because we both fell silent, knowing what was coming. It was mind-numbing. It wouldn't have been so bad in the normal way but I couldn't get the thought out of my mind that I was never going to see her again. In my silence, I had recalled that when I was fourteen years old, I'd seen a film with Errol Flynn in it called *Dawn Patrol*, about the First World War. All the carnage going on in it had frightened me and one particular sequence had stuck in my mind. There was this encampment in a field by a road and a German plane came in shooting the place up and dropping bombs. A man ran to get a lorry and he drove like hell to get out of the camp but as he got to the road he was hit by a bomb and blown up. Now I was a lorry driver, going into war, and that was how I was probably going to die, I thought.

It was a mistake, of course, to go together on that train. We should have said goodbye at home. Anyway, Lucille duly got out at the platform and the door closed solidly behind her. Almost before I released the window strap and got the window down, the train was pulling away. I stretched out of the window as if to stay close to her for a moment or two longer but steadily we drew apart. She was just standing there looking at the ground, not moving – she wasn't going to look in my direction. I suddenly thought, 'I've got to get off … I've got to get to her!' It was dreadful. I half thought of jumping from the train but then the platform ended and common sense got the better of me. The train curved away and Lucille was gone from sight. I still stood there by the window, alone in the entrance way to the carriage and I just wanted to break down and cry. But I didn't. I held myself together. It took an awful lot to overcome those feelings and when I returned to my seat, everyone in the carriage knew exactly what had happened.

I changed trains in London and by the time I got back to Uttoxeter, I was thinking only what a horrible, horrible life it was.

Next morning, we were all mustered at 2.00 am and marched down to the station for trains to Liverpool. It was supposed to be a forty-five minute quick march with all our kit but we had everything we owned tied to us and those of us who had been Concert Party, also carried ukulele, accordion, violin and got knows what else. So we traipsed rather than marched in the dark and as we went along, men began to shed belongings to lighten their load.

On arrival in Liverpool, we saw hundreds of guns and lorries parked up in long straight lines all in desert camouflage, which confirmed our expectations. But when we got closer to them we saw they all had labels on them saying 'Singapore'. We thought this must be a bluff to fool any spies. Little did we know.

We were two days there before boarding the ships. On the first day I was called to the colonel's office and asked if I had got my magic stuff with me. Well, I hadn't. The colonel quickly authorised a spend of £30 – a massive amount of money – and I was told to get whatever I needed within twenty-four hours without taking leave. My only hope was to get hold of a shop in London called Davenports, where I had been buying all my magic stuff since childhood. I booked a phone call and three hours later I was able to get through to them. The shop owner was a severe sort of man, very commercially minded – the kind that wouldn't let you look unless you were going to buy. I explained that I was up in Liverpool and had £30 to spend under orders from my commanding officer. He said gruffly, 'Well, what do you want?'

Not really knowing how to spend such a large amount of money on magic tricks, I thought the best thing to do was to describe myself and remind him how I'd been coming to his shop since I was fourteen years old so that perhaps he'd remember the kind of things I did and know what would be most suitable out of his stock. He said, 'Yes, I think I know who you are, all right,' and so I asked him to put together a box of things and to include a particular trick I had always wanted. This was the piece of paper you could roll up into a tube and after putting a white silk handkerchief in one end and blowing down the tube, you could pull the handkerchief out of the other end, a changed colour. He said, 'Yes, alright, but how am I going to get it to you?' and I had to say I didn't know because we were only going to be there in Liverpool one more day.

He said, 'Is it what I think it is ... are you going abroad?'

I replied, 'Yes, I think so.'

'I'll see what I can do,' he said, and rang off.

By some means or other a large box arrived the following day – heaven knows how with the restrictions there were at that time. This was wonderful! It was more than I'd ever bought on my own and there would be surprises for sure, in what Davenports had put together. I didn't open it though, because it seemed best to wait until we got to wherever we were supposed to be going and then I'd be able to spend some time with it all and *really* start performing. Instead, I put the unwrapped box in the cupboards behind the driving seat of my designated gun lorry and there it would stay until arrival at our destination.

I had booked one last telephone call home for the evening before we sailed. When the time came, the conversations were very one-sided because of course, I couldn't say anything about what we were doing or where we were expecting to go or even that this was my last call. It had to be just another phone call. The news from home was that my twin sister had given birth. I had a nephew! His name was Stuart. Baby and Beb were doing well. I said to Lucille that she should keep her nursing eye on all of them, especially mother. I knew she would feel deeply about my departure.

We, as part of 55th Brigade, boarded the 23,000 ton *Orcades*, on loan from the Orient Line as a troop-ship, and sailed out into the Irish Sea and onwards to the North Atlantic along with three other troop-ships and Royal Navy escorts. As we sailed onwards the convoy swelled to thirteen troop-ships as we were joined by the rest of the division coming from other ports, and amongst us all I counted five Royal Navy destroyers and another smaller ship, which must have been a cruiser. Wherever you looked, from one horizon to the other, you could see ships. It seemed impossible to me that so many ships would be able to keep sailing so close to each other when darkness came. They would be in the pitch-black with no lights anywhere and no radio. How would they not hit each other? To make things even more impossible, we were also heading into a storm.

We were in dire danger all the way, if not from the storm, which lasted for days, then from U-boats and bombers. It was said that the captain of our ship never left the bridge day or night. This trip in the *Orcades* brought my self-preservation instincts to the fore and challenged the determination I'd expressed to Lucille only a few days earlier.

Since childhood, when I had been sick on the ferry across to France, I had been unable to even look at a ship without feeling seasick. But as luck would have it, I went down with pharyngitis shortly after we sailed and was taken to sickbay. So I was laid low yet again but this proved the best thing for me because, lying there in bed, I found I wasn't seasick at all for some reason. Meanwhile, the whole regiment, it seemed, were coming into sickbay, one by one, to get their injections, and I could hear men throwing up all over the place. Even the orderlies were being sick.

When I was back on my feet again, I was surprised to find that I was still not seasick and in fact, I wanted the bad weather to continue because it had dawned on me that in severe bad weather, no one could attack us. My wish was granted as we were buffeted all the way. Because of this, I gradually got my sea legs and before long I was playing silly games on the ship's movement such as standing on the bottom step of a staircase and waiting for the ship to roll, then jumping from the bottom to the top in one go – very clever, but not so clever when the ship rolled a little too far one time and I cracked my head against the iron bulkhead.

Having been in sickbay, I had lost my allocation of space to sling my hammock as the ship was crammed full with not an inch to spare. So I slung my hammock across the bottom stair of a companionway leading up from our mess deck. That seemed a good solution to me because if the ship went down, I'd be carried up by the surging mass coming from below. What's more, I'd brought my trusty Lilo with me from home. My mother had given it to me one summer and now it would be something to go over the side with too, I naïvely thought.

Day and night passed as we pitched and rolled our way along with all the other ships – but to where? Supposedly the desert, but the weather was getting colder, not warmer. Without any idea where we were or where we were going, we found ourselves one morning looking out on a horizon ahead filled with warships. We thought we were done for. We'd run straight into the German fleet.

When we saw aircraft approaching we began diving below to take cover but then someone shouted, 'They're not German, they're American!'

There was then much to-ing and fro-ing amongst our warships and theirs and eventually our ships began to sail away, leaving us with the Americans. It all seemed very odd because as far as we all knew, America wasn't even in the war.

More days passed until we arrived one morning off what we were told was Halifax, Nova Scotia, and dropped anchor. It seemed an odd way of getting to the Middle East, if that was where we were going. We had no idea of what lay in store next but to have a ship under us that wasn't lurching all over the place or the target of U-boats and dive-bombers any longer was a relief. However, there we sat at anchor with nothing to do whilst one or two of our ships went in from time to time and we presumed that we would just wait our turn. To keep us occupied, our colonel had a bright idea. He gave us a lecture on banking and money. He was telling us mainly that we should bank our pay from now on as money would be useless to us where we were going.

After the colonel's speech, to fill some more time I thought I might do some magic – especially as the colonel had said back in Uttoxeter that I would be needed as 'the only man we've got to entertain the troops'.

I and a fellow gunner, Lester Martin, conspired to get something going. His idea was to 'do it properly if we do it at all', and so we set up in front of the empty swimming pool tank on the foredeck, where we thought everyone could gather round on various vantage points – the deck rising towards the forecastle or the bridge deck overlooking the pool, or perhaps even the foremast. Then Lester performed as a sort of town crier, getting everyone's attention, but his clever trick was to go round with the hat saying, 'Pay up some of that useless money and Gus here will do some conjuring!' Well, thanks to the colonel's speech, money rained in on us – straight into the empty pool, which repaid the sender with a loud 'ding' when it landed on the metal bottom. The more the dinging the more the money came in. But Lester had another trick up his sleeve – he got me to stop every short while saying, 'Well that's it ... unless, of course, you have some more money to throw away! We finished up with more money than either of us had ever seen before and very much in need of the banking arrangements that the colonel had been talking about.

Soon after nightfall, we were on our way into harbour and, under the cover of darkness, we were to switch onto other ships and make ready to take part in a most secret convoy. We were to go from Halifax to our destination, still presumed to be the Middle East – in US ships – before America had officially joined the war.

As always, we knew nothing of these things at the time. We just went where we were told. But now it's possible to reflect on it all, as a matter of history.

During the time we had been guarding Britain against the expected German invasion in 1940 and through to the Spring of 1941, the war had gone on apace abroad and the powers that be were despatching forces to Egypt. This was because the Italians under Mussolini had entered the war in June 1940, and by August they had attacked and taken British Somaliland in East Africa, and gone on to invade Greece by the end of October. This put them in a strong position to take control of the passage of ships through the Suez Canal and it gave them access to the oil resources of Iraq and Persia, as it was known then. Now we call it Iran.

However, our armies, which included the Australians, had succeeded against them so that, by February 1941, we had reversed the situation in Egypt and Somaliland. But it was not to last. Germany entered the fray in March and a long period of battles ensued across North Africa and the eastern Mediterranean as a whole.

That was why all the talk had been of us going to the desert and it would have been the case but for developments in the Far East.

Japan had been fighting China since 1931 over territory and this had eventually brought about trade sanctions against them imposed by the United States, because of their refusal to withdraw. By the end of the thirties, it was expected that Japan might drive down into Southeast Asia if they could in order to acquire access to oil and much needed raw materials that they had been unable to secure through trade. The war in Europe gave them that opportunity and when France fell to Germany in June 1940, they found that they had French Indochina within their grasp, giving them a way into our colonies of Malaya and Singapore and the Dutch East Indies, and beyond that, to the oil fields of Burma. In September 1940, they had signed a tripartite pact with Germany and Italy, creating what was known as the Axis powers and then, in April 1941, they had signed a neutrality pact with Russia. The stage was set for grand schemes. Negotiations with the West would be pursued whilst preparations for war would be made in case they failed.

Our convoys of soldiers and equipment that had been going mainly to Egypt had begun being directed to India as well, and with increased urgency as 1941 progressed. This urgency was evident in that these convoys had taken on the designation 'WS' – standing for 'Winston's Special', because Churchill had become personally involved in directing them.

Amidst the relentless progress of war there had come the realisation that Britain and its dominions could not prevail without the might of America. Churchill sought talks with President Roosevelt and they had met for the first time in August 1941, on the President's flagship USS *Augusta*, in Placentia Bay, Newfoundland. Churchill had travelled there on HMS *Prince of Wales*, one of our newest battleships, which represented our fighting spirit and capability well, having played its part in the pursuit and eventual sinking of Germany's newest and greatest capital ship, the *Bismark,* only three months earlier.

Although an apparently good understanding was reached between Churchill and Roosevelt, nothing appeared to come of it because American public opinion was strongly against any involvement in the war. But then events quickly took over and the situation changed.

On 1 September, Churchill, forced by a rapidly worsening situation in the Far East, communicated directly and with utmost secrecy with Roosevelt to ask the US to provide troop-ships and escorts in order that British forces might reinforce the Far East. Whilst Roosevelt was thinking about it, a German U-boat made an unsuccessful attack on the US destroyer *Greer* on 4 September and on the day after that, an outraged

Roosevelt assured Churchill that he would supply the troop-ships he wanted regardless of his nations' reluctance to get involved and without any declarations of war. So it was that on 9 November 1941, six US troop-ships lay in Halifax harbour waiting to carry 20,000 or so British servicemen to their destination, escorted as far as possible by US Navy warships. The servicemen were to be the 18th Infantry Division and the convoy was to be the William Sail 12X – designated 12X rather than 13 for good luck, and 'William Sail' to mask its real soubriquet as one of 'Winston's Specials'.

They brought us in at the dead of night and we transferred lock, stock and barrel, literally – guns, lorries, supplies, everything – by dawn, in total secrecy.

In the cold of that November night, under gloomy dockside lighting, I made my way on foot with the rest of my regiment along the dock and through huge warehouses, to arrive at what seemed to me like a steel wall. It was like the side of some sort of fort. But it was a ship.

It was the biggest ship I'd ever been close to – it was immense and it was the *Westpoint*. It had been the SS *America*, First Lady of the seas, launched only two years earlier as a statement of the new prosperity in America that had gradually emerged to replace the Great Depression of the early thirties. She had been launched by the First Lady of the land, Eleanor Roosevelt, and might have been a serious contender in transatlantic crossings for the Blue Riband, but for the war. Dedicated to the business of first class travel, the SS *America* was launched the day before Britain declared war on Germany and so she never took to the submarine-infested Atlantic. Now she was simply the *Westpoint*, a drab, camouflaged troop-ship, re-dedicated to the business of war.

Drab she certainly was on the outside, but once we were aboard we found state cabins with all the finery you could imagine still in place, including gold taps in the best of them. There was still the gymnasium there, with every possible exercising frame or device, as well as steam cubicles and electrical appliances. There were even shops – just like a small town, and right down below in the depths of the ship, where any pitching or rolling would have least effect, there was the vast swimming pool.

As we boarded through the side of the ship, the gangway party kept asking in their American drawl and unique vernacular, 'Anyone here do conjury?'

The captain's yeoman, who was the person on board that more or less held the position of captain's secretary, was a magician himself and he was looking for anyone of a like mind that he could share the journey with.

I owned up to it and was taken straight up to meet him. Ray Hafler, it was, a very important person it seemed on the ship and the captain had given his permission for him to use his quarters just as he wished, whenever he himself was otherwise engaged on the bridge.

Ray Hafler did a different type of magic to mine. My magic was all close up, sleight of hand stuff but he did mental magic. He would read your thoughts and do predictions and things like that. It was a kind of magic I was interested in but it was a lot more involved and less immediate than sleight of hand. Anyway, we hit it off and were to spend the entire trip exchanging ideas and tricks whenever we could. We had a fine old time of it. Early on, I was doing some tricks with him in the captain's cabin when he drawled, 'Would you like somethin' to drink or anything to eat'? ... What's your favourite?' I responded in what I felt must have sounded like a Noel Coward kind of voice as I said, 'I'll have a Marron Glacé, please,' trying to be cosmopolitan. So he rang a bell and a waiter appeared. 'Boy!' he said, 'Fetch me a Marron Glacé for my guest here.' A large ice cream in a glass, topped with wafer, duly appeared.

This ship was so big and so strange to us that we were given the first week to just walk around and get to know it. It turned out that all the waiters on the ship and all the menial staff such as lift attendants, were black men ... and that was another thing. Going up and down from deck to deck, especially for me having to go up *eight* decks to the captain's cabin, was no trouble at all. We didn't have to go by ladder and staircase – oh no! We went by lift and where there were no more lifts, the remaining ascent would be on marble staircases.

Right down below there were storage facilities as big as warehouses where they would move stuff around with fork-lift trucks. In the shopping area you could buy cigars, ice cream, chocolates – there was nothing you couldn't get there. They had butchers, bakers, dry cleaners, tailors – you could get a suit made! Everything you could want was there, just like that, if you had any money – and my friend Lester Martin and I certainly did, for a while.

And then there was the food. On our first night aboard, we had ham omelettes. Well, we hadn't seen proper eggs in England for two years, having made do with the powdered variety, and as for ham.... We heard that in one of the ships, our commanding officer had become so concerned after a week of luscious food that he ordered his men be fed army rations instead. However, the ship's captain told the officer that his men were 'guests of the US Navy', and would continue to be fed accordingly.

It certainly became a strange existence being in this convoy. There was a war going on but while we were at sea it seemed as though we were no part of it as we suffered none of the privations of war. I began to hope that we would never reach our destination. But of course, there was work to do as well as lookout duties to be done.

Lifeboat drill was the first imperative. At the start of the trip the bells would ring every three or four hours – 'general quarters', as the Yanks called it, and you'd have to go to your designated boat station, which was actually a large life raft. Then, once we'd all got used to that routine, they'd rope off an area of the ship as a no-go area, in order to simulate damage, and you'd have to find another way to your boat station. In the end, we all got to know the ship inside out. I wondered if it was the same on all the other troop-ships.

We were a convoy of six, escorted by ten American warships and an aircraft carrier – quite a fleet – and during daylight hours, all the ships zigzagged about to deter U-boat attacks and to avoid giving away our true course. The aircraft carrier was the USS *Ranger* and it would put up aircraft every few hours to seek out any U-boats in the area. During night-time, the convoy was in total blackout.

Amidst all this activity, we carried out continuous lookout duties and there were Bren gun posts all around the ship. My lookout duties were mostly up in the funnel, where I got a good view equipped with powerful binoculars. The ship had been designed with two funnels, but the forward funnel was a dummy for appearances sake, to make the ship look more imposing. Now it provided a perfect lookout position and I spent hours and hours up in that funnel! Apart from all the manoeuvrings, the thing that amazed me most was the sea itself when the swell was running. It was sometimes so big that the other ships would simply disappear for long moments at a time, even from my line of vision up there in the funnel. The escorting warships, including the USS *Ranger*, seemed tiny in the midst of it all and it looked as though they would completely roll over at times.

But we didn't see any submarines and I often wondered during the trip and many times since, why we were able to proceed day after day across the oceans without ever seeing enemy ships or coming under submarine attack.

These days it is said that the work done by our Intelligence people at Bletchley Park decoding German naval messages may have had something to do with it. It was there, as we now know, that Alan Turing, a Cambridge professor, assembled teams of mathematicians, Egyptologists and what have you, in order to set about the impossible task of decoding messages that the Germans encrypted on a mechanical device called an 'Enigma' machine. By a series of wheel settings, this machine could turn a message into code in over 150 trillion different ways and Hitler steadfastly believed that no one would ever be able to crack the codes it produced.

But six years before the war even started, Polish cryptologists had been reading German messages created on these Enigma machines. The Enigma had been used during that time before the war to encrypt commercial as well as government messages. When war broke out, this Polish apability became accessible to our cryptologists but vulnerability to any change in encryption procedure was a problem. Right from the start of the war, therefore, our people were on alert to get hold of anything that might help understand how changes might be made. Ideally they needed a complete encryption machine to work with but their first capture was only some of the wheels off an Enigma machine. This occurred within the first six months of the outbreak of war. It was February 1940 when a German U-boat on an audacious mission to lay mines at the Firth of Clyde was spotted and eventually sunk by HMS *Gleaner*, a converted survey ship. Most of the German crew survived and one crew member had the wheels on him when he was picked up out of the water. At first they were thought to be just any old gear wheels but fortunately somebody had the sense to send them to what was called the 'Government Code and Cypher School' – the place that became known as Bletchley Park. There, Alan Turing and his cryptographers recognised them for what they really were because they had by then already developed an electro-mechanical device that replicated an Enigma machine to a certain extent, made up as it was with wheels and a plug board. They were hoping that with this device they might work out the wheel settings and plug board connections used by the Germans on any given day. They called it 'The Bombe'.

The code breakers made a step forward in understanding how the wheel settings worked on the Enigma, the Germans made a simple error on 20th April 1940. It was Hitler's birthday and every German unit, wherever stationed, sent birthday greetings to Berlin. These signals always ended with '*Heil* Hitler' and these could be compared with other signals at other times that also ended with this salute. It was a breakthrough for the code breakers. But they still couldn't decipher.

Then, at the beginning of May 1940, the Germans changed their coding procedures. Fortunately, however, another 'capture' had taken place just before that, at the end of April, which resulted in the new naval Enigma settings being worked out again within a couple of weeks. That capture took place off the coast of Norway, where an innocuous looking trawler under a Dutch flag was challenged and boarded by men from our HMS *Griffin*. It was found to be a heavily disguised German armed trawler on its way to Narvik with munitions. When the German crew threw their confidential books, ciphers and charts overboard, they took a few minutes to sink and, in that time, an alert gunner on HMS *Griffin* dived into the freezing sea and recovered the lot. These, together with scribble pads and other paperwork found on the trawler, were immediately sent to Bletchley Park and Alan Turing and his team were able to work out how the Enigma had been set on the day of the capture. But the Enigma settings were changed every day so they still only had a snapshot, and in addition, the various bits of paperwork that HMS *Griffin* brought back from the trawler revealed that the encryption procedures included the use of a set of tables that converted letters into other letters before applying them to the Enigma machine. These were not part of the captured items.

Bletchley Park wasn't able to make any further progress until a further capture was made almost a year later. This was another armed trawler, the *Krebs*, captured off Norway again by the Royal Navy in March 1941. The haul from this boat included the Enigma settings for the whole of the previous month and from these, Bletchley Park created some useable tables. However, it still wasn't enough and they realised that they would somehow have to get hold of a full set of tables and that to do so, they couldn't just rely on another chance capture of a German armed trawler or U-boat. Whatever they did to get it, however, must also not arouse the suspicions of the Germans or else the capture would be worthless. It dawned on the Bletchley Park team that the Germans were using the same Enigma codings on any one day to send messages to *any and all* of their vessels out at sea. Some of these vessels were known to be unarmed weather station 'fishing boats', which we could easily identify. The Royal Navy immediately targeted one of these weather station boats in a location that would be unlikely to raise suspicions if it were 'lost'. This was the *Munchen*, off north-east Iceland, and they captured it in late May 1941. They got from it all the Enigma settings for the following month, which meant that Bletchley Park were able to decipher and give the Admiralty all naval messages transmitted to German U-boats and ships for the whole of June 1941. But then, almost as if the Germans were aware of what had happened, they changed their code tables. In a daring, all or nothing further mission that risked giving the game away completely, HMS *Tartar* was sent to intercept another weather station boat. They came back with enough material to read naval Enigma messages throughout the latter part of July 1941, and to fully build coding tables that enabled them to go on decrypting long after that.

So the likelihood is that from August 1941 onwards, they were able to read all of Doenitz's messages to his Atlantic fleet of submarines and their supply ships, within forty-eight hours of them being sent, which meant that the Royal Navy would have been able to disrupt the capabilities of the German submarines by targeting their supply ships. This seems to be exactly what happened. In October 1941, the German U-boat supply ship *Kota Pinang* was located 750 miles west of Spain and sunk by HMS *Sheffield*. Then, in November 1941, at the time of our convoy, an important Enigma message was read by Bletchley Park that possibly helped us directly.

This was a message instructing *U-126* to meet up with the *Atlantis* supply ship for refuelling and re-stocking at a position 350 miles north-west of the Ascension Islands. Our HMS *Devonshire* was sent into action, locating and sinking the *Atlantis*, but the *U-126* got away and later picked up survivors, who were then delivered to another supply ship, the *Python*. At the end of November, Bletchley Park read the Enigma message for the *Python's* next rendezvous with submarines *U-68* and *U-A*, 750 miles south of St Helena Island. On 1 December, another of our warships, HMS *Dorsetshire*, attacked the lot of them as they lay re-fuelling and transferring supplies. The supply ship was scuttled during the engagement. Perhaps we were saved from a watery grave by this action.

As we sailed on, oblivious to all of this, the duties we had to do were never on such a scale as made any difference to us. The crew that worked the ship, however, did work hard – everything done with meticulous attention. To me, just hearing the endless sound of those engines day and night, and seeing the vast engine room – like a huge factory – made me appreciate how much was involved. There was also the whole business of navigating the ships and avoiding collisions with each other. Refuelling at sea was most impressive, too. How they could do that was beyond me. They did it at full speed with the two ships about 20 feet apart in waves so big it was like riding over mountains. They had huge pipelines going across on ropes and hundreds of gallons of diesel would pass across, making the pipelines jump about while we carried on, flat-out through the water.

We were just passengers and onlookers really – and not very clever one's at times, either.

Late one night, I was coming back below from another meeting with Ray Hafler up in the captain's cabin, and as I was going along the bowels of the ship heading towards my quarters in the hold, I was engulfed by a strong smell of roast chicken coming from a galley. Irresistibly, I went into the galley and saw tables full of roast chickens, all piled up. I asked what they were doing with them at that time of night and was told they were just the day's leftovers. There were stacks of strawberries and gallons of cream, too. Naturally I asked what they were going to do with it all and the answer was, 'Chuck it overboard!' Apparently, anything not eaten in the day would have to go overboard at night to avoid risk of food poisoning.

'Help yourself if you want some,' they said.

Well, I came away with a small sack full of roast chickens, and the flavour trail, as I went below to my quarters, woke up the entire mess. Within minutes we were all scoffing lumps of chicken. But by then, of course, the Red Caps had smelled them too, and they came out in force to see what was going on. Hurriedly, we had to get rid of what was left, and to do so, we had to go up a couple of decks to find a porthole through which we could chuck them because our mess deck was below the waterline. Having got to one, we started chucking the chickens out, one by one. Big mistake!

We found out later that we could have been in terrible trouble and not just because we were not allowed to have any food other than the set meals. The worst of it was that we had chucked stuff through the porthole, piece by piece, which would have created a line of floating food that could easily have enabled any submarine around to guess the probable direction of travel of the ship and of the convoy itself. Submarines would have been on the lookout for anything, any evidence at all of shipping. Even a careless peeling of an orange over the side could give them the information they needed. We could have been court-martialled. The proper way in which the ship got rid of all the leftovers at the end of the day was to collect it all – hundreds of loaves of bread, lumps of meat and piles of vegetables and fruit – and squash it together into large loads using the fork-lift trucks so that each load, when dumped over the side, would sink straight away, leaving no trail.

The disposal of waste in order to avoid food poisoning was taken very seriously on the ship and yet, food poisoning did occur during the convoy, with dramatic effect.

One afternoon someone just dropped, unconscious, on the deck. No sooner had they gone to pick him up than someone else dropped. Men were just dropping like that, suddenly unconscious. The American crew came along each time with stretchers but then one of the stretcher bearers dropped too! It got to the point where our promenade deck, which was probably the largest promenade deck of any ship afloat, was full of bodies covered in blankets. I thought I was going to be next at any moment because I'd just had a bet on with some mates that I couldn't drink five tins of condensed milk in one go. But it made me so thirsty that I'd also gulped down water by the gallon from the drinking water fountains that were available all over the ship. As I was doing so, the Tannoy system crackled into life and a strident American voice hailed out, 'Now hear this! ... Don't anybody drink the ship's water ...' Well, after that I was just waiting to drop dead. Eventually, they pinned down the food poisoning as coming from the first sitting of breakfast. What had happened was that they'd broken eggs into bowls and mixed in the ham the night before as usual, putting the mixtures into the cool room ready for cooking the omelettes in the morning – but they had left some of the mixtures out in the heat of the galley all night. Result – food poisoning – simple as that.

Yes, we were just passengers, disconnected from what was going on in the war whilst weaving our way through the oceans towards, well, towards what? We still didn't know even a month into the trip. We still assumed it would be North Africa. We didn't know anything.

The 7th December found me messing about in the library in the middle of a tremendous storm. The weather had been deteriorating for a couple of days and with virtually nil visibility, there were no lookout duties. The library was a vast room with plush bucket armchairs that you could disappear into. Well, to us irresponsible and somewhat restless passengers, these were a gift in rough seas. A couple of us were in there, feet up into the armchairs, as they careered round the room of their own accord with the violent movement of the ship. It was just like being on the dodgems!

That was the day when the fellow in charge of the library, a cheerful and friendly fellow, suddenly turned very grave. He was an ordinary sailor called Levitt – a name I remember because he said that after the war he was going to set himself up a little business doing things for people, like making certain your wife gets a bunch of flowers on her birthday, and he was going to call it 'Leave it to Levitt'. Now, this sudden change of mood that had come over him made me ask what was up.

'We're one of you now,' he said. 'They've bombed Pearl.'

'Who's Pearl?!' I joked, misjudging the gravity of his mood.

'Pearl Harbor. It's where our Pacific Fleet is based. They've bombed it.'

'Who's bombed it?' I said, showing more concern.

'The Japs,' he said, with disgust in his voice.

'But they're not even in the war,' I said.

'They are now ... and so are we' came his reply, and a dark look came over his face as he stood braced against the movement of the ship, absorbed in thought. Who knows what the implications were for him, his family and friends.

The news of Pearl Harbor didn't seem to shock us like it shocked the Americans. Our view was that we'd been at it for over two years, so 'welcome to the party'. I don't recall it making any noticeable difference to us on the ship. It was, however, a grim reminder of the fighting that we were inevitably heading into. But for now, our only concern was that we were headed for Cape Town, with shore leave in prospect.

Having pulled through the storm, we arrived off Cape Town and were met by HMS *Dorsetshire*. We didn't know, of course, about her earlier action with the U-boat supply ship, but we had heard of her being involved in the sinking of Hitler's flagship, *Bismark*, with three torpedoes. It had been on the Pathé News in the cinemas back in May that year. But disturbing news was to greet us in the next few days, involving the other ship featured in the news about the *Bismark* – the Navy's pride and joy, HMS *Prince of Wales*.

It was now 9 December and we'd arrived at the dockside with the great expectations for going ashore. We were looking down from the top deck, which was so high it was as though we were flying, and we saw hundreds of little cars in hundreds of different colours – something never seen in England, where every car was black or green or some dark colour. We were told that when we got off the ship we were to climb into any car, preferably the first car we saw, and there would be a family member in there who would drive us to their home for a three-day break!

It was just marvellous. The car I selected was a great big open Cadillac, or something like that. I just got in and was welcomed by the driver, who said he could only take one of us and he was happy for that to be me. His family were Jewish and I was going to meet his wife, two young daughters and his son. They just waited on me hand and foot after we arrived and over the three days, they took me everywhere. I tried out surfing and roller-skating and I climbed Table Mountain. They couldn't have treated me better. As Christmas was coming up, I thought I must give them something when I left and so I went to the shops to see what I could get with what little money I had left. A huge 6lb box of chocolates caught my attention simply because we hadn't seen so much as a ¼lb bar of chocolate at home for years. As I was gawping at it, the shopkeeper asked if that was what I wanted but of course, I said that I couldn't possibly afford it. He said, 'Have it, with our compliments,' and he handed it to me. Later, when we all returned aboard ship, we all had similar stories to tell. The shops simply wouldn't let any of us pay for anything. As it turned out, the reason was that a few weeks before our arrival, the *Prince of Wales* had been in and of course, they'd had the whole mob of them in town for three days just like us. News had come in while we were ashore that she had been sunk off Malaya along with HMS *Repulse* – by the Japanese. Over 800 of the crew had died. These wonderful people of Cape Town were offering us their sympathy.

Once we were all aboard again, we found the mood on-board ship had changed completely and we were making a quicker than expected departure. It was the 13 December and we were leaving with four of the American warships but the next day we were met by HMS *Dorsetshire* again and the Americans departed. We continued on our way to whatever the destination would be, five troop-ships escorted by just the *Dorsetshire*.

About a week later, one of our fellow troop-ships, the *Orizaba*, peeled off and then after a couple more days, another of the ships, the *Mount Vernon*, left us as well for some reason. There was definitely something going on, but not for us to know. The remaining four of us sailed on with our protector, HMS *Dorsetshire*.

The *Vernon* had been our lead ship so when it left, the command passed to our captain on the *Westpoint*. In the spirit of camaraderie to celebrate Christmas in the middle of the Indian Ocean, the *Dorsetshire* came alongside us and regaled us with their Marines band, playing music for what seemed all afternoon. It was peacetime stuff and they were in full dress uniform with their white hats and all. They played *Nightingale Sang in Berkeley Square*, *Bless 'em All*, *Whispering Grass* and many others. There we were steaming along, side by side, with all this lovely music going on. Little did we realise, it would be the last proper music that most of us would hear for years, and for some of us, ever again.

We travelled on for another day and then in the early hours of the next morning, our ship and the *Wakefield*, which were the two biggest troop-ships of the four remaining, broke away from the others and started to race ahead, doing a hell of a speed. We were away on our own with no escort and the pace was kept up all day until, by late afternoon, we found ourselves off what we were told was Bombay. Not what we were expecting and the contrast with Cape Town and our 'luxury' troop-ship could not have been greater.

Chapter 7

MAGIC OF THE EAST

The Bombay we arrived at was a nasty, dirty place. I thought there was blood all over the pavements and all over the walls until I found out it was beetle nut. The Indians chewed beetle nut and what they spat out was red. There were beggars everywhere, too. Not long after we had disembarked, I went off on my own while most of my mates went to a cinema because there was a film on called *Puff the Magic Dragon* that wasn't on in England. I hadn't gone very far down the dock road when two little kids rushed up. Each one got hold of my hand and with nail files started cleaning my hands and asking this and that and what money would I give them and did I want their sisters. Then I came across real beggars – the disabled ones. A lot of them had been blinded, deliberately, by their parents, who would pour acid in their eyes and break their arms and legs so that they'd be crawling along the pavement like a spider – legs out here and arms out there, just begging. There were so many of them that they did their begging in shifts – a day shift and a night shift.

I had to quickly learn the 'colonial ways' of dealing with the locals – how I should make them stand to attention when any spoke to me and how I should shout '*Jow*' when I wanted them to go away. 'Treat them like dogs' was the way of it. I didn't quite go along with it and quite soon caused a real rumpus. In the way things were done over there, I had a bearer looking after me – you had to have one – every one of us had one. Wallahs, they were called. They would do all your washing and dressing and they'd clean your teeth for you if you wanted them to. We were supposed to give them the equivalent of a penny a week. Well, I felt sorry for this old boy that was looking after me, so I gave him a rupee every week, which was in those days worth about half a crown. The sergeant-major heard about it and all hell broke loose. He said there'd be an uprising if one of the bearers got more than the others.

We began to settle into the idea of India being our final destination – although 'settling in' it wasn't, because we were out on exercises every day to get us fit again after being at sea and eating so well for so long. Our barracks were at Ahmednagar, which was where Spike Milligan was born. His father had been a sergeant there. One of our other artillery regiments was based at Pune, which was about 20 miles away and I was detailed, one day to drive down to them. In the process I saw some of the nicer side of India. Pune itself was beautiful, really beautiful. All white marble and clean everywhere. It was a glimpse, a final glimpse as things turned out, of how civilised life could be.

But the big thing for me was to try and get the most out of this chance of being in the mystical East – the magician's Mecca, or so I believed at the time. There was the prospect of actually seeing the famous Indian Rope Trick performed, for example, amongst perhaps many others. My notion of how magical this mystic country of the East would be made me feel very small fry setting foot in this holy of holies. However, I was to be quickly disillusioned. No one I spoke to had ever actually seen the Rope Trick, they only told of family members, five times removed, who *used* to do it. The Mango Tree act, in which a small tree would grow from seed in a matter of seconds, was also over-rated because it was actually easily achieved by simple misdirection and with the aid of an accomplice.

Disappointed with what magic there was to see in that part of India, I began showing the supposed magicians some tricks of my own. It wasn't long before they began calling me a 'devil man'. I found that the mere taking of a handful of cards out of a wallah's hair or turban would send him and others tearing off in terror. Teasing the wallahs became irresistible!

In the regimental kitchen there would always be a wallah to do the dishwashing and he would have a huge washing-up bowl filled with hot steaming water like a cauldron. On passing through one day, I stopped and gazed into this cauldron while the wallah was busily doing the dishes and then reached down towards the steamy surface to produce a lighted cigarette. Nonchalantly, I turned and walked away smoking it. Minutes later, I returned, peered into the water again and reached down to pull out another, at which point the wallah began pleading 'No sahib . . . oh no, sahib!' with a terrified look on his face. But I continued and out came another cigarette, which I was about to put in my mouth when the wallah made a run for it, straight out of the barracks, never to return.

The wallah had to be replaced, which meant our sergeant-major was involved and once he knew who was responsible, I was soon up in front of him.

'Any more disappearing char wallahs, Anckorn,' he said, 'and you'll be doing the kitchen fatigues yourself!'

Well I really couldn't resist showing the replacement char wallah the trick and so sure enough, it was kitchen fatigues for me.

As was the case back in England, the sergeant-major and I were once again finding ourselves on collision course and sparring verbally with each other – nothing malicious, just cheek on my part – and he seemed to enjoy it too, such as on parade. On our daily drill parade in India, we would 'port arms' as is usual, which meant we would present our rifles for inspection in such a way that the sergeant-major could see through the barrel to ensure it was clean. When he came to me and looked down it, he pulled back with a jerk and started bellowing: 'Gunner Anckorn! Look down there. What do you think it is in there?'

I looked and to my horror saw a hornet's nest.

'Looks like a hornets' nest, Sergeant-Major.'

'It bloody well is a hornets' nest, Anckorn! When did you last clean this gun?'

'This very morning, Sergeant-Major,' I said.

'Then how do you explain that?'

'Fast workers, Sergeant-Major.'

It was fatigues again for me.

But my cheek nearly got me court-martialled when it came to the official photograph of our troop. They wanted all of us to fold our arms but I said no. Well, I wasn't going to fold my arms and look like an automaton with everyone else!

If India was where we were going to be stationed, I was quite happy and was beginning to enjoy it for all that it was. Yet, after only a few weeks, we were ordered to re-board our troop-ships. It had been organised chaos on the dockside when we had come ashore so we were expecting the same on the return. But when we arrived back in Bombay, there were the American ships as if they had been there all the time. They'd got banners hanging over the side saying, 'Welcome Back Boys'. At the top of the gangway, the sailors were jovially telling us to go directly to our bunks and that tea would be at five. God Bless America!

Still we had no idea of the goings on – where we were now heading or what we were supposed to be doing. More troop-ships joined us too, only this time they were British ships – the *Duchess of Bedford*, *Empress of Japan* and the *Empire Stour*. We also had a Royal Navy ship escorting us out, HMS *Caledonia*. It seemed we were to spend the war forever going from here to there in ships!

Once we were away, our battery sergeant-major mustered us for fatigue detail and announced that he expected us to be at sea for about a fortnight. The fatigue details began with the most arduous at first and as he was about to say who was going to get the worst of it, he paused and the entire troop roared: 'Gunner Anckorn!' Such was my reputation for backchat and banter and where it would get me. But on this occasion, things turned out differently, much to the annoyance of the sergeant-major.

He'd got me on fatigues for the whole of the expected fortnight's trip but on the second day, an officer came up to me to say they were looking for another surveyor for our battery. The surveyor's job is to locate and establish grid references for each gun emplacement so that the officer working out the ranges knows exactly where each gun is. He knew I'd had a bit of an education so he asked me to volunteer, which I did – thinking how it might be useful after the war. The idea was that we would go down to the bottom of the ship where the guns were and start training the very next afternoon by using a gun sight off one of the guns as a theodolite. However, I told him that there was a problem because I had already been given fatigues by the battery sergeant-major. 'Right, I'll sort that out. Do you know where the sergeant-major is?' I told him he was on the upper deck and we both went up to meet him. The sergeant-major snarled at the officer saying, 'Anckorn has already been detailed,' to which the officer simply said, 'Well you can undetail him. I need him for something else.'

The thing was that the next day, when the officer and I went below, we found it impossible to get to the gun sights on the guns, which meant that my training would have to wait until we disembarked again. So, by keeping out of the way of the sergeant-major after that, I had no duties or fatigues the whole trip!

Not long into the trip, rumours had begun to circulate about our likely destination. Some were saying they believed that the mis-direction given on all our vehicles back in Liverpool was in fact the truth. We were heading for Singapore. This seemed likely to be the case when a number of our warships appeared and joined us after the first ten days or so. The HMS *Glasgow* was one of them and then I saw HMS *Exeter*, the cruiser we had all heard about during the *Graf Spee* incident. There were also four larger warships, which we thought were destroyers.

A few days after that, we entered some narrows, which I was told was the Bangka Straits between the south-eastern end of Sumatra and the island of Bangka. The convoy was formed up in single file and we had a destroyer in front of us and a destroyer behind us. It was broad daylight and all guns were manned on the warships as we followed each other into the Straits.

Up above us I could see a lone aircraft, which I was told was one of ours – a Catalina flying boat, which was often used for Convoy escort. As I looked, it dipped its wings and began to fly away from us.

Shortly after that, I saw the guns on the destroyer behind us swivel and I looked up to where they were pointing. I looked up, but before I could see anthing, all hell broke loose on the warships with every gun firing at once. A few moments later we understood why as a stick of bombs fell in our direction. They came down at the back of the convoy and I couldn't see at first whether they'd hit any of us. Once the erupting sea had settled again it was clear the convoy was intact and I searched the sky for more, expecting this to be just the beginning. There was nothing. Our guns fell silent and we just carried on.

It was night-time as we came out of the Straits. Our ship, the *Westpoint*, and another, the *Wakefield*, had moved ahead of the rest of the convoy and we were travelling at full speed, with the *Empress of Japan* close behind. The night was clear, with starlight and a hazy moon making our wake phosphorescent. The visibility was good enough for us to see that land remained in sight. Then at one point we raced through some real narrows as we passed amongst islands that I found out later were the Straits of Durian, just to the south of Singapore. The rush of water as we streamed along reverberated off the rocks in some parts, and at such close quarters, the speed was breathtaking. Whatever our purpose, it was now clearly very urgent.

Shortly after that we were all mustered for a talk by Colonel MacKellar. It frightened the living daylights out of me.

He had a huge map on the wall showing Singapore Island and the Malay Peninsula. On this map were little reds spots all over the place that represented the British Army units on the Malay Peninsula and he highlighted the positions of our 53rd Brigade troops that had already gone in ahead of us. Surrounding these red dots were yellow ones, which we were told were the Japs. He was telling us basically that our forces were completely surrounded by the Japanese and we were going in to join the 53rd and stop the Japs getting into Singapore. He couldn't have been less morale boosting! Perhaps he realised this because he then attempted to reassure us that Japanese soldiers were not up to much, saying that they all had poor eyesight and if we came across one with a bandage over one eye it wasn't because he was injured, no, it was because Japs couldn't close one eye whilst looking through the other to aim a rifle. But then he went on to say that we shouldn't think of being taken prisoner because the Japs would just torture us for information before killing us. He finished with a rousing call to us all to get in there and kill 'the little yellow bastards'! We all left in complete silence feeling totally demoralised as we went down to our mess deck.

We had been given the opportunity to write letters just after we left Bombay and now, as we approached Singapore, I wondered what might happen to the one I had written. Might it ever be sent?

As things were to turn out, the cheery letters written aboard that ship would, for many, be the last they ever wrote.

Bombay Base, India

Dear Mum,

Have had quite a good stay at our last place and now find ourselves at sea again on the same boat in the same bed in the same room! Hope you are all fit and well – I am, and getting quite sun burnt. Let Luce know I am ok as this is the only card I could get and I know she would want you to know first. By now you should have received a few of my letters but of course, through all this dodging about I haven't had any yet. It is very hard writing when there is nothing to answer but we are still in the best of spirits and very healthy and no tropical diseases or anything like that yet. Keep writing to the last address till you get a new one, by that time I will probably have gone right round the world! It's good getting on a boat and meeting old friends again and not having to spend weeks getting to know the place. One thing, we are sure getting tough now but thank goodness there is no chance of a route march tomorrow! We slept last night on a train and the Lilo came in very useful and was like a feather bed! How is the dog getting on? I suppose by now his coat is all woolly again. It seems funny to think of you all in the cold now! All the chaps buy papers here and the first thing they look for is the football news about Arsenal etc., which is always there! The other night I saw a yogi show, which was amazing and contained a lot of magic. He cooked a small rice pudding on my head! Incidentally, I have had the most colossal fun with magic against the natives who are so bewitched by it that they run off – often undoing a turban from which I have grabbed cards and money! That might come in useful one day! Yesterday I sent off a letter and a photo of our troop by ordinary mail. See how long it takes compared with this airmail. Let you know soon all the news.

All my love mums,

Ferg

Chapter 8

THE FALL

There must at this stage be no thought of saving the troops or sparing the population. The battle must be fought to the bitter end at all costs. The 18th Division has a chance to make its name in history. Commanders and senior officers should die with their troops. The honour of the British Empire and of the British Army is at stake.

Winston Churchill, message to General Wavell,
10th February 1942

We rushed down the gangplank amidst the sounds of bombing and destruction. There was a Chinese girl on the dockside and I asked her as we passed how many air raids they'd had. 'Eleven!' she said.

I was so frightened. There was no sign of any of our planes putting up a fight. Ringing in my ears was the colonel's final command to us the night before. 'Go in there and kill, kill, kill! There's no bloody cricket now ... just slash their throats and kill the little yellow bastards!'

This was it. We were finally in this war. It seemed to me that, until now, it had all been a glorious adventure. Right from the start we had been so distant from it all. Here, now, we had landed in the midst of killing. The sudden realisation that they would kill us and we should kill them dawned on me, horribly.

We had been detailed to proceed as best we could to a muster point and then to our billets. Some of us would return later to assist with getting our guns and gear offloaded as there was no dockside labour. Fortunately, the air raid passed without incident to us and we got ourselves away.

The billets were on an abandoned housing estate of neat little bungalows near the Tanglin Barracks, only a couple of miles from the docks. All were beautifully kept and each of different size, it was a case of 'Five of you in this one ... eight of you in that one' as we marched along the road. It turned out that every one of them was like the '*Marie Celeste*' – food still on the tables, cooking left on the stoves and no one anywhere. It felt strange and wrong to be intruding on such normal domesticity, contrasted as it now was, with our hardening hearts and grim determination. We were ready to slit the throats of anyone. Then, for an instant, comedy shattered our resolute mood. We opened a cupboard and out came about eight huge cockroaches. We ran like bloody hell! All the killing gone out of us in that moment!

The following morning some of us were detailed to return to the docks. A party of ten of us went – all gunners.

The scene at the docks was pandemonium with as many people trying to get onto the ships as get off them. The strange thing was that some of them were RAF officers and staff who seemed to be intent on leaving. Otherwise it was women and children. I have learned since then that this was probably the first rush of evacuation of civilians and it started because of information received in Singapore only a day or so earlier by the authorities, about what had happened in Hong Kong when it fell to the Japanese on Christmas day. A nurse had managed to escape from there and told of the widespread abuses and murders by rampaging soldiers.

The dockside was littered with abandoned civilian cars – all in pristine condition and just left where the owners had drawn up and got out. More were still coming and the drivers would throw the keys to any of us nearby saying, 'Take it. It's yours!'

We assisted as best we could with the unloading of our gear but much of our personal belongings had been sent on after us in a following convoy that was yet to arrive. We were told it was on the *Empress of Asia*. As night fell we were told we should remain at the dockside to keep an eye on things and to carry on with the unloading in the morning. I found myself a sleeping position on top of some barrels, nicely sandwiched between two of them. These were next to crates and crates of Merlin engines that we'd brought in along with air frames of Hurricane fighters. You could see the beautifully manufactured engine parts through the crating. They looked huge and somehow deadly. These were well worth keeping an eye on I thought – although I did wonder, having seen members of the RAF boarding the ships to leave.

When morning came, so did the bombers again. This time it looked like they were coming to flatten the docks, there being so many of them – and that's exactly what they proceeded to do.

As the shrill whistling sound of falling bombs broke the morning peace, everyone scattered. Our work party took off towards some surface shelters nearby, but I hadn't caught on that the bombs were heading straight for us and I hesitated. Then, realising there wasn't time to make it to the shelters, I ran and dived into the dock instead. It was a long way down to the water and as I went over the side, I saw a big sign on the railings saying, 'Danger, sharks'! Too late, I was in. Later I was told that being in the dock was the stupidest place to be – not just because of sharks but because any bomb landing in the water would have created a blast wave so strong that I'd have been killed outright.

When the bombing ceased, I climbed out to find everything on fire and destruction everywhere. I ran over to the surface shelter where the others had gone and found they'd had a direct hit. Five of them were dead.

It shocked me so much that I went about the dockside not really knowing what I was doing – just trying to be useful somehow in all the chaos. There was a hose, snaking its way around amongst the debris strewn everywhere, gushing water. I picked it up and aimed it at a lorry that had its wheels on fire. As soon as the water hit the wheels they blew up! Then I dragged the hose over to a warehouse that was ablaze, stacked with tins of food and all sorts of supplies. The roof was burning, so I aimed the water up at it. The jet of water turned to steam on impact with the burning roof, and boiling water showered back down on me. It was total mayhem and everything I did seemed wrong and useless. As for the pristine Merlin engines in their crates – they were all blasted to bits, and through gaps in the billowing black smoke that filled the docks, I saw that the *Wakefield* had been hit right in the middle and blackened men were trailing down the gangplank.

By the time that day was done, I was severely shaken. I'd had enough of it already and welcomed our return to the billets, which had still been untouched. For the next couple of days I managed to avoid fatigues and we were all left to ourselves while, I presumed, we waited for the *Empress of Asia* and the rest of our gear to arrive.

Where we were billeted all was calm and quiet. The Japanese bombers that came over in huge formations, either in a morning or evening, would drop their bombs all at the same time in one big dollop on their targets in the docks or in the town of Singapore itself and then clear off again. Nowhere else was affected. We learned that this bombing style of the Japs had become known as the 'diarrhoea attack'. I got the point.

After these few days of respite, I was collared by one of our Forward Observation Officers, Captain Johnson, to drive him to an aerodrome at Seletar, up in the north-east area of the island. He expected it to provide a good vantage point for looking north across the Johore Straits to the Malay mainland, where the Japs were thought to be preparing for an invasion of the island. Captain Johnson was the officer who had said to me as we left Liverpool on the *Orcades*, when I had to go into sick-bay with pharyngitis, 'We should call you Unlucky Anckorn ... the unluckiest man in the regiment! Everything you do is trouble. I'll bet you're the first to get yourself shot when we get into this war.' It obviously didn't bother him now but the recollection of it filled me with foreboding as we drove with urgency, 20 miles or so across the island to Seletar.

We were travelling in his big Humber staff car and as we passed through Singapore town on our way out, there were Chinese people everywhere, filling the road and blocking our way. I was parping the horn and nudging my way through but Captain Johnson had other ideas. 'Don't bother to hoot, Anckorn, just run them over! Blasted Chinks!'

Finally we arrived at the aerodrome, which looked like it had already been hit by the Japs, but then as we arrived, so did the Japanese again – twenty-seven bombers – lining up for a 'diarrhoea attack'. Undaunted, Captain Johnson directed me to a tall water tower that he wanted to climb in order to make his observations. I watched him as he started climbing up. He was wearing his dress cap with bright red and blue ribbon and highly polished cap badge that glistened in the sun. What a wonderful target he'll be when he gets to the top, I thought. But I had been instructed to take cover, so I dashed to a promising looking place – a huge grassy mound with a door in the front. Fortunately, the door opened and I threw myself inside, slamming the door shut behind me. Instantly, I was in pitch-black and total silence. The door was a really heavy one and it shut out virtually all sound but I felt the ground shake when the bombs landed.

Eventually, the earth tremors ceased and I emerged into a scene of burning, smoking, stinking destruction. A Catalina aircraft was upside down in front of the main buildings and all the other planes that had been standing were destroyed. For a moment or two, I just walked about, trying to take it all in. Our vehicle, at least, was untouched. Looking about, I saw that I'd left the door on the grassy mound wide open so, like a good well brought-up boy, I automatically went back to shut it. As I did so, light shining in revealed the contents of the mound. It was stacked, floor to ceiling, with high octane fuel cans! Another near miss for Unlucky Anckorn, I thought.

The captain appeared from somewhere, unhurt, and we set off at great speed back to Singapore town. I hadn't yet seen a single Jap, but I'd seen plenty of destruction.

The next day, we heard that the convoy with the remaining units of the 18th Division had arrived. However, the *Empress of Asia*, which was carrying our gear, hadn't. The convoy had been attacked just as we had been, only they got a bigger pounding, and the *Empress* had been abandoned burning on a sandbank somewhere out in the Straits. I thought of all the personal stuff I'd had amongst my gear – all the mementos I'd collected so far on this 'great adventure' – all gone up in smoke.

It must have been 6 February when, without any instructions as to where we were supposed to be going, we were ordered to the polo ground outside Singapore town to collect our guns and ammunition.

We got hooked up in convoy and set off – like a herd of elephants 'following my leader'.

As we passed through the town, we became stationery for a while at a part where there was a parade of shops. A man was standing in the doorway of a jeweller's shop with his hands full of jewellery shouting, 'Here, come, take it, take it all – the Japanese are coming and they'll have it if you don't!' I jumped down and he slung some jade necklaces at me, which I stuffed into my pockets thinking 'I'm made! – I'm rich!'

On the move again, we finally left the town behind us and passed through plantations, mangrove swamps and eventually jungle – all the time moving at the slow speed typical of a convoy. It seemed to intensify the heat of the day, which was more sapping than anything we had experienced in Bombay.

The positions we finally arrived at were in the north-east of the island, more or less along the same route I had taken with Captain Johnson the day before. We had joined up with the rest of 55th Brigade, which had preceded us, guarding a stretch of coastline from invasion. It reminded me of doing exactly the same thing in Norfolk. All was quiet, but tense. They told us that there had been Japanese artillery fire the previous couple of days, coming from the mainland but passing over-head to hit a town nearby called Nee Soon and another airfield called Sembawang, as well as Seletar. They had not been able to range in on any of it.

We got ourselves organised and set up. The routine was first to drive the guns to markers placed by our reconnaissance surveyors, who went ahead of us and found the best vantage points. Then, after unhitching the guns and their limbers, which carried the shells, each gun lorry would drive some distance away in order to be hidden in a different location. That way, we reduced the risk of guns being rendered immovable because of lorry damage. Sometimes the lorry driver would stay with the lorry and await instructions and other times he'd go back to the gun. Lorries and guns would be camouflaged amongst the trees or bushes – a difficult task in our case because we had desert colouring – not the best thing in a jungle and rubber plantation battlefield!

Word had gone out that we should watch out for locals who might be giving our positions away to the enemy and for any Japanese infiltrators. Well, most of the troops at that time couldn't tell a Jap from any other Asian. Malays, Chinese, Japanese – they were all just *Asian* looking. With no action going on it just made everyone jumpy. An incident did occur at our gun position. Our lookouts brought in an old man who had wire cutters concealed in his clothing. Our units had been laying communications wire between our positions and our Forward Observation post and so they must have assumed he was up to no good. They brought him in front of one of our officers, but because so much was going on with preparing our positions he just said, 'I haven't got time for that – just shoot him.' So they took him away and called for volunteers to make up a firing squad. Looking at this old, white-bearded, harmless looking Chinese man, I wanted nothing to do with it but others were falling over themselves to volunteer. Anyway, they tied him to a tree and shot him. No doubt they had our colonel's words 'Kill, kill, kill!' in their minds when they pulled the triggers.

Some of our lot decided that they needed some target practice after that and one of them spotted what looked like a chicken, of all things, halfway up a tree. He blasted away at it with his rifle but only succeeded in tearing the tree to pieces all around the chicken whilst it just looked on quizzically. An Indian soldier from another unit near us took the rifle from him and with one shot, blew the poor chicken to bits.

The next day, the killing was aimed at us. Japanese artillery opened up from somewhere over the water. It was spasmodic but persistent all day long. We began to answer back and as I was supernumerary, being the driver, I thought I'd take cover in a field shelter nearby. It was a proper dug-out with a right-angled bend in the entrance way to stop the blasts. Having descended into its blackness, I heard footsteps in the entrance. I prepared my rifle and aimed at the entrance framed by the light. As a shadow threw itself on the wall I half pressed the trigger. Hardly a breath would now fire it. I held my breath. A figure emerged.

'What are you up to, Anckorn?' came the voice of our gun sergeant.

I said I was keeping out of it while I had nothing to do as I'd been close enough already to being blown apart. He said he'd give me something to do and suggested I should fire the gun so that I could tell my mum I'd killed some Japs. The next four rounds were mine after that but of course, we still had no idea if we were hitting anything.

The following day the shelling intensified and we had to move our guns several times to avoid giving our positions away. All day our scouts and lookouts watched for any signs of invasion. Word came that the Japs had crossed from the mainland onto a small island in the Straits just to the east of us but by nightfall they had gone no further and the shelling ceased. That night, I was to remain with my lorry, keeping sentry. Hidden amongst jungle, my beat for sentry duty, according to our gun sergeant, was to be a 50-yard stretch in each direction away from the lorry. It seemed to me that if I simply paraded up and down like that, I would be too easy a target for the 'little yellow bastards'. So instead, I climbed up onto the roof of my lorry where the camouflage 'scrim net' was usually stored and took up a position lying on my belly overlooking the whole 100-yard stretch of my beat. I armed myself with two Mills bombs, my rifle and a machete. Confidently, I imagined myself taking the heads off any Jap that came my way with a single swipe or I would blow them to smithereens with a nicely lobbed Mills bomb. But I was not to be put to the test. The night passed without incident.

At dawn, word came round that the Japs had invaded during the night across the Johore Strait on a 10-kilometre front somewhere over on the west coast, not here on the east. For all we knew they would now also invade here as the shelling started again. But as the day wore on the crescendo coming from the west increased and also spread round to our left, which must have been the north coast. Black smoke was billowing up into the sky, probably coming from the oil tanks at the naval base, we were told. Night-time brought no change. In fact, it got worse, and in the middle of the night, the skyline to the north west of us was glowing red and bright yellow, signifying some sort of tumult.

Then, during the course of the morning, new instructions came and we were on the move again – going west towards the cacophony. The further west we went the more we found ourselves engrossed in the black smoke that was hanging in the air. We now know this came not only from the burning oil tanks at the naval base but also from high octane fuel that had been drained out of huge storage tanks near Kranji into adjacent rivers and set alight. It had been the source of the blaze we'd seen on the horizon during the night. The storage tanks were supposed to have been blown up by Allied troops as they retreated from the area, having been unable to hold back another Japanese invasion from the north. But the engineers tasked with blowing the tanks had lost all their gear in a direct hit on their supply vehicle so instead, a platoon leader called Lieutenant Watchorn, simply got his men opening all the valves while he went off in search of some explosives. The fuel had gushed out into the waterways around Kranji and, when Watchorn came back to ignite it with some explosives, he'd found it had created a huge firestorm that incinerated any of the invasion forces still on those waters. Now the black cloud of smoke that hung everywhere covered us in oily soot when it rained.

We took up new positions to the north of Peirce Reservoir with our guns ranged on an advancing enemy who was by then no more than a few miles away to our north. We opened up and it wasn't long before it became counter-battery work – us firing at their gun positions and them at ours. It was when we had just arrived there that we took our first fatality.

Other drivers and I had gathered for a quick 'smoko' whilst awaiting further orders. While we stood there, an incoming shell sounded like it was heading straight for us. Thanks to the bombardment we'd silently endured over on the coast in the last few days I'd become pretty good at guessing the likely trajectory of incoming shells by the whistling sound they made. This one sounded too close for comfort. I shouted 'down!'

75

and everyone dropped to the ground except for Bombardier Midwinter. When we all got up, he didn't. He was dead.

Throughout that day, we were in action, firing our guns with no let-up and early on we began digging trenches and earth mounds for cover as more and more shelling came in from the Japs – some of it getting very close. Soon enough, there was one that we all instinctively knew was going to be *too* close and we dived for cover. I got behind an earth mound and buried my head as best I could, thinking, 'That's it, I'm dead this time!' But we all survived and when I lifted my head from the earth, there was a can of condensed milk right in front of my nose, fully opened! The explosion must have sent it straight up in the air from where someone had been making tea and now here it was in front of me – manna from heaven! 'Maybe I am dead . . .,' I thought, 'and this is the Pearly Gates – every soldier gets a can of milk on entry!'

That wasn't the only absurdity that day. Sometime later, figures appeared, darting from trench to trench. Unbelievably, it was the local Chinese, selling ice-cream! They were taking no notice of the fighting and probably thinking only of the business they could do. The absurdity of it was later to turn into tragedy because, as the Japs advanced, they decapitated every Chinese they came across and many heads were left on spikes, marking the tracks of their relentless advance.

As the battle developed, our firing positions became compromised by Japanese observation balloons. They simply floated over us, looking down with binoculars and communicating back to their own guns to direct their artillery fire. They seemed to have total freedom of the skies, with no sign of any of our aircraft. It meant we had to move to new positions several times during the fighting and the gun lorries had to be kept close by, ready to move, although eventually we did hide them away.

I was detailed to remain with my gun lorry, hidden some distance away from the guns, and await instructions for our next move. Towards evening, orders came for us to move much further south, which meant taking to the roads again in convoy. Our Signalsman, Bombardier Christian, appeared, telling me we needed to move and fast.

The direction back to the guns involved going round a loop in a river but on his way to me, Bombardier Christian had crossed the loop by a short cut that he'd spotted. Tree trunks had been placed at axle-width to span the river in two places. We thought we'd try the route to get back quicker. Approaching the first crossing place we found that the trees made a track just wide enough for the wheels of the lorry – just! Bombardier Christian climbed out and got across the river on one of the trees in order to direct me from the other side. I made a go of it with the lorry in creeper gear but, before I'd gone too far, I thought it best to see how my wheels were aligned, so I stopped to have a good look. Opening the door, all I could see below me was water. There was no means of stepping out onto anything. So I decided the best thing to do was go back and not risk the lorry. Putting the lorry into reverse, I had to take the chance that if I didn't touch the steering wheel, it would come off the trees the same way it went on. Luckily, it did. Otherwise there'd have been no gun lorry and my gun would have been stranded. We went round the loop after all in sensible fashion.

As we came towards the area in which the guns were positioned, there was a most almighty bang right behind us. Bombardier Christian stood up beside me in the gun lorry to poke his head out of the observation hatch and I called up to him. 'What the hell was that?'

'Look in your mirror!' he shouted.

Behind us was a shell crater. If we had been a few seconds slower, we would have been blown to bits.

I dropped off Bombardier Christian and drove to my gun to make the hook-up. The gun crew told me that we'd been detailed to remain in position as a rearguard while the other guns in my troop moved out. The other gun lorries were setting off and going back the same way they had come to their positions. This involved driving round the perimeter of an adjacent field, keeping under cover as best possible, before reaching the gateway to the road. Meanwhile, our gun sergeant suddenly screamed at me. 'Get that lorry under camouflage!' Looking around to see where any camouflage could be found, I decided on some smaller banana trees nearby and grabbed my machete. I took a mighty swipe at the foot of the first one and the machete passed through with ease, but the tree stayed standing. I raised my machete for a second swipe, whereupon all four trees just fell over. My first swipe had gone clean through the lot, as if they were celery!

Having got the lorry camouflaged, it wasn't long before our turn came to move off. We manhandled the gun off its swivel, got everything hooked up and climbed aboard the lorry. The sergeant directed me to take the same route as the other guns around the perimeter of the field as standard procedure but I objected. I said that I could cut across the field and get to the road ahead of the other guns so that we would be in the right order in the convoy – ours being No. 1 gun. We were always supposed to form up in numerical order because the surveyors would always place us that way, and Command would know which gun was which. The sergeant thought my lorry would never make it in the direction I intended because it would mean going through a ditch and up a 10 foot embankment to get to the road. But I knew the lorry was capable of it – even with the gun and limber attached. After all, it was a Quad, with powerful four-wheel drive. We set off and sure enough, by using the crawler gear, we entered the ditch and rose out again, climbing the embankment to the road with ease. But we arrived at number two position in the convoy. As we proceeded, I indicated to the No. 2 gun in front of me that we should swap places but he took no notice. We drove on and after a while we came to a multiple crossroads, at which the No. 2 gun stopped to check the direction. Suddenly, we were under attack from a Jap monoplane. We saw him turn and start his approach coming in low with a bomb strung underneath his belly. He must have been only 100 feet up as we tumbled out of the lorries and raced towards the trees for cover. Another of our troop and I finished up lying with our heads down behind a tree. The bomb exploded and when the plane had gone I got up, saying to the other man, 'Wow! That was close!' But there was no reply. He remained on the ground, dead. The bomb blast had somehow got him but not me. I had only lost my helmet, which was nowhere to be seen.

The bomb had missed the convoy but the wheels on the limber for No. 2 gun, which was full of ammunition, were on fire, threatening to blow us all sky-high, or so we thought. The driver unhitched the limber and drove his lorry away from the scene, leaving the rest of us stuck behind the burning limber. My crew quickly unhitched my lorry and I drove in front of No. 2's limber while they isolated it from its gun and attached it to me. There were many roads leading off the junction so I just chose one and got the burning limber away and around a corner, separating it from the convoy by trees and bushes. I must have manoeuvred as if my life depended on it, getting away after unhitching it there, thinking myself lucky the whole lot hadn't gone up. I was told later that the limber wouldn't have gone up immediately anyway. There could be fire all round it for hours before anything happened, so there had been no need to rush.

We proceeded without further incident to our new positions several miles or so down the road but when we turned onto a major road, heading west, as far as I could tell, everybody seemed to be going in the opposite direction to us – presumably away from the fighting. There was a lot of military amongst them and I later asked an officer if it meant we were retreating.

'Don't let me hear you say that again, Anckorn,' he said. 'There is no such word in the vocabulary of the 118!'

We had passed round the MacRitchie Reservoir and taken up positions near the golf course and the island's racecourse, which was serving as one of our supply depots.

That evening, we were called to an assembly at the racecourse, to hear from General Wavell, the Supreme Commander of Allied Forces. It was another rallying call. We were told we should consider ourselves the 'death or glory boys', and he ended with an affront: 'Those of you not willing to die are not fit to live!' Willing to die! *Willing?* I thought to myself. Afraid ... certainly. Fearful but ready to die if it had to be that way, definitely. But *willing*? I remember suddenly feeling cold all over.

We didn't rest that night as we seemed to be in the thick of it almost as soon as we returned to our positions, and our guns were firing the whole night long and throughout the next couple of days in what was now a major fire fight with constant counter-battery work and shifting of position and targets. Most of us, by that time, had been without sleep for several days and so I managed to fall asleep right beside our gun, totally oblivious to the violent recoil of the firing gun and the ground quaking under impact of enemy shells. Oddly enough though, when an incoming shell was a little too close for comfort again, I awoke to its sound immediately and got clear with everyone else.

In the early hours of the following day, I was detailed to take a message to our battery commander in the command post, which was far across the other side of a field behind us. To get to his position I had to cross the field under fire with shells landing all around. The field had become pitted with shell holes already and it was a matter of darting from one indent to another in haphazard fashion, making progress broadly in the right direction. The last run was the longest and as I ran, the sound of an incoming shell prompted me to run my guts out until at last, a trench around the command post opened up before me and I dived headlong into it. My momentum was so great that my body went head over heels into the trench, ending with me upside down and legs and torso up over the opposite side. Gathering myself quickly, I scrambled out of the trench and addressed the battery commander. I knew him as a most charming man who was a bank manager in civilian life and now he had become a good soldier too, but when I got to him, his nerve was faltering. He had his pistol in hand and appeared wide-eyed with terror. Beside him, I recognised Sergeant Ludgater holding a Bren gun. The commander reached out with a flask, offering me a drink, which was very welcome but before the spout reached my lips, the smell of whisky filled my nostrils and my respect for the commander evaporated. We had always been drilled to put only water or strong tea in our flasks, as a matter of survival and good soldiering. Now, it seemed, officers would indulge themselves regardless.

Moments later, the battery commander was startled by what he thought was something moving in a nearby tree. He started firing his pistol into it and Sergeant Ludgater turned and emptied his Bren gun into it too. The leafy branches of the tree were shredded, but no Jap fell out of it. It was then that I noticed Sergeant Ludgater was fully spruced up in uniform, which was odd, given the battle going on around us. It turned out that he had been detailed for evacuation later that day. We didn't know it at the time but our High Command had issued orders for parties of men, selected for their specialism and likely future contribution to the war, to be sent to HQ for a 'special mission'. That special mission was to escape from the island by whatever means possible, before Singapore was lost.

Later that morning, my gun took a near miss and was put out of action. I was detailed to go to the ordnance depot back at the polo ground to get a replacement. As we were now fairly close to Singapore town itself, it wasn't far to go, but how I did it without a map, I'll never know. The odd thing too was that I had no fear, despite the intensity of the battle going on and the likelihood of running into the advancing Japs. It really was the case that, in action, as long as there was something to do, there was no fear. Concentration took over. But was I, in General Wavell's view, 'Willing to die'? No, absolutely not! I was determined to fight and to live!

In any event, there was no trouble with Japs or Jap shelling on the way down to the depot and picking up the gun was straightforward. In no time at all, I was ready for the return but as none of us had eaten much for two days and nights, I made a beeline for the canteen before leaving to see what I could find to take back. The cooks had a large dixie tin full of chopped beetroot sitting on a table in preparation for the day's lunch. It was the only thing handy so I persuaded them to let me run it back to the battery, where our need was greater than theirs, I assured them – although beetroot was probably not what everybody was longing for.

With the gun hitched up and the beetroot beside me on the bench seat, I was ready for the off. Then a sergeant-major appeared – carrying a shell.

'You're from the one-one-eight, aren't you?' he asked.

'Yes,' I said.

'Well, you're taking this back with you,' he said, as he carelessly hefted the shell and complained that gun loaders should do their job better in our battery. The shell had been jammed in the breech of the gun that I was now taking back and of course, removing it was no laughing matter as it could explode in the process. Normally, they would have carefully followed a set procedure for removing the shell and then the cartridge would have been separated off so that the bags of cordite could be extracted and the shell made safe. But he was about to hand me the complete shell, cartridge and all, and as he hefted it, I could see from the nose cone that it was primed to go off on impact, too.

'I'm not!' I said. 'That thing's fused for impact – you don't expect me to drive with that?'

'You're taking it, and that's an order!' he bawled, adding, in his bloody-mindedness, that it would teach us to be more careful.

'I'm not, and that's a fact!' was my insolent reply, and I started to drive to the gate.

Somehow, when you're in action and your life is at stake, instinct takes over and rank doesn't come into it any more. On top of that, I had always been of a mind that if something didn't make sense to me, I simply wouldn't do it, no matter who was telling me. It must be an Anckorn family trait as my brother was the same and my twin sister would argue the hind leg off a donkey. But now, I was about to get my comeuppance.

When I stopped at the gate the sergeant appeared again, cradling the shell in his left arm. He simply came up to the lorry, opened my door with his free hand and dumped the shell in my lap. Slamming the door shut, he walked off without a word.

Dumbfounded and not wanting to disturb the damn thing, it seemed the best thing to do was just drive. So off I went – gingerly, carrying the live shell in my lap and chopped beetroot on the seat beside me.

On the way back I spotted bombers in the sky – but not heading in my direction. I kept my eye on them. A neat formation of twenty-seven again – did they always come in twenty-sevens? Further up the road there was one of our anti-aircraft guns, which fired a single shot as I passed. I presumed it was a ranging shot because nothing happened and the aircraft continued. Then suddenly, the lead bomber exploded and every kind of coloured light came out of it, as if it had been packed with Verey lights or something. It was like a firework display. The plane then went straight up, vertical, before flipping over onto its back and falling, head-first, like a stone – flat-out – must have been 200 miles an hour when it hit the ground. Wham! As he was coming down, all the other bombers appeared to turn around and go home. I'd heard that the lead bomber in a Jap formation was always the master bomber who gave the orders to the others in 'follow the leader' fashion, so without him, presumably, that was it, they'd have to go home. I cheered out loud in my cab at such good shooting by our lot.

I'd gone another couple of miles and was nearly back to our gun position when I became aware of people diving into ditches along my route. I'd decided before this trip that if I saw men diving into ditches like that, I'd stop the lorry and do the same. But I couldn't see any more aircraft around so I just carried on. The fact was, the bombers were behind me and I was their target! Whether it was the same formation of bombers I'd seen earlier or not, I'll never know, but with complete mastery of the skies the Japs could probably just look around for their targets at will. I was a sitting duck, still in desert camouflage, wandering along the road, trailing a gun. When the bombs started falling and exploding behind me, my foot went to the floor on the accelerator but it was no good – I got the lot – a diarrhoea attack!

The noise was deafening and absolutely terrifying. The lorry was lurching about and metal was flying around my cabin. I had thought the cabin of the lorry might give me some protection but now it was more like a biscuit tin, tossed around on the road by the erupting earth and skewered in a thousand places by shrapnel. Suddenly there was a voice and it was shouting, 'Stop! Stop the lorry! Stop the lorry!' It was my own voice. Ever since seeing one of my fellows get shot driving his lorry and watching him as he careered onwards into a ravine, I'd told myself that if it ever happened to me, I'd stop the lorry somehow, no matter what. But after kangarooing down the road like some demented victim of prey, the lorry juddered to a stop on its own, arrested by the weight of the gun behind it.

Instinctively, I thought to get out and away from the lorry and as I moved to do so, I saw through my side window an image that has indelibly planted itself on my memory ever since. In a strange, mystical slow motion, I was looking at a bomb coming down less than 10 feet away – so close, I could have put my hand out and caught it. The rivets on it were plain to see and Japanese lettering, too. I saw the tailfins and a long spike on the front of the bomb as it went into the ground. I saw the bomb begin to explode as flames shot out the back of it. Unbelievably, I saw all this and in that instant, thought, 'I'm dead!'

It's true what they say. Parts of your life do flash before you. For me, it was my fourth birthday party. I was at home and could see myself and my twin sister amongst guests, sitting around the table. Each one of us had a large glass with different coloured jellies in and some had cream on top. The piano was there and my mother standing by it. I looked at the dress she was wearing. I saw that our patterned curtains were drawn and there were little flickering flames of the candles on the table. In this deathly reverie, I heard myself saying 'poor mum' out loud.

There was a deafening blast as the lorry lurched violently again and I was engulfed in what sounded like metal hailstones from what must have been an anti-personnel bomb. I knew I was getting wounded but it didn't seem to hurt.

The bombardment went on and on and on and I began to pray that something would get me straight in the head and make it quick. Then the mayhem stopped and instead of wanting to die, I wanted to live again!

The air was thick with dust and the lorry was leaning over on the passenger's side. I looked at myself and it seemed I was still in one piece. Then I realised the shell was no longer in my lap. I looked about franticly and saw at the back of me, a huge hole, going up through the lockers and the roof. Surely the shell couldn't have gone off and left me in one piece? That sergeant at the depot must have been pulling my leg, but how come this hole? I moved to open my door and get out but found my right hand hanging off. There was no pain but it was completely unresponsive and I could see that something had gone through my arm as well and opened an artery. Blood was everywhere. I knew I must get out quick and so I lay over on the seat and kicked at the door with my feet until it swung open. Legs first, I dropped out into swirling dust not knowing where I'd be landing. Before I hit the ground, my left leg was jolted up suddenly and a spasm of pain went through me. Something had penetrated the back of my knee and a strange thought came into my head –'they're actually attacking *me*! They're trying to kill me! They're *supposed* to kill me!' A gunner like me is usually some distance away from direct action and so this very personal reality of killing had never dawned on me. The horror of it propelled me onwards, despite my injuries. Somehow, I was up on my feet running at full pelt away from the lorry through thick smoke and dust not knowing where on earth I was going and as I went, it felt as though I had an orange box wrapped round my left foot. It must have been the effect of the bullet or whatever it was. Then, out of nowhere, one of our gun sergeants appeared. He ran alongside me shouting 'Where are you going?' and took hold of my arm. 'I don't know!' I shouted back. Then he seemed to veer off and disappear into the smoke, whereupon I fell straight into a monsoon ditch and passed out.

It has never been particularly significant to me but it was pointed out sometime later that I'd been bombed on Friday, 13 February at 1300 hrs! Well, the number thirteen had always been my mother's lucky number and so it was for me, it seems. Had it been any other day or time of day, perhaps the bombing would have been the end of me.

As it was, I lay there out cold and during this time, there was all sorts of goings on, apparently.

The whole event had occurred near enough to our gun position for my troop to see what happened. So near, in fact, that once the bombs had stopped falling and the smoke and dust had thinned out a bit, some of the men ran down to the lorry – but I doubt it was out of concern for me. No. Besides checking the gun itself, which turned out to be useless, they probably just wanted their gear out of the lockers in the back of the cabin. When they got there, they found all the lockers smashed up, blood all over the place and lumps of purple soft mush sliding down what was left of the windscreen. One of them was apparently physically sick and when they returned, they'd said to the others, 'Poor Gus. He got a right packet! Not much left of him and what there is – well, it's all over the cabin.' They couldn't have known it but what they'd actually seen, of course, was the beetroot that I'd collected from the ordnance yard, mixed with all the blood that had gushed from my arm and wrist. They obviously didn't see me lying in the ditch.

However, Bombardier Porter, from my battery, did. He wasn't with the others. He had been nominated for the same 'special mission' as

Sergeant Ludgater and was on his way to headquarters in Singapore town when he came across me lying in the ditch. Seeing that I was seriously wounded and likely to die, he took my dog tags, both of them, in order to report my status. It was his report that eventually filtered back to my parents almost a year later, when they were notified by the War Office that they had received an unconfirmed report of me being wounded on 13th February 1942. The War Office note went on to say that, whilst endeavours were being made to confirm the report and the nature of my injuries, they would continue to post me as 'missing in action'.

Bombardier Porter himself went on to make a successful escape a couple of days later, along with two dozen others in a group led by Lieutenant Mickey Burrows, one of our officers. They were a group of hand-picked specialists, mostly from my regiment, who were considered valuable to the war effort elsewhere. There were also five Intelligence Corps personnel. A detailed log was kept of their hair-raising escape, which began when they made a break for it at 6.30 am on the morning of 15 February. They had commandeered a leaky lifeboat off a naval training ship and rowed themselves out until they came across a small steam launch, which they likewise commandeered and immediately set about getting going. It took the engineers in the group, one of which was Sergeant Ludgater, half the day to get enough steam up. Meanwhile, the rest of the group went about pilfering coal from neighbouring craft and food from dockside warehouses. Finally, with barely enough steam, they weighed anchor and made their way in fits and starts out to sea, leaving Singapore, a blazing ruin of a place shrouded in black cloud, behind them. They eventually made it to Sumatra and after further adventures, staying only just ahead of the Japs, who were by then invading Sumatra, they put to sea again and were luckily picked up by one of our warships. Ten days later, they were in Bombay.

By some means or another, men from my battery did find me before it was too late. I regained consciousness whilst being dragged back to our gun positions by Bombardier Buck. Once there, he got me strapped up with a tourniquet and a lorry arrived out of nowhere, driven by our gun sergeant. He was going to take me to a field hospital but they couldn't get me inside the lorry for some reason, so instead, they decided to lay me in the slot between the wing and the engine housing. Gun Sergeant O'Neill then proceeded to drive off at full speed. The pain was just awful and I kept trying to distract myself from it. It seemed odd that the sergeant was driving – he should be working the guns, I thought – but perhaps more of them were out of action by now. He was crunching the gears and straining the engine as the journey went on and on, during which I drifted in and out of consciousness. Suddenly, machine-gun fire started coming at us from the roadside and something

84

cut my nose and thudded into the engine next to my face. The lorry shuddered to a halt. We were at a standstill in the middle of the road with bullets coming at us from all over the place. None of this seemed to worry me – I was out of it, half dead anyway.

But then I felt myself being manhandled again, off the lorry and into a Red Cross ambulance that had drawn up, despite the mayhem. Inside were four other wounded men. We had an Indian driver who slammed the thing into gear and raced off as fast as he could. Within seconds, it seemed, we were being shelled and then the ambulance swerved violently before coming to a stop. The other four wounded opened the doors and cleared off, leaving me inside, scarcely able to move and looking out on an open field near some housing that we had come to rest in. The shelling had stopped and there was no sign of the driver. Time passed and despite the open doors, the heat inside became intense under the blistering afternoon sun. My breathing was getting faster and my mouth stuck together when I swallowed. It felt like I'd been placed in an oven. I attempted to move and get myself out of it. But then the Indian driver suddenly appeared, thrusting something at me and shouting, 'Water, sahib, water!'

He lifted my head and something wet went down my throat. As I drank and felt the spillage going over my face, my mind was spurred into life with an hallucinatory thought, 'The driver is Gunga Din!' and I began reciting to myself the words of the poem that I'd learned by heart as a child:

> 'E lifted up my 'ead,
> An' e plugged me where I bled,
> An' e gev me 'arf-a-pint o' water-green.
> It was crawlin' and it stunk,
> But of all the drinks I've drunk,
> I'm gratefullest for the one from Gunga Din.

With the words going round my head, I must have passed out again because the next thing I was aware of was being dragged across a street that was lined with buildings. I must have looked like a dead chicken when a little Indian boy came running up to me and put his face right up to mine. 'Hello!' he said, with a big smile across his face. When we reached the kerb of the pavement, my feet clanged into it and pain shot up my body as the dragging continued until we entered a building that turned out to be a huge post office filled with wounded men. A surgeon was using the post office counter as an operating table and perhaps because I was bleeding so heavily, they lifted me straight onto it.

'I'm sorry, son,' I heard the surgeon say, 'I can't save your hand, it's got to come off.'

I mumbled back, 'Well get on with it and save me.'

An orderly put some gauze over my face and splashed ether on it, at which point I reacted violently, shaking my head to get clear of the suffocating gauze. Then the orderly seemed to recognise me. 'Aren't you the conjuror we saw in Liverpool?'

Still spluttering, I said that I was and the orderly immediately appealed to the surgeon. 'You can't cut his hand off, Sir, he's a conjuror!'

Before I blacked out, I heard the surgeon say, 'Well, I'll see what I can do.'

Whatever he did I wasn't to know, as the next time I became properly conscious again, I was in a crowded hospital ward with my arm strapped up and hung from a hook above my bed. On the end of my arm all I could see was a large dressing like a huge boxing glove. I didn't know if it was an hour, a day or a week later.

It was, in fact, the morning of the 14 February and I was in the Alexandra Military hospital. The ward was crammed with wounded. So much so that men lay on camp beds either side of me. I was desperate to know if I still had my hand or not, because I couldn't feel anything on the end of my arm and I couldn't see anything either with the arm being held up in the air by the hook. I asked the man on my right.

'Have I still got a right hand – can you see for me?'

He struggled to get himself up and eventually he was able to see.

'This little piggy went to market . . .' he started but he didn't need to go on. The relief in my mind was sensational!

Time passed with comings and goings of staff in the ward and I drifted in and out of consciousness. There were increasing sounds of gunfire and explosions each time I awoke but nothing seemed to matter anymore and I began to think I must be dying. But with each bout of consciousness, pain was intensifying – as well as my thirst.

A couple of times when I awoke, there didn't seem to be any staff anymore and then I caught sight of an orderly coming down the ward, hurriedly putting up blackout boards on the windows even though it was daylight. The sound of shelling and gunfire was all about. Someone else was running up the ward. I heard myself making a sort of growling noise and a voice next to my bed was calling out, 'Doctor, Doctor . . . do something here . . . he's bleeding like hell!' My blood had apparently been dripping down on the man below me. The running footsteps arrived at my bed and my strapped-up arm was lowered from the hook and the tourniquet was adjusted. Excruciating pain rushed through my upper body as my arm was placed across my chest, and I passed out again.

It must have been around this time that Japanese soldiers made their entry into the hospital grounds and into the hospital itself.

86

It is now well recorded that about 100 soldiers in full battle gear assaulted the hospital, just before 1430 hrs that day, firing at those who came out of the hospital to protest Red Cross immunity and bayoneting staff as they came across them. When they arrived in the theatre block, they set about killing indiscriminately, including a patient under anaesthetic on the operating table. One of the surgeons, Captain Smiley, took a bayonet in his chest but it was deflected from his heart by a cigarette case in his breast pocket. The soldier thrust again but the captain this time deflected it with his arm and it went into his groin. Two more thrusts followed, knocking the captain into an orderly and they both fell to the ground with Captain Smiley on top. He whispered to the orderly to play dead and the soldiers left. After they'd gone, the orderly tended to the surgeon's wounds and he not only lived but immediately got on with helping others who were still alive.

For my part, I woke to the sound of heavy footsteps and the sight of a military person striding down the ward. Up to this time, I had still never seen a Japanese soldier but this certainly wasn't one of ours.

I turned to the man beside me.

'Is that a Jap?' I asked.

'Yes,' he said. 'They've taken over the hospital.'

'Oh,' I said, but then drifted off again.

Re-opening my eyes at whatever time it was later, I saw more goings on. This time, a group of wounded were struggling along the ward, bound together with what looked like barbed wire and followed by a soldier with fixed bayonet. I turned again to the man on the floor beside me.

'What's going on?'

'They're taking them out to shoot them,' came the reply.

'Oh,' I said again, none of it registering properly with me in my delirium.

It was noticeable that the battle noises had diminished, although there was still gunfire now and then. The ward was quiet and I was holding in my pain, listening and trying not to make a sound. Suddenly, I could hear many feet coming into the ward and a kind of thumping noise started.

'What are they doing?' I asked the man next to me.

'Bayoneting. They're bayoneting everybody,' he said calmly.

I listened again. There were no cries, no screams, nothing. Just thud ... thud ... thud.

I didn't feel fear and I don't think the man next to me did either. I just thought, 'I'll never be twenty-five,' for some reason, and then, 'Poor mum'.

The thuds went on ... thud ... thud ... thud ... I didn't mind dying, but I didn't want to see them do it me so I pulled my pillow up with my good hand and got my head under it. Then I must have drifted off again because when I awoke next, there was silence again in the ward. I turned slowly to the fellow on the camp bed next to me but he was dead. Lifting my head, I could see the other beds still had their occupants, but there was no movement. I remember thinking, 'So this is what death is like ... I must be dead.'

Nobody knows why I wasn't killed like all the others but the assumption is that, when the Japs came to my bed and found blood all over my chest and down on the floor and my face covered – like a corpse – they must have thought me dead already and passed me by. In any event, I was still losing blood and because of it, I must have become unconscious again, staying that way for some time because the next thing I knew, I was lying on the floor of what turned out to be the Chinese High School.

There was a mass of us there on the floor and once again I turned to whoever was next to me.

'Where are we?' I said.

'We're in the bag,' came the reply.

I'd never heard that expression before so I tried again.

'Where's that?'

'We're prisoners. It's all over,' came the answer.

My dulled senses scarcely understood the enormity of meaning in these words. It was 15 February. Singapore had fallen. The citadel of the empire had been ravaged. The proudest of armies had been brought to its knees.

Chapter 9

CAPTIVITY

The Japanese did not take Singapore Island. Malay Command lost it.
B.P. Farrell, *The Defence & Fall of Singapore*

The officer commanding all Allied forces in Malaya and Singapore was Lieutenant-General Percival. He was a man of much achievement and distinction but a man that could be described as more analytical than imposing of character and perhaps also as a man more gifted in dealing with situations than capable of changing them. He ordered the surrender, believing that there was no longer any hope once ammunition began to run out and once the besieging forces had contaminated the water supply, blown up fuel dumps and cut power supplies. He would have realised that, with complete freedom of the skies and, so it seemed, the sea, the Japanese could easily reinforce their situation and revise any temporary victory that might be achieved by the Allies. He believed that to continue the fight would have meant slaughter for the civilian population as well as the army. The decision was his. General Wavell had left the scene and set up camp in Sumatra.

Surrender came as a great shock to us troops and to civilians alike. History tells us that it was also something of a surprise to Lieutenant-General Tomoyuki Yamashita, commander of the invading Japanese 25th Army. He had been expecting to have to fight to the death in the streets of the city.

It must have been a severe setback too for General Wavell, who, as we now know, issued orders to Percival only five days earlier that were unequivocal:

It is certain that our troops on Singapore Island heavily outnumber any Japanese who have crossed the Straits. We must destroy them. Our whole fighting reputation is at stake and the honour of the British Empire. The Americans have held out in the Bataan Islands against heavier odds and the Russians are turning back the picked strength of the Germans. The Chinese, with an almost complete lack of modern equipment, have held the greater part of their country against the full strength of the Japanese for almost four and a half years. It will be disgraceful if we yield our boasted fortress of Singapore to inferior enemy forces. There must be no thought of sparing the troops or civil population and no mercy must be shown to weakness in any shape or form. Commanders and senior officers must lead their troops and must if necessary die with them. There must be no thought or question of surrender. Every unit must fight it out to the end and in close contact with the enemy. Please see that the above is brought to the notice of all senior officers and by them to the troops. I look to you and your men to fight to the end and prove that the fighting spirit that won our Empire still exists to enable us to defend it.

In the event, our superior strength stood for nothing. Commentators since the war have concluded that Singapore was lost due to prevarication, dispute and constant friction between our commanders, as well as with and between the civil authorities, even before the battles started. There was a moment, before the Japanese invasion fleet had barely set off, when history could have been written differently. 'Operation Matador', as it was known, was a plan for a pre-emptive denial of the Thailand coastline to the Japanese such as to prevent them getting a foothold there and access to Malaya. Despite endless equivocation, our forces were ready and waiting to move into Thailand and secure areas around Singora and Patani, where the invasion was expected to come, but even as the Japanese were known to have set off, there was still no green light from London. At almost the last minute, London did give the green light but Lieutenant-General Percival failed to give the order to advance and so the die was cast against us.

Throughout the battles that followed, our forces were never co-ordinated properly and so their potential was dissipated. In addition to this, the morale that had been there in our troops at the beginning of the campaign was ill-founded. It was rooted in a misplaced belief and trust in our innate superior fighting capabilities, which meant that the scale of suitable extra training for jungle warfare was inadequate.

Historians note also that 'Fortress Singapore' was no fortress at all because the northern defences of the island had never been completed, even though the project to make Singapore the central core of British Imperial defence in the Far East actually began in the 1920s. The fact was, we couldn't afford to fully fortify Singapore after the debilitating cost of the First World War. Unbelievably, the reality of this and its implications were only brought to the attention of Churchill in the last few weeks before Singapore fell. It was on 21 January, just over three weeks before the fall, that General Wavell sent him a devastating message:

> I am anxious that you should not have false impression of the defences of Singapore Island. I did not realise myself until lately how entirely defences were planned against seaward attack only.

In his memoirs Churchill was bitter:

> I ought to have known. My advisers ought to have known and I ought to have been told or I ought to have asked. The reason I had not asked about this matter amid the thousands of questions I put, was that the possibility of Singapore having no landward defences no more entered my mind than that a battleship would be launched without a bottom.

It is now a matter of history, of course, that what we witnessed was not just the loss of Singapore but the crumbling of the British Empire.

The immediate issue for the conquering Japanese was that they suddenly had a vast number of prisoners on their hands, which they weren't expecting. This was a new and strange situation for them, having fought their way right down the Malay Peninsula at lightning speed to take Singapore in just nine weeks. They themselves had no concept of being a prisoner or indeed of being out of action because of being wounded. Their troops were indoctrinated with an ancient belief system that manifested itself in the military concept of *bushido* – the will to fight to a glorious death for the honour of the Emperor. That zeal must have been at its peak on the eve of their assault of the strategic Bukit Timah Hill and on the following day, the 11 February, because that was their *Kigensetsu* day – the anniversary of the foundation of the Japanese Empire 2,602 years previously. Anyhow, their zeal took them to victory and left them with something like 120,000 prisoners of war to deal with. They probably detested the very sight of each and every one of us. Perhaps our own General Wavell shared that view after his final rallying call and earlier invective, 'If you are not willing to die, you're not fit to live!'

Within hours of taking control of Singapore, the Japanese decreed that the vast British military establishment at Changi, covering almost 10 square miles of the easternmost tip of the island, should become a gigantic prison camp in which the majority of the captives would be concentrated. The order to move to Changi was given on 17 February and for three solid days a procession of defeated men trudged wearily out of Singapore town and along the 16 or so miles of road out to Changi. I wasn't one of them. Those who couldn't walk were dealt with differently.

I don't really know how long I was on the floor of the Chinese High School with the other assorted wounded. All I know is that we stayed there until the day some Japs came in and started taking us out. I was picked up and thrown onto a lorry with the others. They drove us up to Changi and on arrival, we were each thrown off the lorry onto the ground next to others on stretchers. By now I was in a state of hypersensitivity. If someone had so much as dropped cigarette ash on my foot it would have felt like a bomb. I just knew I must get attended to or that was it. I was dying. But there was no point in expecting anyone to come to me as it seemed everyone had worries of their own. We were all exhausted, thirsty and hungry.

So I picked myself up as best I could – crawling around with my left leg not working and my right arm still smashed. I must have been like a spider with a broken leg. While I was crawling I came across our divisional commander, Major-General Beckwith-Smith – the man who had so heartily approved my joining the divisional concert party in England and so enjoyed my magic show that he called me 'his conjuror'. He would often salute me in jest before I saluted him! The last time I'd come before him was to receive a medal for winning the half-mile race in the brigade sports day, at which he had said to me, with that deep, shoulder-bobbing laugh of his, 'Another of your magic tricks eh, Anckorn!' Now here I was, barely able to crawl, and there he was, sitting on a bench by himself, very dishevelled and disconsolate.

When I reached him, I said, 'Hello, Sir'. But he didn't even look at me. He remained motionless, staring into the distance – not with it at all. What struck me most was his loneliness. No other officers were anywhere to be seen. He seemed lost.

Singapore must have been a personal disaster for Major-General Beckwith-Smith – 'Becky', as we called him. He had been made a general and given command of the 18th Infantry Division after having done such a good job commanding the 1st Guards Brigade as part of the British Expeditionary Force that fought in France at the beginning of the war. The Guards distinguished themselves in their rear guard action during the eventual dismal evacuation at Dunkirk. Under his leadership, the 18th Division soon distinguished itself too, competing with other infantry divisions in training exercises. The result was that the 18th got the first assignment overseas for a fully armoured division and that was to be North Africa. But en route, the destination had switched to being Malaya and Singapore, and he would have to face yet another 'fighting retreat' situation – more hopeless than Dunkirk. Nevertheless, it was the firepower of the 18th that gave Yamashita something to think about in the final days and hours of the battle for Singapore. On the day I had gone for the replacement gun and the next two days after that, while I was drifting in and out of consciousness from my wounds in the Alexander Hospital, Becky had them firing at full pelt, and in the final hours of the 15 February, he had ordered them to fire off everything they'd got. It gave the impression that the Allies were far from surrendering and hardly short of ammunition. But to no avail. When it was all over Becky, had sent a message out to us all – a message I never got to see:

> No Commander has led a happier and more loyal team into battle. The division was sent into a theatre of war for which it was neither trained nor equipped, to fight a clever and cunning enemy who was on the crest of a wave. It was sent to fight a battle already lost and had to pass through troops whose morale had been badly shaken. It had to endure long periods of hardship without food or rest, yet it fought with great courage and tenacity, inflicting heavy losses on the enemy. Every man, and I know he will, should rightly hold his head high, knowing that he has upheld the best traditions of the British Army. During the 18 months I have been privileged to command the division at home and overseas, it has carried out every varied and exacting task it has been called upon to undertake and now I can only dedicate the rest of my life to help in every way the Officers, Warrant Officers and men of the 18th Division. God bless you all and bring you safely home when victory is finally ours, with the knowledge that you have played your part in its achievement.

To me, he seemed a broken man and what's more, it was to be the last I'd see of him. Some months later, he was bundled off, along with all the senior command, to Formosa. But he died of diphtheria within a few months.

I continued crawling around looking for faces I knew for the next two days, sleeping wherever I finished up on the ground. I couldn't help thinking how like those beggars in Bombay I must have looked. Eventually someone found me – one of our gun sergeants. He took hold of me and got me to the sergeants' mess that had been set up. It all looked very proper with swing doors and all that. I was beginning to feel half alive again as he walked me into the building, but when we went through the swing doors, one of them swung back and whacked me on my injured arm and wrist! It opened it all up again, with blood everywhere, which meant I was hurriedly taken to what had become the hospital wing of the camp called Roberts Hospital, where I got the first real treatment for my injuries.

The first thing they did at the hospital was put me in the gangrene ward. It was like a cheese factory – the smell was disgusting. I didn't realise I'd got gangrene but my whole arm was gangrenous when they 'unwrapped' it. Once again, it looked like I might lose my hand, and now, possibly my whole arm. But they had another solution. They filled my wrist and arm with maggots!

The back of my hand was completely open with all the tendons exposed. So what they did was put eight maggots in there and plaster over it. They also plastered up the compound fractures in my arm and left the whole lot to sort itself out. Probably a week later, they opened it all up again. The maggots had cleaned up the mess completely. All you could see was beautiful red meat, like in a butcher's shop! But then they had to get the damn things out and they had gone right up my arm by now, to near my shoulder, where I could feel them still wriggling. The doctor got a pair of extra-long forceps and stuck them into my arm through the open wound. Each time he thought he'd got one he'd actually got hold of a tendon, causing me to yell, 'That's me! ... not the bloody maggot!' Eventually, all the maggots came out, but in twelve bloated pieces.

It was all worth it. My wrist and arm healed well over the following weeks. On one of his rounds the medical officer proclaimed cheerily that I was making good progress and my arm was definitely saved. In the manner of a shopkeeper having given good service he asked, 'So, is there anything else we can do for you?' I replied hesitatingly, 'Well, I've had no bowel movement for probably three weeks now ...' to which he replied, 'Anckorn, you haven't eaten anything worth calling food for the last three weeks, what do you expect?'

That was indeed the situation generally now. Nobody had eaten much in the last three weeks. The camp had apparently run out of any canned food that had been found or brought into Changi with our arrival or that had since been grabbed from bombed-out houses or warehouses. The daily diet in the hospital had become just one little biscuit with a bit of raspberry jam on it, and all day long, we would crave for that biscuit. Eventually, rice started to be issued to the camp and I had a visit from my friend Fred Coles, who had been our brilliant accordionist in the concert party back in England. He came to see me on the first day rice was issued. He'd put a portion of his rice ration in a little tobacco tin and brought it to me. In my weakening state through lack of nourishment, lying there in the hospital ward, this meant a great deal to me and I remember thinking as he left me, 'Well, whatever our situation, you can't get a better man than that!'

Things did 'improve' once rice was being issued but the overall amount of food available to feed all the hospital patients was woefully little. I believe it meant that all they had to dish out per man per day was:

8oz of rice
1/6oz of tea
2/3oz of sugar

1/2oz of milk
1/2oz of cheese
1oz of vegetables
1/6oz of salted butter

When I was eventually discharged from Roberts Hospital, I made my way back to the sergeants' mess to find out where I was to be billeted. Our regiment had been allocated to a number of bungalows that stood on the Roberts Barracks grounds in Changi. On arrival at my designated one, I immediately asked after friends to see where they may be and in particular, Bombardier Christian, because the last I'd seen of him was when he had come to say goodbye to me in the battle. He had been detailed to go and fix a communication wire that the Japs had cut and he didn't expect to survive.

My housemates directed me to a bungalow nearby where he was known to be, although nobody had actually seen him for quite a few days. When I arrived at the house, some of his fellows were around but there was no sign of him.

'Is Bombardier Christian here?' I asked.

'Broom cupboard!' came the answer.

Half thinking they were pulling my leg, I went to the cupboard and on opening it, found him in there but in such an emaciated condition that it shook me. He had been such a healthy man with a good solid physique and now he was reduced to a skeleton. His face was sunken, making his prominent white teeth stick out a mile and his eyes peered out from deep, darkened sockets. These were the signs of dysentery.

'Chris ... it's me, Gus,' I said. 'What are you doing in there ... come on, get out of it!'

'I've had it. I'm dead,' came his barely audible reply.

'You're not dead, Chris, you've just got dysentery ... now come out of there and we'll get you seen to.'

'Leave me,' was all he would say and so in the end, I did, thinking he would come out eventually, in his own time, and his mates would get him to the dysentery ward of the hospital. But I never saw him again.

The days that followed were to make such an impression on me that it led me to develop a code of behaviour for myself that I would stick to for the rest of my captivity.

The Changi camp was not just one barracks but a site made up of four separate barracks. The 18th Division was in the Roberts Barracks and the Australian 8th Division had been put in the Selarang Barracks about a half-mile away from us. At that time, the camp was somewhat free and easy – we could more or less roam about as we wished and visit other areas at will. It meant that, setting aside food shortages, life at the camp could be tolerable and considering we were no longer fighting, it seemed we didn't have to worry about being shot, shelled, bombed or bayoneted. I managed to convince myself that if this was where we were going to have to be for the duration of the war, all would be well as long as we all held on. But as I went around the place, I felt increasingly separate from others the more I observed behaviour that indicated otherwise. What I was seeing would scarcely have seemed possible only a few weeks earlier.

When rice first became available, it was dished up in large mess tins, one for each bungalow. This was portioned out near as damn it equally to everyone but on occasion, there was a tiny bit left. On one such occasion, our NCO said, 'Who wants this?' and no one showed any interest as the stuff was so awful anyway, but when he slung the mess tin down on the floor, a fight started. Two of my housemates were literally at each other's throats, rolling all over the floor like a pair of dogs, just for the few grains of rotten rice that were left. I resolved there and then, that would never be me – I would discipline myself to never expect more than I got and to be detached about what I did get. The image of Fred Coles came into my mind, offering me that little bit of his rice. That would be me too, not this business, fighting like dogs.

Later, rice was dished out from the central cookhouse in our area and we would all queue up to get our small bug-infested ball of disgusting rice. There was method in eating it. To get the bugs out you held your plate out in the sun and the direct sunlight made the bugs crawl out of the rice ball to the side of the plate. In the meantime, you had to keep the flies off – one fly on your food and you'd have to chuck the lot away because of the high risk of dysentery, or worse. Our cooks could never judge the right amount of rice for everybody and often there would be some left over. The Malay cooks would shout what sounded like 'Leggies', which was actually '*Lagis*', meaning 'more', and another queue would instantly form. This second queue became known as the 'Leggies' queue or just the 'Leggies', for short. So often, men would take their first portion and simply go and join the back of the same queue again hoping it would become the Leggies. Having wolfed down their first portion, they often became distraught when it turned out there were no Leggies. Observing this, I resolved that I would always make a 'meal' of the first portion, eating it grain by grain and treating each grain as a 'mouthful' in itself – to be looked at and savoured as if it were from a box of chocolates.

As we could move around freely, most of us did just that. But I became aware of so many men just wandering aimlessly, looking downcast and with increasingly starved bodies, looking skeletal. You could almost see their spirit dying as the days went on. So many looked in a dreadful state with faces almost as sunken as Bombardier Christian's had been and with a pallor that often had me thinking, 'Poor fellow, he must be dying.' Then, by chance, as I was going about, I found a broken piece of mirror, which I picked up, thinking it would come in useful. As I did so, my face was caught in it and I was horror-struck. My face was as bad as theirs. It was unrecognisable! I left the mirror where it was and resolved I would avoid ever looking at myself again. As long as I could feel alright and keep my mind off things, that was all that would matter. As I carried on I also decided that I would not wander around as I was tending to then and as most men did. No. I would look for a place I was going to walk to and even if it was just a tree, I would walk over to it, in a straight line, with purpose and with my head up. Mentally, I would always be leaving one place and going to another.

There were made-up roads through the camp, still in reasonable condition after we'd cleared them. One day I came across a fellow sitting on the roadside curb with his head in his hands, looking very despondent. I made it my purpose to walk over and join him. We chatted. He had been a concert pianist before the war and had regularly done recitals at the Wigmore Hall and had played at the Albert Hall too. By way of conversation, I asked him how he rated himself.

'Horowitz. Vladimir Horowitz. He's the only man that can show me a thing or two,' he said pensively.

But our chat was only reminding him of how things were and how they should be for him now, if it were not for this war.

'I can't put up with all this, here,' he went on. 'I simply can't live without my music.'

With my belief that 'all would be well' if we could all just hold out, I started talking about our division getting the theatre in Roberts Barracks functioning again and the programmes of lectures that had been started, too. The theatre was a massive hall and rooms were plentiful. We got talking about subjects that interested him and I found we had a common interest in languages. We both spoke fluent French and he was just as fluent in Spanish. His other interests were astronomy and navigation and he began to think of going to lectures on these subjects if there were any. But music was his lifeblood.

It seemed to me an odd thing that men like this were out here at all and involved in fighting. He was a slight, physically insignificant man, so obviously an artiste and a thinker, not a fighter. But of course, he was a Territorial, like the rest of us in the 118th, although he had been seconded to us from another regiment. Territorial units tended to be 'hand-picked' for interesting men that could get on with each other, not necessarily men that could go into battle. So here was this man, Reg Renison, accomplished concert pianist, serving in the war as a Signaller – and now a prisoner of war. We struck up a friendship that was to carry us both through the months ahead.

The theatres on the Changi site – there were several of them – were quite quickly brought into service and by the time I had come out of Roberts Hospital, productions had already started. I heard that in the Australian sector, there was a conjuring act going on so I made it my purpose to go down to see the show. The man I met and got to know there, Syd Piddington, was in many ways the exact opposite in nature to my new friend, Reg Renison. He had been an accountant before the war, but now, finding himself amongst so many people of such diverse talents and with time to get to know them, his mind was opening up more and more to the options in life and the possibilities for him, other than being an accountant! He wasn't actually a conjuror; he had simply offered his services to the formative concert party there, based on what he'd done years ago as a schoolboy – which wasn't much. Although he'd been on stage a few times in the concert party and done some tricks, he was rather thinking of dropping the conjuring, preferring to be involved in stage managing the shows and taking minor parts in plays. Unfortunately, he had quite a stammer, which limited his scope for stage work – but his mind was completely unlimited. We got on like a house on fire from the start. He enjoyed talking about the people he was meeting in the camp and about their experiences, interests and knowledge, and in the months that followed, we were to meet up many times and talk for hours.

The freedom of movement we had during the first few months in Changi couldn't, of course, last. The Japanese Command gradually pulled out their own troops, presumably for more fighting elsewhere, and replaced them with Sikhs from the Indian divisions that had fought with us. Large numbers of these Indian troops had defected after being taken prisoner, to join an embryonic Indian National Army that the Japanese were encouraging as part of their plan for a 'Greater East Asia Co-Prosperity Sphere', within which Asians were to co-operate with Asians and the old Colonialists, us British and the Dutch, were to be subordinated. Orders went out that the Sikh guards were to be saluted whenever and wherever they were encountered. The various areas of Changi were sectioned off and special passes were required if we wanted to go from one area to another. These passes, in the form of special armbands, were only available to those with approved work or business to do. This severely restricted my movement as I was unfit for any kind of work at that stage but one day, I found an armband lying in a gutter. That evening I used it to go and see Syd Piddington. At each checkpoint I was surprised to find that the Sikh guards just looked at me and laughed, whilst waiving me through. I used the armband a few times before finding out why it was causing such hilarity. The Japanese characters on the armband said 'Prostitute on business'.

The Sikhs made the most of their new status. It was a turning of the tables for most of them – having been the oppressed they had now become the oppressors. It was while passing through a checkpoint one day that I got my first 'bashing' from them. The guard seemed pleasant enough but asked if I spoke Urdu. Well, I'd learned something of the language during our short stay in Bombay, so in my naïve way I said yes, I did. Wham! The guard must have assumed that if I could speak his language then I must have been one of their white oppressors.

During these times, my physical condition was still a problem even though I was forcing myself to get around. My left foot was dragging because of the metal that was still lodged in the back of my knee and my right hand was dysfunctional. The wrist had been getting worse in that it would not rotate properly so there wasn't a lot I could do with it without rotating my whole forearm. In the end, it meant another spell in Roberts Hospital. The surgeon who attended me this time, Major Nardell, found that a spur of bone had grown in my injured wrist, causing the limitation of movement. He would have to remove it. While I was waiting for the surgery, I received an amazing gift with a note attached, wishing me luck. It was from the man I'd befriended on the roadside kerb when he was so despairing – Reg Renison. The note was addressed to 'Gnr Anckorn' in 'the better off ward'.

My dear Fergus,

The enclosed is a pretty crude substitute for a silver horseshoe and blue ribbon yet imagine it of gold and trimmed with diamonds it couldn't be symbolical of more sincerest good wishes for the complete recovery of your wrist.

It has long been my custom to pray to the good Lord on your behalf but I will redouble all efforts to pester not only Our Lord but all the appropriate saints, principalities and powers that they may both restore you the full use of your hands and preserve you from any conceivable risk of catching any 'extras' while you are in dock.

Mind you behave yourself – at least I shan't have to envisage you making eyes at pretty nurses!

Keep your pecker up old chap and God Bless you.

Yours affectionately,

Reg

When the operation took place, for good measure he also came to watch while I was put out with some anaesthetic. He said that the surgeon used a broken blade off some sort of band saw and he held it in both hands to saw away at the spur until the bone was flush.

All went well but then I did catch something 'extra' – dysentery.

It meant that they moved me to an isolation ward some distance away in the old Changi Gaol. Luckily, it turned out to be bacillary dysentery – the type that doesn't kill you – that's if it was dysentery at all. In any event, I was back in Roberts Hospital after a week.

The next job was to get the shrapnel or bullet or whatever it was removed from my knee if possible so that I might walk without tripping up all the time on rough ground. The surgeon working on me this time was Major Smythe – I called him 'Butcher Smythe' – a swine of a man. He said he would get the bullet out under general anaesthetic but then attempted it under a local. But the local didn't work for some reason. After cutting open the back of my leg, he set to work with a pair of ordinary pliers to pull the metal lump out. I yelled as I went into agony.

'What's the matter with you?' he said.

'I can feel it!' I shouted.

'No you can't,' he retorted as he continued to grope with the pliers until he found the thing, got hold of it and started to pull.

'What am I doing now then?' he said.

'You're pulling my kneecap out! Leave it alone you bloody idiot!'

'Shut up,' he said, 'or I'll give you a general to shut you up.'

I was desperate.

'You can give me what you like but you're not bloody touching me again,' I told him.

So he brusquely sewed me up again and there the lump of metal has remained to the present day. What seemed to have happened was that bone had grown around it making it impossible to remove by any means other than by cutting into the bone. I learned to live with it and to avoid tripping up by passing a piece of rope down under my left foot and holding the ends together in my left hand so that I could easily lift the foot when needed.

After all these treatments, I was glad to be left more or less to my own devices in a wing of the hospital that had a veranda where patients could sit out. It was while I was sitting out on that veranda that I witnessed a scene of irrepressible colonial spirit!

The veranda overlooked one of the checkpoints between designated areas and an officer of ours was passing through. Whilst the Japanese Command had ordered all badges of rank to be removed right from the start, it made no difference to us because we knew who was who. This was a colonel and he was a small, shrunken figure of a man. He walked straight past the Sikh guard as if he wasn't there, whereupon the Sikh guard demanded a salute but the colonel simply continued on his way, ignoring him. The Sikh quickly went up to him and delivered a resounding slap on the colonel's face – this being the specific punishment authorised by the Japanese. Well, the colonel turned on the guard and belted him so hard in the face that the man collapsed in a heap. At which point the colonel yelled, 'Don't you ever strike a British officer again, you bastard!'

When I finally left Roberts Hospital, I got involved in earning some money in order to buy food. Five cents per day I earned. My injuries kept me away from any physical activity but there was one activity the Japs would pay for that we could all do – catching flies. This was their way of fighting dysentery and their calculations were that with so many prisoners in Changi, if each prisoner were to catch just ten flies per day, dysentery might be eradicated. The scheme was that all flies caught should be brought to an incinerator, where a Japanese guard and a British sergeant would count them and record them against your name for pay purposes, before disposing of them. They would then pay us every ten days, so we could earn fifty cents every ten days.

The scheme worked so well that we eventually found ourselves short of flies to catch. Rotten foodstuffs thrown out of the cookhouse was the easiest source of flies but when that began to fail, the latrines were the place to be and we'd squat there until the requisite ten flies were caught. I saw a business opportunity. Thinking myself very smart, I collected maggots from around the latrines and started a fly farm – selling the flies to the lads as they were produced so that they didn't have to go and squat in the latrines. But I wasn't the only clever dick. Sergeant Fairclough was our man in charge of recording and tipping the flies into the incinerator, and he saw an opportunity too. He made a trapdoor in the incinerator so that when he chucked the flies in, they came out the back, untouched, into a box. He then sold them to the lads.

After a while the Jap guard suspected something was going on because the flies began to look like they'd been dead a long time! So I had another idea. Perhaps I could manufacture flies that would look more recently swatted. I got an old tyre that was lying around and stripped off some of the rubber. This would do to make the bodies of the flies and I dipped one end of each tiny body into palm oil to replicate the little red head of the type of flies we were catching. Then I used a piece of cellophane to make tiny wings, which I stuck on with rice paste. Hey presto, they passed muster! Mass production followed and all was well until a smell of burning rubber hung in the air around the camp. This was quickly traced back to the incinerator that my flies had been sent to and so production ceased before the Japs worked out what we were doing. That was the end of that business enterprise.

By the time I had come out of Roberts Hospital the second time, my friend Reg Renison had got involved in forming a camp orchestra and was wrapped up again in his beloved music. Instruments had been found or made up in sufficient number to justify an orchestra and a concert piano had even been found from somewhere. Reg was going about with a pair of mitts on his hands, despite the heat, as this kept his fingers in trim, ready for playing. He had also made himself a short rubber keyboard, which he used to exercise his fingers whenever he got the chance. He was hoping to put on a performance of one of his favourite pieces, Rachmaninoff's *2nd Piano Concerto* and as there was no sheet music for it, he wrote the whole score out himself, for each and every instrument, from memory. When enough had been written for a rehearsal, he invited me to come along to hear it. His players were all officers so I suggested it may not be acceptable for an ordinary gunner such as me to attend. He wouldn't hear of it and so I duly attended. I was stunned. This small, insignificant little man walked into the rehearsal room, straight up to the podium in front of all his seated players. They remained seated, so he tapped his stick vigorously.

'It is customary, when the conductor enters the room, for the orchestra to stand. We will start again.'

He went out of the room and re-entered a moment or two later to see each man stand as requested – officers, all of them. They were in the palm of his hand.

Whilst some sort of order had come into our lives at Changi, instigated by the efforts of our own senior officers, the Japanese authorities still had problems in dealing with so many of us. Matters came to a head in what is now called the Selarang Incident. In the strange way that the Japanese did things, a command had been issued from Tokyo that all of their subjects in captivity should sign a 'no escape declaration'. Perhaps they thought this would reduce the numbers of guards they needed. Having cooped us up on the 10 square miles of the north-east tip of Singapore Island that was Changi Barracks, the Japanese had assumed that escapes would be rare, as there was nowhere for us prisoners to escape to without being easily recognised and recaptured. But escape attempts were numerous and this must have been the case everywhere in their new empire. So every man was to sign a 'no escape declaration', which read:

I, the undersigned, hereby solemnly swear on my honour, that I will not, under any circumstances, attempt escape.

Their demand was put to our Lieutenant-Colonel Holmes, who commanded all the British troops billeted in the Roberts Barracks area, and to Brigadier Galleghan, who commanded all the Australian troops who were billeted at the Selarang Barracks area. It was, of course, derided and rejected.

So, the Japanese decided they would apply pressure. They ordered all British POWs in Changi to join the Australians in their barracks at Selarang and to muster in the parade square. This was an open parade ground area approximately 200 yards square surrounded by a series of seven, three-storey barrack blocks that were normally home to around

1,200 men in total. We were all marched out of Roberts Barracks, not knowing where on earth we were going until we were directed into Selarang. There, some 17,000 of us were gathered and there we were to remain for as long as it took for us all to sign the declaration. Every inch of the place was occupied, including the rooftops, and in our case the whole of the 118th Regiment of near 700 men was put in one barrack block. There we squashed ourselves together and slept on top of one another for lack of space. But no one complained – we were not going to let the Japanese see our spirit broken. During this time, everything that had to be done was done in the square. Deep latrines were dug through the asphalt in the centre of the parade ground and a makeshift hospital area was set up under whatever canvas or other material cover could be mustered. Surgeons carried on their work dealing with amputations and medical staff continued to treat dysentery cases. Cookhouses were set up for the little food that we were allowed but there was hardly any water. At every possible exit from the square, Sikh guards were positioned with machine-guns and orders to shoot anyone who even put one foot over a line they had made on the ground.

The whole situation was a seething mass of humanity doing absolutely nothing except queuing up for the latrines. I got myself out of the barrack block during the day and moved around as best I could. On one of the mornings, I came across a man attempting to clean his teeth with water he'd got from the only tap in the square. He'd gone to the side of the square with his mug of water and his toothbrush, intending to straddle a gully there and spit out his toothwash. He didn't realise that this 'gully' was meant to be the boundary line for the square in that part, and which, if strayed over, constituted escape. He was shot before my eyes by the Sikhs manning the nearby machine-gun.

We were held in the Selarang Square for four days before eventually being told by Lieutenant-Colonel Holmes that it was alright for us to sign the document as we would be doing it under duress. As usual, most of us had no idea what had been going on over the previous days or why it had been decided we should sign. It was only after the incident was over that I got something of the story – from the Australian CO, Brigadier Galleghan.

Shortly after 'the signing', the Japanese allowed groups of us to go down to a beach there at Changi to clean ourselves up – like a ghastly school outing! I found myself walking along next to the Brigadier. He told me that after the first three days of refusal, the Japanese carried out an atrocity to see if that would change our minds. Lieutenant-General Fukuye, who was in command of all POWs in Singapore, ordered that four Australians, who had previously been recaptured after trying to make an escape, should be taken and shot in front of their senior officers. Brigadier Galleghan and Lieutenant-Colonel Holmes, as well

103

as other officers, were taken down to the beach where the four men were lined up with their backs to the sea, in front of a firing squad. The execution was to be carried out by Sikhs, who were former Indian division troops known to our officers, who had, like the many others, deserted their allegiance to us and were now allied to the Japanese in the Indian National Army. The execution was appalling. The Sikhs fired a number of shots into the men, but not to kill them. They had fired into parts of their bodies to fell them. Then they slowly walked up to the writhing bodies and shot them repeatedly at point blank range until all movement ceased. This atrocity did not, however, succeed in changing minds. It was medical staff that did that the following day. They reported that men were beginning to die in the square due to the conditions and that many more were likely to die if the situation went on much longer. This was because Lieutenant-General Fukuye had turned out the very sick who had been in Roberts Hospital, and they were in the square along with everyone else. It was because of this rather than anything else apparently, that our commanders decided to give the order for us to sign the no-escape declaration. Lieutenant-Colonel Holmes told us that he would take full responsibility and there would be no repercussions.

It took nearly the whole of the next day for us to file past the tables on which the declaration forms were stacked and to sign the statement. Most of us inserted fictional names and made unrecognisable signatures. We were then allowed back to Roberts Barracks, where we found that the place had been looted in our absence.

The incident had taken all of us to new depths of squalor and degradation and shown us what the Japanese were capable of in their treatment of prisoners in this new Co-Prosperity Sphere of theirs. Little did we know, but worse, far worse, was yet to come for many of us.

A vaguely satisfying postscript to the atrocity occurred after the war. Lieutenant-General Fukuye was brought before a war crimes court and found guilty of the murder of the four Australians, whereupon he was taken for execution on the same beach at Changi and in the same spot where those men had died so horribly.

To all of us, the workings of the Japanese mind were unfathomable and often ridiculous – right from the start of our captivity. They also had a vindictive streak that led them to mete out gratuitous humiliation whenever they found an opportunity. This was often evident in the way they handled 'tenko' – the assembly and roll-call of prisoners, which they called for every morning and evening. What some Japs did was to come along during the afternoon with their car or truck and take one of us for a drive into town, where they'd give their captive food. Then they'd take him back to the camp after tenko in the evening. Of course, the rest of us would have covered for the missing man by one means or another and that gave the Japs an excuse to give the officer carrying out the roll-call a 'bashing', because they knew he was lying. The bashing would be a heavy slap across the face while the officer stood to attention. Apparently this was a normal form of punishment in their own ranks and the person being bashed was expected to take it without flinching.

I got my first Japanese bashing when I was still crawling around after being deposited in the camp at the start. I was dragging myself across the parade ground when a Jap shouted 'Oi!' and made a gesture with the back of his hand, which I took to mean 'get moving ... get off the parade ground.' It didn't mean that at all. In fact, it meant the opposite – 'come here!' When I tried to shuffle off, he shouted at me again and the more he shouted, the more quickly I tried to get away. So he came and bashed me with a long rod.

Because of the way the Japanese behaved towards us, we never knew what to expect next, and suspected everything they said. The biggest question for all of us was where they were really sending the thousands of prisoners that were leaving the camp from time to time and for what purpose. Whilst I had been in Roberts Hospital, I heard that around 3,000 had been taken 'up-country' and that was in addition to a previous 3,000 taken earlier up to Burma. The Japs said that prisoners were being sent to 'better camps', where living conditions would be easier and more food available. After the Selarang Incident, we imagined they were being taken away to be shot.

There were also big influxes of prisoners. After the Selarang Incident, as it had become known, Dutch prisoners started coming in from Java and Sumatra and whilst many of them were said to be in transit to Japan or other destinations, many remained in Changi and were accommodated in their own area near to us at Roberts Barracks.

I made it my purpose to see if Frans Bakker was amongst them. He was the friend my twin sister and I had made at the swimming pool in Dunton Green just before the war. He had fallen in love with her but had then taken himself off somewhere, with no further word forthcoming.

I made frequent visits into the Dutch camp but no one knew of a Frans Bakker. What I did find, however, was that the Dutch were starting their own concert party and they had an illusionist who was supposedly the nephew of Houdini and who had formed his own troupe. He called himself 'the Great Cortini' and his act was called 'Cortini's Magical Eye'. His troupe referred to him as 'the Professor' and when I went to see if I could meet him, I was told by his troupe, 'The Professor is resting at the moment. You'll have to come back later.' Well I did go back later and had a good chat with 'the Professor'. He invited me to join his show as a conjuror after showing me what he could do by way of conjury with a billiard ball – which wasn't very much! The trouble was that I had not done any conjuring since the bombing, and really, I still only had proper use of my left hand. So when it came to my first performance on his show, I dropped the billiard balls!

For all of us remaining at Changi, the semblance of normal existence increased as time went on, even though that existence continued to be on starvation rations. Red Cross ships did bring some alleviation but there had only been one allowed in as far as I was aware and what supplies there were had been mostly taken by the Japanese, it seemed. There was always hope that another Red Cross ship would arrive one day laden with desperately needed vitamin-rich foodstuffs, medicines and longed-for mail from home, but none came as the months went by.

Our officers had imposed a disciplined structure to the day as soon as they could after we'd all cleared the place up and settled into Changi at the beginning of our captivity. That, and the daily working parties coming in and out of the camp, kept many of us routinely occupied. It was not enough, however, for one of our officers. He would have had any of us who were not on working parties digging holes and filling them in again if he could. What he did start was PT first thing in the morning. Not a bad idea with a regiment of healthy, fit men needing their muscles toning but we were, by this time, a bunch of skeletal, vitamin-deprived waifs on the verge of going down with heaven knows what kind of previously unknown affliction. For my part, I remained on doctor's orders while my injuries took many months to heal.

Outside the daily routines, we made life tolerable for ourselves by concentrating on other essentials – sport, education and entertainment. Cricket matches were held on some Sundays and the 'test matches' between ourselves and the Australians drew crowds – even the guards watched. We had Sergeant Geoff Edrich as our captain – he of the famous Edrich cricketing family. We also had Lester Martin, from our 118th – reputedly the most athletic man on the island, according to some medical staff. During a match, you could almost imagine you were back in England except that play here was not only interrupted by rain but also by exhaustion, given the physical state of most of us.

To exercise the mind, what had started as a few lectures from time to time developed into a sort of university, drawing on the huge amount of knowledge and skills amongst us. The Changi library still had most of its books and more had been found in various houses around and about so as to make it possible to circulate books amongst those taking part in any particular course subject. By the end of 1942, Reg Renison was giving music orchestration lectures, as did Denis East, who was a member of our original concert party as well as former band leader and 1st Violinist to the London Philharmonic Orchestra before the war. Denis also started a band in the camp called the 'Nitwits'. They put the

106

spirit into the Roberts Barracks area at Christmas time by wandering around, playing Christmas tunes and encouraging carol singing.

It was entertainment that gave us all something to look forward to most days, and it was odd how the worse our situation became in the camp, the more frequent and better the shows became. There was both the equipment and the talent for it.

One of the theatres there was called the Windmill Theatre, set up in what was the old NAAFI. Our Lieutenant Mackwood, who had put on our divisional concert parties at home, put on a well-known play there called *I Killed the Count*, which he re-wrote from memory, and he played one of the leading roles as Rene La Lune. There were still the ten of us from our 18th Division Concert Party, although I wasn't taking much part while still trying to learn how to do my conjuring with only one fully functioning hand. The Dutch illusionist, the 'Professor' Cortini, performed with us. He wasn't, of course, a professor of any-thing. In fact, he was hardly educated at all but he *was* a first-class illusionist. As the theatre facilities were so good we'd put on full magic shows, with the Professor's illusion act – sawing people in half and things like that – and me doing a limited amount of conjuring. One show we did started in a macabre tone in keeping with our surround-ings. The lights would go down and the curtains would be partially opened with the Professor standing there between them. But as you looked he would gradually turn into a skeleton – a complete skeleton – and then he'd turn back into a man again, bow and disappear behind the closing curtains. That illusion was made possible by Ronald Searle, who of course is now well known for his sketching. He drew the skeleton backcloth.

There was another theatre on the site, which we called the 'KoKoNut Grove' because it was away amongst the coconut trees, and this had a wonderful proscenium stage that meant really professionally produced shows could be put on. The officer in charge there was Jack Stephenson, who became something big in the BBC after the war. The Australians had their own theatre too, and their professional producer was John Wood, who also went on to become important in Australian broadcasting.

The best theatre of the lot was the one we called the 'Changi Palladium'. It had been a proper cinema before the battle and we found it more or less intact, with stage equipment and lighting, too. What wasn't there or what had been damaged was easily replaced out of bits and pieces 'liberated' by working parties coming back and forth from Singapore town or made up out of debris and scrap that was lying everywhere around the camp.

Some of the shows demonstrated enormous skill and improvisation in the props department. I vividly remember one set even now. It was a night-time, New York City backdrop that had lights in the windows, traffic lights flashing, illuminated road signs and, most impressive of all, twinkling stars in a night sky. We could have been in the West End!

Distracting as these entertainments were, there was no getting away from the grinding hunger that beset us all. The daily menu for months on end was nothing at all:

Breakfast: Rice pap and polishing. Mug of raw tea.
Lunch: Plain rice plus a ball of rice with something green mixed in with it. Mug of raw tea.
Dinner: More rice. Mug of thin broth of some kind. Mug of raw tea.

The rice polishing was like ground pepper in texture, which we were told by doctors we must eat as it contained vitamin B. The only way of doing so was to mix it in with some of the tea, weevils and all.

Little though this was, I was sharing mine with a little doggy that I'd come across and befriended – 'Jessie', I called her. She went with me everywhere and I trained her to stand on her hind legs in the cookhouse queues when there were peanuts for sale so that men would feed her. She used to come with me when I went to see Syd Piddington in the Australian area or to see friends I'd made in the Dutch area, and she would sit and wait for me at the checkpoints sometimes if I wanted her to.

But food was so short that sharing it with Jessie was not altogether a good idea. I was finding it almost impossible to stay awake during the day and I began to fear that if I let myself fall asleep, I might never wake up. So I decided to take up refereeing basketball games for the Dutch to give myself something to attend to. They had games every evening and it was a game I knew well, having played it at the commercial college in London before the war. It worked. The concentration needed kept me awake – and alive! But then I managed to stumble on a pothole along the touchline and break something in my ankle. The only remedy was for me to retire to my billet and lie on my back for weeks with my foot stuck up against the wall until gradually, the swelling subsided and whatever it was reset itself sufficiently for me to walk again.

Just as I was getting back on my feet, Jessie went missing.

During my enforced inactivity while my ankle repaired itself, Jessie had stayed with me, which meant she wasn't getting her 'beggings'. I had become so worried as to what I should do with her that it was a relief in a way when it appeared she had taken herself off.

Once I was getting about again, I was pleased to be invited by some of the Dutch prisoners to have a meal with them one evening. The Dutch, generally speaking, fared better than ourselves and the Australians because many still had their own money and were able to buy what little extras there were to be had. They'd got a few of us together for this meal, which turned out to be a veritable 'feast' with meat in it, too. It was a Dutch sergeant that had prepared the meal and afterwards I asked what the meat was. Tentatively, the Sergeant replied, 'It was dog, Gus.' Then he added, 'Your dog, I'm afraid. We thought it was just a stray, because there are a few around here as you know. But then after we'd despatched her, somebody came and told us she was yours.'

I heard the next day that the sergeant had been imprisoned by his officers for eating Jessie. She had obviously made a big impression on people in this place where there was not much to like.

Food of any kind continued to be the focus of all our interests and, around that time, I got another invitation. It was from Sergeant Stanbridge, the sergeant-major whom I'd cheeked for so long and on so many occasions in our battery. It had always been in good humour and he had always played up to it too, so there was never any ill feeling. He said, 'Do you want to come and see my garden?' It was as if we were in England! I couldn't believe it. He took me to an allotment of land that the Japs had allowed for cultivation several months earlier as a way of easing the food problems. They may have allowed the cultivation but it was up to the ingenuity of the prisoners to find something to plant. My sergeant-major had got what he needed from the one and only Red Cross supply that came in. There had been tomato jam amongst the supply because doctors knew how vitamin-rich it was and how tomato can be boiled, fried or processed in any way without losing those vitamins. But this sergeant-major of mine knew of another benefit. He'd carefully collected the pips out of the jam and planted them, so that now he had some healthy looking tomatoes just beginning to ripen.

We had all adjusted to this captivity in our own ways and so life just went on. At first, many got by on the thought that 'it would all be over by Christmas', while others just hoped the war would sort itself out while they were held at Changi, so that they would never see action again. There was a kind of stability. As far as I was concerned, it was a horrible sort of limbo.

The idea that we would 'all be out of there by Christmas' had died as Christmas 1942 came and went. It had probably died earlier than that because we heard from somewhere or other that an attempted landing of a large force of our troops in France, called the Dieppe Raid, had failed and nothing positive had been heard since. As the Japs were continuing to send prisoners up to Burma and Thailand we assumed they must be expanding their empire too, and there was no word of any counter-attack by the Allies, anywhere. As far as I was concerned, surviving each day was the only thing that mattered and beyond that, my only thought was how to get a message home that I was alright. I had no idea what my parents may have been told about our situation or about me. Our officers couldn't be sure what information was getting back to London, if any. I feared they could have heard that I'd been killed in action since my 'dog tags' had been taken off me by Bombardier Porter on his way to making his escape and I presumed he handed them in somewhere if he'd made it.

Communications seemed impossible. There was no means of sending a letter or a card out and Red Cross parcels and mail came in only rarely. Nothing so far had come for me. Then several weeks into the turn of the year, the opportunity to send a postcard home came up. The Japs were sending more of us up-country and men were leaving in batches almost every day. Whether it was because of that or not I don't know, but we were issued with blank postcards by the Red Cross and told we could write no more than twenty-five words plus our name, number and the date. Mine read:

Dearest Mum, Dad,

Hope you are well, happy. My love to Luce. Best wishes other Anckorns, Robin, parents. Usual cheery spirits. Don't worry.

Ferg

I wondered as I wrote it whether they would ever actually get the card but at least there was a chance and then they would know I was alright.

As the regular departures of men continued, word had got around that they were going to Thailand to work on some sort of a railway that was being constructed or repaired up there and the idea of there being more food and better conditions as the Japs would have us believe was, of course, suspect. It seemed a bit of a lottery as to who went or who stayed but it turned out that our own officers had some say in the matter – as I was to find out when my 'Anckorn awkward streak' got the better of me and I found myself in trouble again.

We had a particular regimental sergeant-major, a swine of a man. When we were first taken prisoner, his idea was to put himself in control of things whenever he saw the chance. 'We don't want fellas fighting over stuff – cigarettes, for example. I suggest you hand in all your cigarettes and I'll keep them in a store. When you want them, you draw them.' So he got everyone's stuff and proceeded to help himself whenever he felt like it. Well, he didn't like me. I had been giving him lip. I couldn't stand the man. Unfortunately, he also picked up enthusiastically on the idea of PT for everyone before breakfast and eventually, he was gunning for me.

When it came to it, I said to him, 'I can't do PT because of my wounds,' and I handed him the medical officer's note. He brushed it aside and ordered me to be on PT parade the next morning. I turned out for PT as ordered but I told him I was not going to take part.

arents, Wilfred and Beatrice Anckorn.

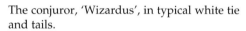

Gunner Anckorn 947556, October 1939. Just signed up.

The conjuror, 'Wizardus', in typical white tie and tails.

erviceman Anckorn, Britain at war.

Gun, limber and lorry. The full works: training in Wales, 1941.

SS *Westpoint*, launched as the luxurious ocean liner SS *America* only days before war broke out in Europe.

'V' Troop, 483rd Field Battery, the 118th Field Regiment RA (TA), Ahmednagar, January 1941. Fergus is centre of the 4th row from the front, arms unfolded.

Scene of a massacre. Alexandra Military Hospital, Singapore.
(Courtesy of the Trustees of the Imperial War Museum)

Memorial plaque in the grounds of Alexandra Hospital.

ALEXANDRA HOSPITAL

In 1938, the British built this as a military hospital. Japanese troops attacked the hospital on 14 February 1942 in retaliation against retreating Allied soldiers who had fired at them from the hospital grounds. They killed an estimated 50 staff and patients. The following morning, the Japanese soldiers killed another 150.

After the war, the hospital reopened as the principal British Military Hospital in Asia. It was handed over to the Singapore Government on 10 September 1971. It reopened as Alexandra Hospital, a civilian hospital, on 15 September 1971. Since April 19... the hospital also serves as the Alexandra campus of the National University of Singapore's medical school.

NATIONAL HERITAGE BOARD

Rice trucks used to take POWs up-country. (*Sketch by fellow POW, Will Wilder*)

Wampo Viaduct under construction on 'Death Railway'. (*Sketch by fellow POW, Will Wilder*)

Unloading sick and dead from riverboats, Chungkai 1943. (*Sketch by fellow POW, Jack Chalker*)

Cleaning out tropical ulcers with an old spoon and no anaesthetic. (*Sketch by fellow POW, Jack Chalker*)

Colonel 'Weary' Dunlop (facing) and Captain Markowitz (back view) operating together, Chungkai, January 1944. (*Sketch by fellow POW, Jack Chalker*)

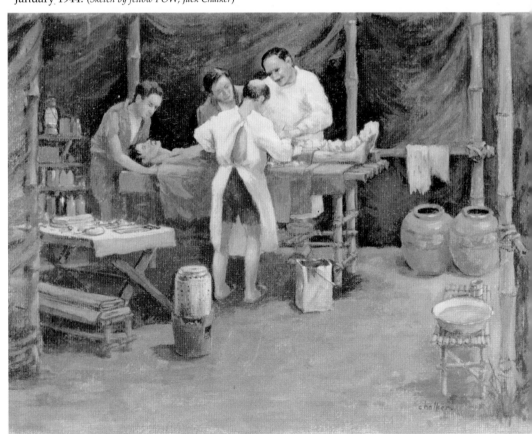

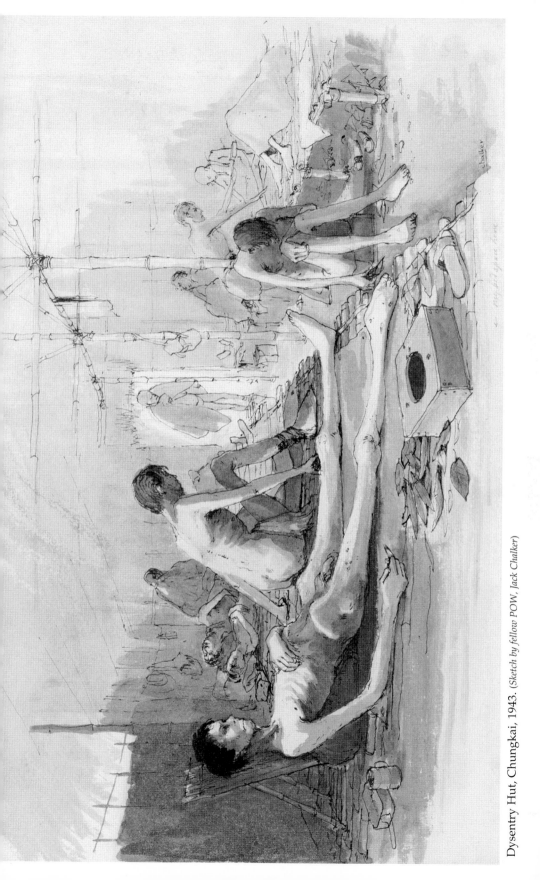

Dysentry Hut, Chungkai, 1943. (*Sketch by fellow POW, Jack Chalker*)

IMPERIAL JAPANESE ARMY

I am interned in **NO 1. P.O.W. CAMP THAILAN**

My health is excellent.

~~I am ill in hospital.~~

I am working for pay.

~~~~

Please see that......**YOUR HEALTH + LUCE**is taken care

My love to you **Ferg.**

STILL **SMILING**

Getting a message home. Encryption by shorthand.

Watch bezel found in the jungle put to good use. The picture fitted perfectly.

View from the bedspace of a typical attap hut.
(*Sketch by fellow POW, Will Wilder*)

...oncert party, Nong Pladuk, ...944. (*Programme produced by ...orman Pritchard*)

ACE CONNOLLY and his KINGS of SWING

BOB GALE   LES KENT   JACK BIET
ERIC GIBBONS   HARRY PRINS
JIM WILDEBOER   BUNNY AUSTIN

CARSON (SAM) EDWARDS and his HILL-BILLIES

LES KENT   VIC LIVERMORE   GEORGE DAVIDSON
BOB CHRISTIAN   FREDDIE HALBARD   BUCK MORTON
LEN FRENCH   TOMMY BURTON   GEORGE EAVES
GEORGE GREATHURST   GEORGE TEMPLEY

JOE HILL   FREDDIE HALBARD

'Any more for   'if I had my way' &
Sailing'   Was it Real!'

BANJO BOB with LES KENT and JIM WILDEBOER

'HELLFIRE'   sketch

with
CAPT. MARTIN   Lt. HUNTRISS
Lt. LOWDEN   Lt. CHISHOLM

WIZARDUS   JACK and JUDY

Magic & Mystery   'Memories'

LES. COX   COMPERE

"On the Spot"

A play in two acts
with   by Bob Cole

BEN   DIAMOND   RONNIE PARR
RAY FAIRCLOTH   BOB   GALE
LES   COX   BOB CHRISTIAN
OSCAR STINSON   DARKIE PINNOCK
ALBERT   RYAN   VIC LIVERMORE
NORMAN PRITCHARD   TOMMY KIRK
JACK FRAZER   SAM JACKSON
ERIC GIBBONS —— ACCORDEON

Stage Manager   JOHN LOWDEN
Props by   CAMERON and Co.
Producer   J. D. V. ALLUM
Assistant Producer   NOEL WOODS

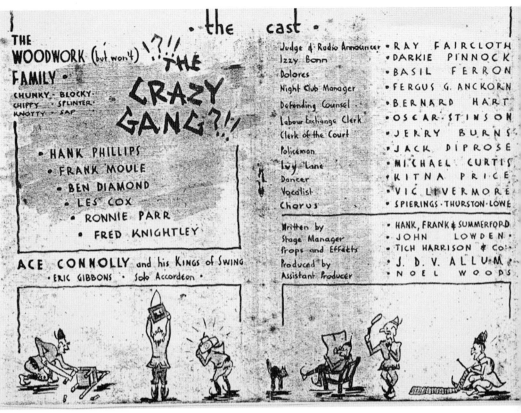

Concert party, Nong Pladuk, 1944. (*Programme produced by Norman Pritchard*)

Buried alive! Allied bombing of 'Hashimoto's railway yards' at Nong Pladuk. Five bombs went astray

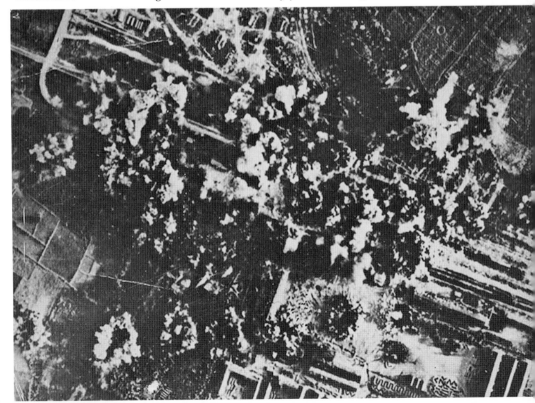

Identity bracelet made by Jack Biet. Inscribed by using a nail.

End of captivity, August 1945. The salute was taken at Ubon by Lieutenant-Colonel Smiley.
(Courtesy of Philip Smiley)

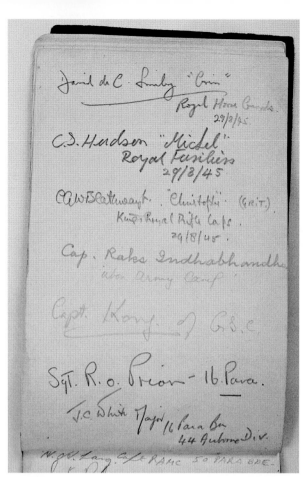

Signatures of Force 136 members who liberated Ubon POW camp, August 1945.

Colonel David Smiley. This photograph was taken in 1960 when on operations in Yemen. (*Courtesy of Philip Smiley*).

On the way home, 'fattened up' and re-issued with battledress, Suez, October 1945.

Lucille.

The troopship *Orbita*, October 1945.

Children's Party

GIVEN BY

THE LORD MAYOR

AND

LADY MAYORESS
Sir Bernard and the Hon. Lady Waley-Cohen

The Mansion House
Saturday, 7th January,
1961

Fergus performing at the Lord Mayor's children's party, the Mansion House, London.

Police Special Constabulary, Fergus Anckorn, Commandant, West Kent 'D' Division.

Associations provided an outlet to talk of shared experiences.

Body language says it all. (*Courtesy of the Japanese Embassy, London*)

Gunner Anckorn: proud to have served.

Fergus Anckorn – still smiling.
(Toby Philips Photography)

'If you want to complain, you do PT first and complain afterwards,' he said.

Clearly he wasn't going to listen, so I got a bit more emphatic. 'If you think I'm going to lose my bloody leg for you and then complain later, you're wrong. I'm not doing the PT. Look at me ... this leg, this foot, this arm!'

His only reply was, 'I don't care. You do what you're told.'

I continued to argue and when the PT started I just cleared off. So he put me on a charge.

When you go on a charge, you have to be dressed in your best uniform, and you have to have your cap on. You then stand outside the guard room until you are called. When you enter the room, the first thing they do is knock your cap off to humiliate you. Well of course, I could only turn up with no hat, no shoes and virtually no clothes because everything had been lost when I was bombed and the battle-dress I had been wearing was torn off me by the medics.

'Where are your clothes?' said the sergeant-major.

'I haven't got any, Sir. All removed in the field hospital after I was bombed, Sir.'

Persisting with his King's Regulations approach, he went on, 'Where's your cap?'

So I told him I hadn't got a cap either. At which point, he gave me his cap and told me to put it on. Then he called me to attention and barked out an order to step forward, followed by the usual 'Left right, left right' but I couldn't even walk properly so I came in as best I could with my left foot dragging and only my left arm swinging. He stepped towards me and I presumed this was going to be the humiliation ritual, so I grabbed the hat off my head and impertinently threw it on the floor saying, 'There! I've just saved you a bit of work.'

Regardless, the charge officer started the proceedings. 'Right, 947555 – you are charged that, contrary to military orders and good discipline, you failed to obey a command ...'

'No, that's not me,' I interjected.

'What do you mean?' came the sharp reply.

'947555. That's not me. My number's 947556, so I don't think you can carry on with this hearing.'

He couldn't, of course, because the record would show he was charging somebody else. As he started to correct the number, I repeated myself, 'I'm sorry, Sir, you can't go on with this.'

'You have just agreed that your number is 947556.'

'Yes,' I said, 'but that's not the person you're charging. You said you are charging 947555. I'm quite certain you're getting this wrong.'

'Nevertheless, we'll carry on,' he said emphatically, but as he started to read out the facts of the case, I interrupted again – very brazenly.

'Lies,' I said.

'Shut up.' He rebuked. 'You'll have your say in a minute'.

But I was seething. The situation was absurd in the extreme. Here we all were, prisoners of war, many dying of dysentery, half-starved, half-naked and, above all, humiliated by a capitulation that, to most of us, remained inexplicable and probably more to do with poor command than anything else and yet this idiot was trying to throw the book at me.

'I'm not going to stand here and listen to these bloody lies!' I said.

'You'll do what you're told,' came the reply.

And so he went on with the charge and at the end of it, he followed procedure by setting out the punishment and asking, 'Are you going to accept this punishment?'

'No, Sir, of course I'm not,' I said.

'Well you will have to go in front of the CO if that is the case.'

My next words produced utter consternation. 'I'm not accepting anyone's punishment. I've got a chit here from the MO, but this bloody fool ...'

I was in mid-sentence, pointing to the sergeant-major, when the charge officer shouted: 'Do you want to go in front of the colonel, then?'

To which I said impetuously, 'Yes, and when I do, I'm going to refuse his punishment too because I want this to go to a court martial!'

Well, it was all ridiculous, but there it is, it happened. I was ordered out again with the sergeant-major snarling like a dog as I went and the very next thing was, sure enough, a re-run in front of the colonel. This was 'Peanut' MacKellar, the very same who had told us we should 'Kill, kill, kill!' as we came into Singapore. We called him 'Peanut' because of his stature and because we thought he was nuts.

He started the proceedings but I stopped him immediately. 'Before you go on, Sir,' I said calmly, 'I'm not going to accept any punishment you're going to give me. I want a court martial.'

'You can have a court martial sure enough when you're back in England,' he retorted.

'So be it,' I said.

He thought about this for a second or two and his face took on a look of dark determination. 'Right. There will be a court martial convened here, tomorrow. You are dismissed.'

Well, normally, as far as I understood things, for a court martial to be convened there had to be a general, or at least a brigadier available to hear the charges. Our general, Beckwith-Smith, had, by this time, died in Formosa, where he'd been sent by the Japanese along with Percival and all the other senior staff. So, I presumed, as there was no one of suitable rank available, they must have decided that it was permissible for someone to be given the rank of brigadier for the purposes of a court martial. Having found a suitable candidate who would accept this role, the court martial proceeded as planned.

When this newly appointed brigadier heard the charge and saw my condition he rounded on Colonel MacKellar. 'You're a bloody fool, man. I've got no time for bloody fools, here of all places. This court martial is closed!'

A victory for common sense, you might think, in absurd circumstances. But my fate was sealed by this outbreak of 'Anckorn stroppiness'. Right from schooldays, I was always happy to do what was required, but if anyone messed me about, it just raised my hackles. This reactionary streak had become accentuated since we went into action. The fact was that nobody seemed to give a tuppenny damn about rank when lives were on the line. As far as I was concerned too, as a driver responsible for the movement and safety of my gun and my detachment, if orders made sense, fine. But if not, I would argue and try to get done what I believed was best.

The outcome of my stroppiness on this occasion was that the snarling sergeant-major came straight for me when the next cull of prisoners took place, sending more of us up-country. 'Right! You're going to do some real soldiering for a change, Anckorn,' he said. 'You're going up-country with the Japs and you're probably going to die there.'

Well, one thing was certain. It was very definitely the last time I would say 'No!' to anybody, for a very long time.

The fearful contemplation of whatever would await me up-country was fortunately relieved the next day by the arrival of Red Cross mail and my first ever letter from home in over a year since we had landed in Singapore. It was from my mother and her opening words were like a soothing balm: 'My darling boy ...'

I noted the date she had written the letter – July 1942. Did she know, somehow, where I was and what had happened? I read on. No. It was evident they all knew nothing.

We are all well ... Lucille ... Fag ... Beb ... and baby Stuart is now eight months old ... a sunny little chap.

My mind went back to that day, now so long ago it seemed, when we boarded the *Orcades* at Liverpool and I'd made one last telephone call home to hear that Beb, my twin sister, had given birth to a little boy and she was going to call him Stuart. I read on about Lucille working towards her nursing exam finals and my brother Gordon giving up journalism and taking up engineering instead. 'It's what he always wanted to do,' my mother was saying and she went on to say about my school friend Robin, that he was 'forging ahead' too. Then the smell of summer was almost real to me as my mother told of how she was making jam from the fruit in the garden and asked if I remembered when Lucille and I stayed up late finishing the jam-making for her the previous summer. My father had added a half page to my mother's words giving me news – crisp and factual, as always – ever the journalist. He'd sent a photo to the mother of Bombardier Christian – someone had seen Chris and reported him well. I remembered how I'd seen him – a retched skeleton, crouching in the broom locker, wasted by dysentery and ready for giving up. My father went on with a message from Beb ... she had named me a godparent to baby Stuart. Another reason, I resolved to myself, that I would survive all this, no matter what lay ahead. I must see my godson.

Throughout my time at Changi, as the days and weeks and months went by, my consolation had been that I was at least alive. I could not have told what day, or what month, or even what year it was at times. I had found that my body could recover itself if I just willed it to and let it. I had seen myself akin to Jessie, the doggy I'd befriended and trained – just an animal, taking whatever came, whatever happened, without complaint – just staying alive, day by day, week by week, month by month, grateful for whatever food came my way and accepting of whatever hardship befell me.

But now it was time to say my goodbyes and I found myself wanting to take with me some reminder of all those fellows who suddenly seemed to have meant so much to me in Changi over all those months. Who knows if we would ever see each other again? So I made myself an autograph book out of bits and pieces I'd found here and there and into it went well wishes from many of them, creating memories that are still there to be read in that book as it has survived to this day.

There are good wishes from the surgeons who saved my hand – Julian Taylor who 'did what he could' amidst the mayhem of battle after the bombing, and Major Nardell, who, along with his 'old firm of ward U2 at Changi', collectively finished the job as best they could.

Members of our concert party are in there too – Aubrey King and George Wall, both wonderful singers, and Cyril Wycherly – such an unremarkable little man if you met him – just a scruff of a boy still, but he could play any tune you liked on the piano. Then there's Lance Corporal Thomas with his bogus quote in Latin saying, 'A good charoot is better than a bad cigar.' Thomas was an artist and a brilliant impressionist. He was the one who mimicked Edward VIII simpering over Mrs Simpson as well as the stuttering of his brother who succeeded him when he abdicated to become King George VI, doing it so convincingly that the act had been banned. Derek Cooper is in there, another artist but also one of our funniest stand-up comedians. He wished me 'a future free of regimental sergeant-majors' and he drew a picture of me and my big mouth to make the point. Ronald Searle drew a picture of his hairy self for his good wishes. Then there are those who said their goodbyes with poignancy. Colonel D'Aubuz, who had been a former ADC to Lawrence of Arabia and for whom I had been writing memoirs in shorthand while at Changi – my damaged hand gripping a ball with a pencil stuck in it, as that was the only way I could do it. He recited from Rupert Brooke, evoking a better place for us all:

> *And think, this heart all evil shed away,*
> *A pulse in the eternal mind no less*
> *Gives somewhere back the thoughts by England given;*
> *Her sights and sounds, dreams happy as her day,*
> *And laughter learnt of friends; and gentleness,*
> *In hearts at peace under an English heaven.*

My friend, Reg Renison, sent me on my way with a reminder of our shared enjoyment of languages, hoping we would meet again soon:

Vaga siempre con Dios, querido amigo … no le olvidare hasta que encontranemos otra vez.

(May God always be with you, dearest friend … not forgotten until we meet again.)

Whether I would meet any of them again was yet to be seen.

March 1943. Farewells from Changi before going up-country

May your hand never lose it's cunning!

From the Old Firm of Ward U2 Changi Hospital

115

18th Div: CONCERT PARTY. CHANGI 1943.

Here's wishing you all the best
your sincere Friend
Aubrey King

May your future be
free from R.S.M.s
Derek Cooper.

"Melior est bonum cherootum quam malum cigarem"
(Virgil)

Oliver Thomas.

.... in your palace, and almost forgot
it was a prison. — James Elroy Flecher
Julian Taylor
March 1943. London.

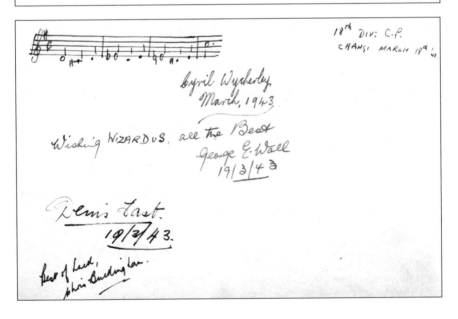

18th DIV: C.P.
CHANGI MARCH 18th 43.

Cyril Wycherley,
March, 1943.

Wishing WIZARDUS, all the Best
George E. Wall
19/3/43

Denis Cast.
19/3/43.

Best of Luck,
John Buckingham.

116

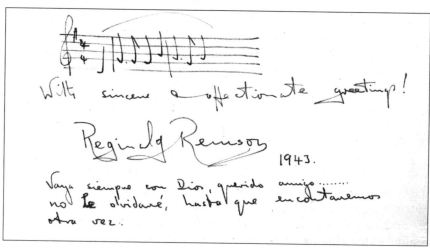

Chapter 10

JOURNEY TO HELL

We walked to the station in Singapore, probably a thousand of us, mostly barefooted.

I still had no clothes, like many others, but before leaving the camp, I had found a pair of swimming shorts, Jansens. So I travelled in those. I had few possessions. These were gathered in a small bag and amongst them was the autograph book that carried the good wishes of my friends and fellows in Changi and another small notebook I'd made. Inside this I kept a tiny photo of Lucille and me, which was one of the Polyfotos we had got when we were engaged and which my gun detachment had recovered from the gun lorry after the bombing, along with some of their own kit. Most precious of all, though, was my half-farthing neck chain and the gold ring on my finger that my mother had given me at embarkation. I'd covered this with a filthy bandage to avoid it being seen.

We were chivvied along by guards saying that we were headed up-country to a Red Cross camp where conditions would be easier and we would get more food and water. On arrival at the station we were herded into a great long train of closed steel railway trucks, with sliding metal doors in the middle of each side. They were normally used for transporting rice sacks. Each one was about 20 feet long and half that in width but there must have been about thirty of us crammed in my truck when they slammed the sliding doors shut. It was standing room only with a bail of straw in the middle for us to take turns sitting on. We didn't know it, but we were going to be cooped up like that on a journey of over 1,200 miles, taking five days and nights.

We rattled along through searing hot days and freezing cold nights with hardly a word spoken – a sorry crowd, dysentery-ridden and ill-tempered. Against Jap orders, we had the doors partly open and some lads got themselves out of the truck and onto the roof to breathe fresh air and be cool during the day, but they weren't allowed back in at nights, so they had to suffer the cold as well. Fights broke out over who would sit on the bail of straw. Going to the loo was accomplished by someone holding you by the arms and feet whilst you poked your bottom out of the open doors.

There were few stops. A main one was at Kuala Lumpur, where the engine must have re-watered or something and where they extracted any of us who'd died from dysentery. I just gawped at the wonderful domed railway station while the doors were opened. Another place we stopped at much further along the journey seemed to be in the middle of nowhere.

It was early morning, dawn just breaking, and through a little gap between the doors, which were now closed, I saw a beautiful bay with waves lapping the beach and palm trees all along, just like a picture postcard. It was an indelible image of serenity in glorious colours, enlivened and made vivid by the rising sun. There was a man working his land with an ox, too, and mist was rising in swathes of white. It was just beautiful. There was no war in this place for this man. Yet here we were, filthy, smelly, starving and dying as we travelled along, prisoners of war being treated worse than that man's ox, on a journey that seemed to be going on forever, to a destination unknown, in the hands of people that had the power of life or death over us. But strangely, this little glimpse of life lifted me completely. I renewed my determination to live, come what may, and I would find out, after the war, where this place was and I would come back! I felt the gold ring on my finger under the grimy bandage and I swore to myself that I would see my mother again. Then I felt the half farthing on my neck chain, remembering the promise I'd made to Lucille, and I swore again that our two halves would one day be reunited, whatever happened.

My reverie ended abruptly when the train lurched and we grinded on our way again, the track then taking us away and back into the jungle. Our destination turned out to be a place called Ban Pong. It was a jungle town with lots of huts and houses surrounded, as far as I could see, by banana plantations and jungle.

As soon as we were off the train, the Japs put us to work unloading rice sacks from some of the wagons. They were about 1cwt each. Very, very, heavy. The idea was that each of us should take one sack, step over the rails and carry it to the warehouse, 20 or so yards away. A Jap slapped one on my shoulders and suddenly I just couldn't move. I couldn't get one foot off the ground. It was as if my feet were screwed down. Fortunately, Lester Martin from my battery, who had become a good friend of mine during our Changi captivity and who was still as strong as a horse, pushed his way over to me and took the rice sack off my shoulders. He just hopped over the rails with it and over to the warehouse, dumped it and came back to help with others. This was a man that nearly died from diphtheria in Changi after the fall of

Singapore. Here he was now, fit as a fiddle as he proceeded to help lift the sacks for everybody else in our truck who couldn't. He took thirty in the end and the Japs let him get on with it because even they realised they had 1,000 men on their hands, many of whom were just about finished and about to die on them. After that we were taken to a camp where we stayed for three days while we recovered some strength.

It was a camp of great long bamboo huts with roofs made of *attap*. Each hut looked nearly 100 yards long with the thatched *attap* roof coming almost down to the ground on each side. Inside there were rough wooden platforms on each side running the whole length of the hut and these were to be our beds. These 'beds' were infested with all sorts of bugs and the eaves of the roof were infested with mosquitoes. The worst of it was that the camp was waterlogged. It looked as though it had been built in a padi field and because the latrines had not been dug deep enough, our huts were swimming in excrement. If any of us had actually believed we were being sent up-country to where conditions were better, all those illusions were now completely dashed. The only saving grace, as far as I was concerned, was that this camp had no fencing around it – only the plantations and jungle. The reason for this was apparently simple. Why would anyone make off into the jungle and attempt escape through dense undergrowth where a sense of direction would be lost before you'd travelled half a mile and through which any other civilisation could be hundreds of miles away for all we knew? For me, however, it was different. I was fascinated by the jungle and drawn to it. I had no fear of it; in fact, I found myself revelling in its promise of wilderness. I loved the sounds and the smells and all the creepy crawlies. After being held in Changi and cooped up on the train journey, this opportunity to roam was a great release. Once in the jungle, I found I could take my bearings on trees or plants and mark my passage as I went so that it wasn't difficult to retrace my steps. I felt I could go in and out as I pleased.

So, during this time, I managed to get away from the vile and virulently infectious camp more than once.

On the last of my excursions, I came upon a hut and a Thai girl attending two goats. There was a well nearby and I signalled that I would like some water. She showed me how to draw the water. It was cool and plentiful so I thought I'd wash myself, too. I had resolved to keep myself clean whenever possible, no matter what, as part of holding on to my self-respect. This was just wonderful as clean water was in very short supply at the camp. Refreshed, I said goodbye and retraced my steps.

Almost straight away on my return, I was told to assemble with a group that were moving on again. Having nothing you would call belongings to gather up, I was ready in an instant. It was then that I noticed that my gold ring was off my finger and remembered that I'd put it in a coconut shell on the side of the well at the girl's jungle hut, while I washed myself. In my mind's eye, I saw my mother giving me that ring and I felt suddenly very sad and stupid.

We were taken to a line of trucks on the railway, pulled by an army lorry. The Japs had fitted the lorry's wheels with steel flanges that enabled it to run on railway tracks as well as the road and so, pulled by this contraption, we continued our journey.

We came to a place called Kanchanaburi, which became known to us, with our trait for shortening names, as Kanburi. It was quite a big place and here, after the degradations we'd suffered in the squalor of Ban Pong and the preceding long journey cooped up in the rice wagons, we were greeted by Lieutenant-Colonel Toosey from our 135th Field Regiment and a few of his officers, all looking spic and span and very much in charge. They brought sanity and dignity suddenly back into the proceedings and Colonel Toosey made a point of shaking all of us by the hand as we passed, telling us there was a 'meal' waiting for us and that we would have a dry place to sleep that night. They showed us to our huts, where we joined with others – 200 to a hut, just as it was in Ban Pong, but at least here it was dry. I went to my 18 inches of bed shelf and stretched out with an overwhelming sense of relief at this great improvement in our conditions. The 'meal' was a rice cake and a mug of tea but this, together with the welcome we'd got, was enough to give us back our self-respect and to get us feeling more like a unit again.

Lieutenant-Colonel Toosey was a remarkable man and the troops talked about him a lot. In the last days before the fall of Singapore, he had been told by the High Command that he should make his get-away along with other officers that had been identified as important for continuing the fighting elsewhere. He refused, saying that he preferred to stay with his men and that Command could not order him to abandon them. From that moment on, his single objective had become one of getting his men through whatever lay ahead of them and to get them all home at the end of it all, no matter what. Over the years of captivity that we were now to endure, there would be many instances of him standing up for us in the face of barbarity, often standing between a soldier who was to be beaten and the guards, telling them that he was the senior officer and that they should deal with him, not the soldier. Later, it became known to everyone that it was he who was instrumental in getting food supplies and much needed medicines into the camps in areas where he had any influence and it was he who had got the Japs to accept that there should be better hospital huts. He could make people go along with him and his resilience gained respect from the Japs so that in the end, they always took notice of what he had to say. It is a fact that without him, even fewer of us would have made it back home.

The place we were in was definitely not a place 'where conditions would be better and food more plentiful', as the Japs had said at the outset. We were here as forced labour to build a railway that would go all the way to Burma, branching off from the Bangkok line that we had come up on from Singapore. The history books now record what this was all about.

The Japanese armies had occupied Malaya and Singapore, and with 'free passage' through French Indochina and Thailand, were moving onwards to occupy Burma by the middle of 1942. However, their ability to supply their armies in Burma by sea was hampered by constant attacks on their shipping and their ability to supply them overland in the north along what was commonly known as 'the Burma Road' through China, was hampered by Chinese resistance. This left Bangkok as the only possible vantage point from which supplies might be sourced, but there was no overland route from there up to Burma. The possibility of a railway across the peninsula across Thailand, or Siam, as it was known then, had been considered many times long before the war and a survey had been conducted as early as 1912. By the mid thirties, after more surveys, a possible route had been identified but the project was abandoned by the authorities in Siam. The terrain was extremely difficult, consisting of dense jungle, jagged mountains and many waterways. On top of that, the monsoon weather conditions were at their most extreme in that region because the land mass caught the full brunt of weather systems sweeping in across the Bay of Bengal during the months of May to November. It was believed that any attempt to build such a railway would involve great loss of life, as well as huge financial cost. In the period before war broke out, Japanese engineers had also looked at the project and decided that it could be done but calculated that it would take five years. However, after the fall of Singapore and their conquests throughout Southeast Asia, they found themselves with such a huge number of prisoners – whom they held in the greatest contempt – that they thought it could be done a lot quicker than that if they were to use the prisoners as forced labour. So they set about building this impossible railway, regardless of the cost in human lives. Their target, given the exigencies of war, was to have it completed in less than eighteen months. The result was that over 60,000 POWs were sent up to work on the railway, of which around 30,000 were British and the rest were 13,000 Australians, 18,000 Dutch and 700 or so Americans. In addition, it is believed they enslaved over 270,000 Burmese and Thai natives, so that in total, something like 330,000 souls laboured on that railway. The death toll of known individuals was over 85,000 by the end of it and there were many, many more who died, simply unknown.

My first working party was at Tamarkan, where we were building bridges to cross a huge river – the Mae Klong River. One bridge was of bamboo and the other of steel. This project was the subject of the film *The Bridge on the River Kwai.*

Our first working parties were on the bamboo bridge but we were soon moved to the steel bridge where they were driving the piles into the river bed to carry the bridge frame. The pile driver, held in a bamboo 'A' frame, was driven by ropes that hundreds of us would systematically pull and then let go in order to raise and drop the weight. It must have been somewhat similar to the slaves building pyramids in Egypt, I thought. The work was relentless and we worked to Tokyo time, which meant that we started at probably five in the morning and finished at sundown.

About three weeks after we had arrived there, some of us were detailed to return to Ban Pong on a working party. I was full of hope that it might give me the opportunity to go back to the hut in the jungle and see if I could recover my gold ring.

While we were there, I took my chance and set off into the jungle, confident of my ability to find my way and sure enough, before too long, there was that hut again. As I approached, the girl must have seen me coming because she came out holding one arm up in what I thought was a wave. When I got closer I could see she had my bandage and the ring in her hand! Unbelievable, if it hadn't actually happened. This girl could have sold that ring and the money would have kept her and whatever family she had for years.

Later, we were returned to Kanburi and to the bridge work at Tamarkan. Then, after a few more weeks, we were to be moved again, further 'up-country' and into the real hell of it.

Chapter 11

SUPIDO!

Nowhere in the world was sadism practised with greater efficiency than in the Japanese Army.

Edgar Snow, *Red Star Over Asia*

They had a train of open low-loader steel trucks to take us from Tamarkan and we were to set off around the middle of the day. Sitting on them would have been like sitting on a frying pan as they had absorbed the heat of the tropical sun by then, but fortunately, there were some bits of rice matting.

We travelled slowly along newly laid railway track and during the journey, the train stopped on a curve in the line surrounded by dense jungle. It was a chance to get off the hot plate because the guard was out of sight round the corner and so I jumped down into the undergrowth. There, I spotted a humming bird feeding from a blossom. He didn't move and let me go right up to him to see his magnificent plumage and wings flapping like the blazes. No fear of humans, obviously. I found that was the thing about virgin jungle – the wildlife had not experienced humans and so they seemed to hold no fear of us. The contrast with my own existence couldn't have been greater. I didn't realise how rare this sighting of a humming bird was at the time. Once again, this image of something wonderful was going to be something for me to hold on to as we descended further into a living hell of human atrocities.

The train began to move again and I climbed up just in time to be where I should be when the train straightened out, bringing us into view of the guards again. These guards had brought a couple of pigs with them. The pigs had no protection from the hot steel plates of the truck and so they gradually cooked alive on their backsides and hind quarters. The Japs used their battle knives to slice pieces off and eat them as we went along. The pigs were perfectly alive. I began to wonder what lay ahead for us.

We didn't know it, but orders had gone out from the Japanese high command at this time for the railway to be completed in double-quick

124

time. The situation, as history now tells it, was that the Japanese were about to take Rangoon and their need for the railway to re-supply their forces was even more urgent. The railway had been planned to be completed by December 1943, but now they wanted it finished by August. For us, it was the beginning of what we came to know as the 'speedo' period. 'Speedo' was our interpretation of the word 'supido', which was what the guards incessantly screamed at us as we stumbled about our tasks in the monsoon-soaked virgin jungle, plagued by malaria, dysentery, tropical ulcers and beriberi.

We had moved to a camp 40 miles north of Tamarkan to a place called Wang Pho, or Wampo, as it is often written. Here, the railway had to be built into the side of a cliff to form a viaduct running alongside the Khwae Noi. The conditions at Tamarkan had been slavery alright but now we were to find out what slavery really meant. Fourteen-hour shifts, day and night, and all on 60 grams of rice a day.

An embankment had already been built up by the time we got there and now they had started building the structure of the viaduct itself, using huge teak beams that had been brought up from a place at the junction with the Bangkok line called Nong Pladuk. The offloading and movement of the teak beams was done with elephants ... and by us. The Japs reckoned that what an elephant could do, we should also be able to do and had us in lines of seven each side of the beams, strapped up with rope slings and bamboo poles, hauling them along.

These guards at Wampo drove us with sheer brutality. Written instructions had apparently been issued to them saying that if necessary, they could kill prisoners who failed to work, without reference to higher authority. We were being shoved, punched, butted, kicked and bashed with sticks, even while working. Black humour was our only defence. When they singled out any of us for a special bashing we used to say that person had 'qualified'. They'd bash you in all manner of ways but you had to hold yourself up because if you fell to the ground there was a chance the guard would kick you to death. You had to try and judge it because some guards would finish you off in a screaming fit if you fell, while others would walk away. It became so commonplace to 'qualify' that we all developed techniques for surviving it. Mine was just to repeat to myself, over and over, 'Do what you like but you're not going to kill me. Go on, smash my teeth in, break my arms ... so long as I am alive at the end of it!' One fellow I saw 'qualifying' took a hell of a beating and eventually fell to the ground. He took a kicking but the guard then walked away. I went up to him and he spluttered, 'How did it look? I thought I got it about right, didn't I?' He could have been a stunt man.

The brutality wasn't only towards us. One guard even had a go at an elephant. It was a funny thing about these elephants. If they were tasked with pulling two teak logs, that's what they would do and they would repeat it endlessly. But if they were then suddenly given something in addition to the two logs, they wouldn't move, even if it was something relatively trivial in weight that had been added. Well, one day this happened in our working party and a guard decided to make the elephant move. He took a heavy tool that had an iron spike at one end and hit the elephant between the eyes with it. The elephant roared and started onto him. The guard turned and ran for his life. The elephant chased him, teak log and all in tow, as he crashed along at full pelt. Even with the load, the elephant gained on the guard, so he ran down the embankment towards the river. The elephant followed and down they both went – the elephant sliding on his bottom like in a Walt Disney picture! They crashed into the river below and the elephant set about squirting water at him through his trunk. The terrified guard swam to the other side to get away. A few days later, true to form, when the guard was back on duty, the elephant spotted him and started after him again. The guard had to be sent away in the end.

As we became increasingly starving and exhausted over the weeks that followed, we desperately looked for food whenever possible. Some of our chaps decided one night to see if they could kill one of the water buffalo that sometimes came to a water plain nearby. It wasn't long before they found one and they attacked it but, being so weak, it took them an hour or more to kill it. They then hacked off great lumps and took them back to camp, where the cookhouse made a soup out of it all. There was enough for it to be dished out to everyone in the camp but the cooks made sure that when they ladled it out, the meat lumps stayed behind so that they would get the best of it. It lasted us quite some time as it was dished out sparingly. One day, I came back to the camp for some reason while the working parties were out and one of our officers came up to me and said, 'Anckorn, do you want something more to eat while you're here?' and he took me to the officers' hut. They'd got a load of the soup on the go, with plenty of meat in it, too. I told him to stick it. Men were starving to death and dying of exhaustion out there, yet here they were looking after themselves very nicely, thank you. I wanted none of it.

It might have been on that day that I took the opportunity to go down to the river and wash myself. The monsoons had not yet started and so the waters were shallow and clear. I'd got a mess tin lid from somewhere so that I could throw water over myself. As I stood on the riverbank I took the half farthing and chain from round my neck and put it in the tin lid to give it a good clean first as it had gone green and mouldy, and then I let it soak under the water on the river bed. I was just washing my arms when a Jap guard saw me and shouted after me. My reaction was instant. I grabbed the mess tin lid, chucked the water out into the river and got moving back up to the camp – clouted all the way by the guard with a stick once he reached me. I suddenly realised I had chucked the chain and half farthing out with the water. Next day I got a chance to break away from my working party again and go down to look for it. But it was nowhere. That was the end of it. Lucille seemed further away than ever.

Under the manic control of Japanese railway engineers as well as the usual guards, the construction of the Wampo Viaduct went on apace. In their way of doing things, the viaduct structure had to be erected before being treated with hot creosote. We would have done it the other way round. The way they did it meant that we would have to climb the structure once it was built to apply the creosote.

The day came when a Korean guard came up to me and ordered me up the viaduct structure with a bucket of the hot creosote. I indicated that I couldn't climb with only one good arm and a gammy leg. He simply screamed at me and went off to get a stick to bash me with. Meanwhile, I thought I'd better get on with it.

I cradled the bucket in my injured arm and set off as best I could, using my good arm to hoist myself up the wooden ladder and my injured arm to hook onto the struts whilst also holding the creosote. The stanchion I was climbing was a good 100 feet high. My progress was slow and accompanied by shouts of 'Supido!' from the guard below. Vertigo, which I'd developed since the bombing and which came on even at low heights, was making it increasingly hard to take each step and the world began to swirl around me. After what seemed an age, I got myself to the top. But having got there I had come to a delirious halt, unable to move. It wouldn't have made any difference if God himself had spoken out of the sky and ordered me to creosote that wood, the vertigo had completely taken over. The whole world was spinning. The guard was still shouting – his voice getting nearer and nearer until he was there with me on the platform, shrieking in my face and jabbing at me. As I couldn't respond he grabbed the bucket of hot creosote from the crux of my arm and threw the lot over my head. Fortunately, I had a banana leaf hat on my head, which protected my face, but I was aware of my shoulders and chest suddenly roasting.

The next thing I knew was that I was in the river below being washed by fellows from my working party. I never knew how I'd got there – whether I had climbed down or fallen down – until only recently, in fact. On a trip back to Thailand with other ex POWs, one of them told me that he had been there when it happened and saw how some of the working party had climbed up and got me down because I had completely passed out up there. Heaven knows why I had not fallen off the structure or why the guard had not kicked me off – it would have been typical. These guards could do as they liked with us – as long as the same number of bodies was brought back to camp each night as went out in the morning. It didn't matter to them if we were dead or alive. No questions were asked.

It was therefore even more amazing that the Japs then had me taken away by boat to another camp downriver. It seemed the Japs took a different attitude to visible injuries as compared with weakness to work through illness or starvation. As I was taken to the boat I was saying goodbye to the men in my working party and saying, 'I'll be back ... I'll see you soon.'

One of them replied, 'No you won't, Gus, we'll all be dead, more like!' It was Lester Martin, the one who'd carried everyone's rice sacks off the train at Ban Pong – strong as a horse. Well, they were. All of them. Dead within weeks. If I hadn't been badly burned, I'd have been dead with them.

Chapter 12

LIVE OR DIE

It was night-time and pouring with rain by the time I arrived at the other camp. It seemed the monsoons had started early and it rained without ceasing, hour after hour. There was no one around to say where I should go or what I should be doing and I was just lying there in the mud on the riverbank. At least the rain was washing me and soothing my back and shoulders.

I crawled to the nearest hut and got myself in out of the rain, under the bed shelf that ran along the open side. Just then a voice called out, 'Hey! Get out of there, this is officers only.' It seemed ridiculous to me that anyone should have preferential treatment given the circumstances we were all in and even more ridiculous that officers should try to separate themselves from their men. I just said, 'Move me then! I'm no trouble to anyone – just trying to get dry for a bit.' 'Bloody cheek!' and various other mutterings was all I heard in response and they left me alone. During the night I thought I was having a nightmare as I experienced awful sounds of screaming but woke up to find it was two rats having a go at each other – on my chest!

In the morning I got myself into a one of the other huts and so began my time at this camp, which was called Chungkai.

It was a strange camp at that time, with no sense of order to it – unlike Tamarkan, where Colonel Toosey was in control, and unlike Wampo, where there was forced labour, day and night. Here there seemed to be no great demands on us and I wondered, in fact, what everyone was doing there. While recovering from the burns, it didn't really matter to me, of course.

During this time however, Chungkai was receiving an ever increasing number of sick, injured, exhausted and emaciated bodies brought down from the railhead and jungle camps, on long punt-like river boats they called *sampans*, and unloaded at the riverbank. This was the result of the Japanese *Supido* drive to get the railway built ahead of schedule. It

129

seems that my incident at Wampo was just a small taste of what those I left behind and those further up the railway track had to put up with.

Lieutenant John Durnford said it well in his account, *Branch Line to Burma*, published not long after the war:

> As the cry of 'Speedo, speedo' went up from the engineers waving their metre sticks like the Egyptians their whips, so the working parties dwindled in numbers through sickness and death … Another day from dawn to sunset, another metre, another kilometre, another life lost, so that they call it now 'the Railway of Death', reckoning a life expended for every sleeper laid.

More and more men were being dragged up from Singapore and Java to replace the many that were dying or being disabled as slave labourers, pressed into work in what had become a perpetual rotation of day and night shifts. But the Japanese Command had begun to realise the limitations of pressing sick men into work as it meant their railway would not get built by the end of the monsoon period, which was when they now expected an Allied counter-attack through northern India and Burma to begin. So they had decided that certain camps down-country should be designated hospital camps and those unable to work could then be shipped off as more able bodied men came up in their thousands. I had been brought up from Singapore in a consignment of 5,000, and following us in April were another 7,000 and yet another 3,000 shortly after that. All were dispersed over the railway to work as slaves in the monsoon conditions. Chungkai and Tamarkan were two of the designated hospital camps and so the steady flow of sick and damaged men back to these camps was destined to become a flood.

Bodies were laid out where they were offloaded and each regiment was expected to look after its own if casualties could be identified, but if not, bodies were left there until someone decided what to do with them. It had become a daily event to have bodies arrive and so there were always people down at the riverside. One day, I was down there when a *sampan* came in with its load and amongst them was someone I knew very well. It was the sergeant-major who had commandeered men's cigarettes, clothes and other possessions back in Changi, pretending it would be for the general good if he were to act as distributor, but then he had plundered what was collected for himself – the very man who so vindictively assigned me to go 'up-country' after failing to get me court martialled for refusing PT while I was still virtually crippled. Now he himself was reduced to a dreadful state and it crossed my mind that I should roll him into the river and be done with him. There was satisfaction though in the fact that he had been brought up-country after me and probably sent to one of the nastiest of camps that we were hearing about, beyond the viaduct at Wampo. Anyway, we brought him up to the huts and gradually he came round. Unbelievably, within five days he was back on his feet and in no time at all, he was declaring himself senior amongst our lot in the camp and trying to charge any of us who transgressed King's Regulations! I thought, 'No need for me to do anything – you've got it coming to you mate, from all directions, sooner or later!'

With the influx of more and more sick, diseased and wasted bodies, Chungkai struggled to adapt itself to its new purpose as a hospital camp and medical staff found themselves constantly at odds with Jap ways of thinking. To a Jap, if you couldn't work you should be left to die. It seemed that what the Japanese Command had in mind when they said 'hospital camp' was actually 'cemetery'.

Julie Summers recalled in her biographical book about Colonel Toosey, *The Colonel of Tamarkan*, the colonel's own account of this mentality and its implications:

> The Japanese despised ill health considering it a sign of weakness. The doctors received no support from them and often had to make desperate decisions when faced with impossible demands for fit men for working parties about whether a man could or could not go to work. The doctors became front line soldiers in the war against inhumanity, indifference and neglect. They were not fighting the Japanese; they were fighting the attitude of the Japanese.

This attitude also dictated that the sick should receive only half-rations and insofar as the Japanese were holding to the principal of paying POWs any sort of wages, the sick should receive none. It also meant that medical supplies were virtually nonexistent.

Treating the sick demanded courage, extreme ingenuity and resolute management under these circumstances. Tamarkan was the first to reorganise itself into a hospital camp and there, Colonel Toosey dealt with the half-rations issue by requiring all able bodied prisoners to give up a spoonful of the 60 grams rice ration each day for those who were hospitalised. He partially addressed the funding of hospital needs by deducting one third from the officers' weekly pay. This eventually became the way things were done at Chungkai, too. In the first few months after I had arrived, the camp had seemed to have no purpose, and it was generally 'every man for himself'. But later we had a new commander in the camp – Lieutenant-Colonel Owtram – and things changed. From being a camp with no purpose, no order and no discipline, Chungkai began to focus on treating the sick, saving lives and burying the dead.

It was, of course, the skill and ingenuity of the medical staff that saved the lives. In Chungkai there was a remarkable man, a Canadian – Captain Jacob Markowitz. He had been the first person in the world to carry out a heart transplant long before the war and now, having been caught up in the fall of Singapore like all of us, his surgical and medical skills were saving hundreds of lives. He had to deal with the results of beatings, as well as the illnesses and infections. Tropical ulcers were a common problem. These started as cuts from sharp bamboo splinters, which then festered in the tropical heat and became chronic due to malnutrition. The ulcers eventually became so deep that flesh gave way to bone and in the end, gangrene would set in and amputation would be needed. Markowitz was known in the camp for being able to amputate a leg in less than ten minutes, and that was with make-do anaesthesia and a makeshift saw. He and his orderlies had no real equipment so they just had to innovate. They used broken bottles as funnels and whipped coagulating blood with bamboo sticks to keep it useable. They would scoop out tropical ulcers with old spoons and bandage you up with much re-used strips of old shirts. Jungle medicine it was but no effort was spared to save lives in that camp.

Markowitz himself was a quiet little man. He used to walk about the camp, on his own, slightly hunched, and I noticed he would have his thumbs held inside his hands with his fingers curled inwards too. I guessed he was trying to prevent his fingernails from picking up infection. He was accompanied in his daily work by an artist, Jack Chalker, who made anatomical drawings of all the operations and procedures. Jack had been working further up-country with another surgeon, 'Weary' Dunlop, who became legendary for his work up there and who later came to Chungkai. But Jack had his face flattened by a Jap guard with a shovel. After that, he'd been sent down to Chungkai. He had joined up on the same day as I and we had been friends ever since, although we had not been in action together. Now here he was working with Markowitz. His drawings were much acclaimed after the war and they made him a Fellow of the Anatomical Society in recognition.

As Chungkai filled up with the sick and disabled, they were spread throughout the camp so that just about every hut contained some of them and a full range of dreadful afflictions had to be coped with. In addition to the tropical ulcers, there was the ever present dysentery, malaria and dengue fever, as well as various conditions caused by avitaminosis, including scurvy, beriberi and pellagra. Impetigo was common and so were many bed bug infections, as we called them – scabies and typhus among them. On top of that, many of us had various forms of the skin infection called tinea, which caused compulsive itching, severe soreness and painful cracking of the skin in the most

132

sensitive parts of the body. As if that wasn't enough, the whole sorry camp became a quagmire under the incessant rain during the monsoon season.

Sleeping in the huts was impossible with the rain pouring off the *attap* roofs and splashing up from the mud below onto the bamboo slats that formed our beds along the two sides of each hut. There was a job in the camp, of preparing the dead for burial. A little hut, 8 feet by 6 feet, came with the job for storing the bodies. It was a job that we had instigated, not the Japs, and so any of us could volunteer for it. I did – as a means of getting somewhere dry.

Inside the hut was a place for laying a body out and a basketful of rice sacks. The job was to put one rice sack over the feet and another over the head and sew them together in the middle. That made them ready for the burial party. There were around nine or ten deaths a day but sometimes as many as fifteen, so that there was no room left in the hut for me, and I would have to sleep on top of the bodies before they were taken out the next day. I had sunk to the point where all it meant to me was that I was out of the rain and the mud. It meant nothing to me even when the bodies groaned due to air being expelled from their lungs as I turned over on top of them in the night. I had become hardened to it all.

Along with the task of preparing the dead for burial there was another. It was to take amputated limbs out from the main hospital hut where Captain Markowitz was doing his work and bury them. Like the bodies of the dead, these limbs were not buried particularly deeply because none of us had the strength to dig deep graves. One day, when I had buried a whole leg in the customary manner, I noticed a dog that had been around the camp making his way to the burial area. Shortly afterwards he returned, scampering through the camp and making a beeline for the jungle – with the whole leg in his jaw.

At some point during that monsoon season, the Japs gave us three little pigs as a 'gift', saying if we fed them, we'd have lovely porkers by Christmas. Feed them? With what? Well of course we took the pigs and fed them by sharing our 60 grams of rice a day with them as well as with the sick and we fed them anything else we could get our hands on. To keep them out of the rain, we built a little byre out of bamboo. Sometime later, there was to be a visit to the camp by a Japanese general. Everything had to be spick and span for his visit and for the inevitable propaganda pictures that would display the camp as idyllic. Despite the monsoon conditions my task was to clean up these pigs. They had of course been in the mud and pouring rain so the Japs gave me a scrubbing brush and hot water – two things that we never had. So I scrubbed them and made them lovely and pink – and then I had to keep them out of the mud until the General arrived. I was darting about keeping them in the byre until the General finally did arrive. The pigs were standing there, panting after all the running around but still pink and respectable looking, and there was I in a clean pair of shorts that the Japs had given me for the occasion. Of course, the general and his propaganda entourage never looked at the pigs and after they had left, the Japs came to take the shorts off me again. Looking at those pigs, clean and dry in the byre, I said under my breath to myself, 'I wish I were a pig!' This suddenly shocked me. I had just expressed envy of a pig. It made me say out loud, 'Fergus Anckorn, you've just wished you were a pig! Right, that's it. It's upwards from now on, you sink no lower!'

There and then, I revised the code of behaviour I had set for myself back in Changi and I was going to stick to it, no matter what. Firstly, I would shave myself every day with whatever I could make or get as a shaver. Secondly, I would make sure I washed myself well every day. Thirdly, I would never meander around the place aimlessly. Even if I had no purpose of going from here to there, I would walk as if I had. Fourth, I would keep a smile on my face at all times – even when I was going to sleep. This was especially important to me because I didn't want my face becoming contorted into the painful grimace that was so common on sleeping faces there in the camp.

As my burns gradually healed up, I was able to do more light duties around the camp and worked with the medical staff treating our various afflictions. One of these was beriberi, which is a vitamin deficiency complaint. The name beriberi actually means 'I can't, I can't', which is a literal description of its debilitating effects. If it doesn't actually kill you through eventual heart failure, it leaves you with severe muscle damage and sometimes complete loss of use of your legs.

One of the medical officers taught some of us to give massage treatment to beriberi sufferers using coconut oil. He had found it was possible to get sufferers back on their feet with regular massaging. We were given a small bottle containing coconut oil for each session and we had to hand back what we didn't use because he knew we would drink it otherwise.

After giving one of these treatment sessions, I was returning my bottle when I passed a line of eight or so bodies lying on the ground. They had been brought up from the riverbank after the latest *sampan* delivery. Amongst them was someone I thought I recognised. I went to him and asked if his name was Cliff Swan, hoping it was because he and I had become the closest of friends as gunners in the same battery.

He whispered, 'Yes, who are you?' and I said, 'It's Gus. Gus Anckorn,' but he just said, 'Oh,' and looked at me without recognition. Either I was now unrecognisable myself or he had lost his mind. It was getting towards nightfall and returning the bottle meant a long walk across the camp so I said I'd have to come back in the morning to see him. When I returned, there was a gap where he had been and I asked those of the others that could talk what had happened. The Japs had come asking if any of them were engineers and Cliff had said he was, even though he wasn't, and they took him back up-country to work. The next time I met up with him was after the war and he told me how that event had turned out well for him. The work was light – working on the various bridges along the railway just tightening bolts and things and moving from place to place as a small specialist working party. He thought it was probably thanks to his sudden impulse to say yes to the guard that he survived. He just wanted to get away from the camp because he believed he'd been left there to die. That was a big difference between him and me. He made a decision even in that dreadful and weak condition no matter what the consequences. Fortunately it did turn out well for him. I, on the other hand, found myself never knowing what best to do. It seemed to me that the situation was too chaotic, unpredictable and dangerous so I never *decided* anything. I let things happen. My thought was that if I made a decision and ended up in trouble, I'd never forgive myself. It was the same when it came to throwing in my lot with others in the camps. I didn't want to be bound to others and have to go wherever they went and do whatever they decided to do. I needed to be a free agent and just take whatever happened in my own way without trying to change the situation. I was *me* and whatever happened to me, well alright, that's what was in store for me ... I wouldn't be blaming anyone else. Drifting along with the tide rather than fighting it seemed the better thing to do. Just get through each day and be grateful for waking up each morning was my internal mantra, along with a grim determination to see my fiancée, Lucille, again whatever happened.

There was a large Dutch and Javanese contingency in Chungkai as there had been at Wampo and at Tamarkan. In order to exercise my mind, I had started learning Dutch back at Changi after the Dutch arrived there in late 1942, and now on the railway, I continued my learning by trying to get on working parties with the Dutch or by finding a Dutchman to work alongside whenever I could. The working parties at Chungkai involved comparatively light work and it meant there was more of a chance to talk while getting on with it. My Dutch speaking was coming on well, to the point where I could spend time in the Dutch sector of the camp making conversation. Once when I was there, I heard a voice I recognised. I looked and there was one of the Dutch prisoners having a blazing row with a sergeant-major of ours.

The Dutchman had his back to me. It was not only the voice but also the bandy legs I now recognised. The man was Frans Bakker – the boy my sister and I had befriended at the Dunton Green Lido and who had gone off without saying anything, during the summer before war broke out. We assumed he'd gone back to his father's horticulture business in Holland, but it had all been a bit odd. Now here he was – and ever the businessman, he had set up a laundry business in the Dutch quarters. His hut ran next to the first of the British huts and he had made a washing line, strung up between his Dutch hut and the British hut. One of our sergeant-majors had wanted it down. After the blazing row, it stayed where it was.

Generally, the Dutch didn't make themselves very popular in the camps. Back in Java, when the Japs took over, they had told the surviving soldiers and civilians alike to go back to what was left of their homes and wait for orders. This gave them time to prepare for whatever would happen next and meant they were able to liquidate what assets they could and gather money, clothes and supplies to take with them, wherever the Japs were going to send them. Eventually, of course, they were shipped across in batches to Singapore and onwards. When their fighting units arrived in Singapore as prisoners, you would not have believed they had fought as bitter a battle as we had. We had finished up blooded and in tatters and our existence in Changi in the months that followed the fall of Singapore made our appearance even worse. The Dutch, by comparison, had marched ashore in spick and span uniforms with impeccable military drill. Our lot, never having seen a Dutch uniform, thought they were Germans with their generally loud behaviour and strange guttural language reinforcing that notion. They had been designated a separate area in Changi right from the start and their separateness persisted by their behaviour.

Now, in the camps along the railway, the Dutch kept themselves to themselves, often able to buy food from locals and carrying on little business enterprises amongst their own. Here in Chungkai, one of their businesses was confectionary – making 'peanut stars' out of Gula Melaka, a sugary substance that comes from coconut trees. Another business was making cigarettes. They had a long table sorted out that ten workers could sit around and they'd made special tobacco rollers for each worker to use. The tobacco leaves came from a local abandoned tobacco plantation and they had got some decent paper from somewhere to roll the tobacco into. They would tie up the finished products in bunches of five and go round the camp at night selling them.

Frans's own laundry business was doing rather well. For five cents, Frans would launder shirts and shorts or whatever, and he would give them back the next day, clean and pressed. He'd always had a supply of soap with him so the wash was easily done and he would have the items dried in half an hour on the line in the baking sun. Then, to press them, he would roll them out and sleep on them overnight.

Frans's face lit up when he recognised me and he immediately took me to meet his friends. 'Here is the boy I was telling you about,' he said. 'It was his sister I fell in love with.' He turned to me to translate what he'd said but I stopped him saying that I had understood because I had been learning Dutch. He joked, 'Oh yeah? You Anckorns think you can do anything … well, I'll test you …' and he reeled off a long sentence that was simply, 'If you think you can speak Dutch then pass me those shoes from under the bed shelf.' So I did and it got raucous approval from his friends. From that moment onwards I became welcome amongst the Dutch, which was something I valued right through captivity.

It was wonderful to meet up with Frans again and we had a lot to talk about.

That night there was a flood expected from the river as it was in spate due to the monsoon. It was decided to put sentries out to warn the camp if it looked likely the river would break its banks during the night. The plan was to have sentries doing two hours each throughout the night, up on a hillock that was a good vantage point. Frans and I offered to do the whole night so we could have a good talk together. We climbed onto the hillock from where, sure enough, we could see and hear what the river was doing and we sat there all night chatting. He had enlisted in the Dutch forces as a gunner, just like me, and had become a machine-gun sergeant. The battle for Java and subsequent fall was just as bad as Singapore, he thought. He told me how he had left England with the secret intention to get a position and earn enough money to be able to come back and propose to my sister. He had gone to Java and was working on a plantation there until he had to enlist. He hadn't known quite how to write to my sister after that. Now he wanted to know everything about Beryl and what she had thought, but I had to tell him that she had taken up with someone else, thinking he had deserted her.

We were obviously chatting too much as neither of us saw or heard the river seeping surreptitiously into the camp. We only became aware that the river had burst its banks when pandemonium broke out in the huts as people became aware of the rising water level, which must already have got to about three feet deep in places. So much for our sentry duty.

Monsoons create exactly the right conditions for the deadly disease of cholera and it had struck in the jungle camps up at the railhead in June. It sent shock waves through all the camps – ours especially, as we were likely to receive cholera cases amongst the daily toll of wasted bodies. The Japs were scared stiff of it and immediately did everything possible to distance and separate themselves from prisoners, including putting lime boundary lines around their huts. We heard stories of their dire procedures for dealing with cholera victims at some of the remote camps up-country. They would mark out an area away from the huts, where the victims would be taken to die. They would have prisoners build pyres out of dry wood and place victims on these whilst still alive. They were then left, vomiting and delirious in the full glare of the sun with no food or water. When they were dead the Japs ordered prisoners to set light to the wood. There was a particularly nasty incident we heard about that took place at one of the camps up near the railhead when cholera took its first victims. There were three or four of them and the camp commandant ordered that graves should be dug and the bodies placed in them, covered with lime. As the graves were being filled in, one of the victims moved and one of our officers called for a stop to the proceedings. The Japs refused and so he demanded that the man should at least be shot rather than buried alive. The Japs again refused so the officer grabbed one of the Jap's guns and shot the poor man himself.

At Chungkai, the medical officers had prevailed better against Jap barbarity. An area of the camp was marked out and fenced off, but in that area, small huts were built to house the victims and shade them from the sun. A pile of dry wood was placed underneath so that when death came, the whole hut would go up in the cremation. In the meantime, a volunteer would look after each man in the hut, giving him water and what food he could eat. It was simply stunning that men would put themselves forward like that as volunteers and so starkly different from the behaviour of the Japanese.

Such was the Japs' fear of cholera that they had their own medical people eagerly giving out injections in our camp. On the day they did this I was to go on a working party up to Kanburi, about 7 kilometres away. We were inoculated before we left in the morning.

To get to Kanburi, we had to walk down a long road that crossed others in four places. At each junction, the Japs had set up an inoculation unit and they were injecting everyone that came along. Although we said we'd had an injection already, they just carried on, so that we finished up getting four more injections – which meant that we each had five in total by the end of the day. I thought perhaps five would be more preventative than one but then, that night, symptoms of cholera started to appear – stomach cramps and a high temperature. Having seen how our cholera victims were dealt with, I was determined not to get laid out on a pyre of dry sticks and so I took myself off into the jungle and found a patch of open ground with a soft bed of under-growth and lay down, thinking that was it, I was going to die. A dreadful weakness seemed to come over me and movement became impossible. Well, I must have passed out because the next thing I knew, the sun was shining down and jungle sounds were all about. This must be heaven, I imagined. Then a piercing trumpet call broke into my reverie and with consciousness coming back I realised it was *tenko* – the morning roll-call. Leaping to my feet, I cursed myself for still being alive. It wasn't cholera at all, just the reaction to all those injections!

By comparison with Wampo, Chungkai was actually something of a haven. Not only were the working parties doing lighter work, but also there were new camp routines to get involved with once we had become a hospital camp. One daily routine I got myself into very quickly was the foraging of firewood in the jungle. The cookhouses and the hospital used vast amounts of wood for their *kwalis* – large wok-like bowls for cooking and boiling water in. The wood had to be got from the surrounding jungle and, as time had gone on, all the nearby dead wood had been taken and it was necessary to forage deeper into the jungle each time to pick out the dead wood from the green. They called the working parties *'maki'* parties – *maki* being Japanese for 'firewood'. We were given a bamboo token by the Japs as a 'warrant' for the activity and sent off into the jungle to get what we could. There was no time limit other than roll-call at the end of the day, which meant you could get away into the jungle and spend most of a day there sometimes. My *maki* party routine was to spend the first few hours collecting the wood and burying it where I could come back for it later. Then I'd go off and explore. It was such a place to be, noisy with animal life, mysterious and just lovely. To me, it wasn't the 'green hell' that others were enduring up-country. The Wampo Viaduct had been yet another bad thing to happen to me that turned out to have saved me from a lot worse. This was now a great privilege – who else back at home, had ever experienced a real jungle? It was simply entrancing.

I found I could have fun watching the monkeys. They would follow me, up in the trees, jumping from branch to branch as I made my progress below. These were Rhesus monkeys and they loved water. Down by the river they would play games with each other running down tree branches to the water and diving in on top of each other. They would push one another under the water and try to stop each other from coming up again. They seemed to be able to stay under the water for ages. Often one would dive under the water and it would be two minutes or more before two little trapdoors opened on the surface – the monkeys' eyes!

The monkeys were very useful companions in the jungle. If I came across something that looked as if it were edible, I would take it and then find a place where I could lie down and wait for the monkeys to come down. They'd come down to see if I was still alive or not! When they were near, I'd roll the thing towards them and if one picked it up and ate it, I took it that I could too. I learned how to get the monkeys to come right up to me and take things out of my hand – the secret was never to look them in the eye. In the animal world that was a threat.

Of course, the same applied to the Japs – you never looked them in the eye either, for the same reason.

Returning to camp was like a return to hell, by comparison with the freedom of the jungle. As always, our only personal space was on the bed shelf. We each had a short section of the bamboo slats that ran along the whole length of the huts on each side, like a shelf. The slats were quite springy but they were full of bed bugs. Bed bugs and mosquitoes were our nightly bed partners, as well as other assorted insects. My defence against them all, especially the mosquitoes, was to make a sleeping bag out of my blanket. I made a needle out of bamboo and used thread from rice sacking to sew up the blanket into a body bag, leaving a flap at the top that could be pulled over my head once I was installed inside. Then I made some eyes in the lip of the bag and sewed buttons to the flap so that, when inside, I could button myself in. Completely encased, I could rest at ease – putting up with the heat as a lesser of the evils to cope with.

Then one day I managed to get hold of a mosquito net and settled down that night thinking how fortunate I was and how cool it was compared to being in my sewn-up blanket. It had this lovely almond smell, too. The sense of good fortune, however, only lasted until it became apparent that the almond smell came from the nests of bedbugs in the corners and folds of the net. They started to drop down on me during the night like paratroopers! The blanket proved the better option despite soaking it in sweat every night.

I did find another answer to beg bugs and mosquitoes eventually. I managed to catch a chameleon in the jungle. It was strange. Having caught him, he would never leave me. It seemed that he accepted me as his master, like a pet dog would. At night, I would put him on my chest and nothing would touch me. Whenever a mosquito or a bed bug did appear, out would come his tongue and he would have it. In the day-time, he would sit on my shoulder and sometimes on my head and he'd have all the flies that came anywhere near me. We became real mates! Every morning, I would take him out to find dew on the leaves. Holding him in my hand, I'd take him up to a leaf with a dew drop on it and he'd put his tongue out and collect it. We would go from leaf to leaf like that and then I'd put him back on my shoulder and away we would go.

Once the sun goes down in the jungle, it becomes dark almost instantly and on moonless nights it would be pitch-black in the huts. It meant we had to use our ingenuity if we were going to play cards or have a game of make-do draughts or chess. Here again the jungle provided the answer. Six fireflies in a bottle made a very handy lamp!

During the months since I had recovered from the creosote burns, I had begun to do magic again. The guards at Chungkai were not

140

so driving on the working parties as those up at the railhead and so during our ten-minute breaks, which we got every couple of hours, it was possible to distract them with magic tricks. I would pick up stones and make them disappear or turn little ones into bigger ones or make sticks pass through each other. It was just the run of the mill stuff that I could do using mainly my left hand for the action and the injured right hand and forearm simply for holding things. They loved it and often we could make a break last for twenty minutes.

One day, a Korean guard whom I'd never seen before came up to me in the camp. He must have seen me up-country or back at Tamarkan. Anyway, he said in broken English, 'You have beautiful hands,' and I felt immediately apprehensive. He went on, 'You magic man.' And I replied, 'Yes'. 'Me too,' he said. 'You come our hut tonight and do magic.'

Still very apprehensive but not wanting to upset the Korean guards unnecessarily, having felt the results up at Wampo, I duly went to the hut that night. It was on stilts, 10 feet off the ground to avoid the flooding that we had now found the camp was prone to in the monsoons. I was given food and cigarettes and, sure enough, we exchanged tricks. Tomimoto was this guard's name and he turned out to be a very decent chap in every way.

Things were going well until late in the evening when we heard the loud voices of some Japs coming towards the hut. They'd obviously got happy on something and were now returning to this hut that Tomimoto shared with them.

'I'll go,' I said, but he insisted, 'No, you stay, you are my guest!' Well, his hut mates arrived and of course, a furious row broke out over my being there. Tomimoto gave as good as he got, which enraged the Japs to the point where one of them took his bayonet and rammed it straight through him. In a split second, I took a giant leap out of the window into the pitch-black night. From 10 feet up and with still only one leg working properly, I somehow landed safely and scampered back to my hut as fast as I could. That night I lay listening for the repercussions. Nothing happened and nothing was said by anyone to anyone. Until sometime later.

I was outside my hut getting the bugs out of my bed blanket when a guard came over and stood near me. He seemed to be just watching what I was doing but then he spoke quietly to me. 'Your friend ... he paradise go.' Then he just mooched off and that was that.

Not long after that incident, my magic was to bring me close to death again – only this time it was my own life at stake.

The Japanese camp commandant was a man called Osato. He liked magic. He would have seen me around the camp doing the odd trick and things and, for all I knew, he might also have been told about Tomimoto. One day, he came up to me and, in a mixture of broken English and sign language, told me I should do some magic for him but said nothing more.

This was a man who at times seemed to have some compassion in him but at others was utterly ruthless and savage. I had seen him one day, walking across the camp with a black dog he'd got from somewhere. The dog was on a lead made out of some rope and was walking quite happily alongside him. Then Osato stopped walking and took out his gun, cocked it and pointed it at the dog's head. He fired, but missed because of the gun recoil. He cocked the gun again, fired and missed a second time. The dog meanwhile was now looking up at him wondering what he wanted. Osato cocked his gun a third time, fired and the dog fell into the dust, blood pouring from his broken skull. Osato threw the rope over him and walked off.

Then, on another occasion, there was a line of about six of our men stood outside his hut with six guards opposite them. Osato came out of his hut and gave a little nod to the guards, who then set about beating the men up with bamboo sticks. An invitation to do magic for this man was not good news. Nevertheless, later that day, through one of our interpreters, I was summoned to his hut. The interpreter was one of ours but virtually Japanese in looks and everything. He came with me.

In the hut, to get started, I picked up something from the table in front of the commandant and did some business with it. He nodded in a gesture that to me was like God saying, 'Well done', and he signalled 'More! More!' with those inimitable hand movements, which at home would have meant 'clear off ... shoo', but out here, as I'd learned in Changi with a bashing, meant the opposite. So on I went with the tricks – each one now being followed by the Pidgin English command, 'More-one!' from Osato, until he'd had enough.

Osato was just like the guards I'd done tricks for – each time wanting to know how the trick was done and wanting to see if they could do it themselves. It was always enough to show them only part of a trick before their attempts to do it proved unsuccessful and they would give up. But their insatiable appetite for magic remained.

Well now, of course, I was buttonholed by Osato and was sent for whenever he was bored or couldn't sleep or something and in fact, often I did perform until he fell asleep! I was getting called out more often than our interpreter liked and it came to the point where he said, 'Look, it's alright for you but I'm already on the go all day and half the night and now with this Osato business, I have to go in with you while you do magic for him.' So I suggested he should teach me to do the act in Japanese. All I needed were the phrases ... take a card ... look at it ... remember it ... put it back ... shuffle the pack and so on, as well as numbers. So he did and we went through trick after trick with me listening to him repeating everything in Japanese and noting down the words in shorthand so that I could rehearse them later. Shorthand was perfect for this because it is based on sounds, which meant that my scribbles enabled me to accurately repeat the word sounds each time and it wasn't long before I had it all off-pat. The interpreter – or interrupter, as we called them – could now get his sleep.

A day came when Osato said to me, in his mixture of broken English and sign language again, that he wanted me to do a special trick for a visiting general. Well, whenever possible, it was a good idea to do a trick that involved food because the chances were that I'd get to eat it afterwards. In their view, anything we touched became contaminated and so I'd be told to take it away. A particular trick came to mind involving eggs that I thought I could do despite my still gammy right arm and hand. Eggs were gold dust in the camp because of their nutritional value. Officers and others, such as the Dutch prisoners who had money, could buy eggs but in our hut, eggs were a rarity. When we had first arrived at Ban Pong and later Kanburi, I had managed to get a number of eggs off some local market girls by taking just one egg from their basket and making it disappear, whereupon they had me do it again and again until all the fellows I was with, as well as myself, each had an egg. I hadn't tasted an egg since then.

I signed back to Osato that I had nothing to do special tricks with and he replied, 'You speak,' which was his way of saying, 'tell me what you want.' Straight away I said, 'Egg'.

Osato took a pencil and slip of paper from his pocket and wrote on it. He then thrust his arm out at me with the paper in his hand and said, 'Take!'

So I 'took' ... and went off to the Japanese cookhouse and gave it to the cook there. He looked at it and then at me and finally asked me what I wanted. I suddenly realised that Osato hadn't asked me how many eggs – so he probably just scribbled down 'egg', which was what I had asked for. Quick as a flash I said, 'Fifty eggs', in perfect Japanese and he went and got them – to the order of the commandant!

Away I went back to my hut, where my fellows and I set about making a huge omelette with the fifty eggs. I needed a couple of eggs for the trick I was going to do but I thought I would not waste good food on a trick. So first, I got a bamboo thorn and cut holes in the two eggs and emptied them out ready for the omelette but I needed one of them to appear to be a complete egg in the trick so I had to be sure I could make up artificial contents for it before cracking the remaining eggs into the omelette. There was a kapok tree nearby, from which I was able to take a substance that was just like cotton wool, and I got some red palm oil and mixed the two in a small amount of water. The result was a yellowy green substance that looked just like the yoke of a duck egg. Then I got some coconut oil to make do as the albumin and put it, together with the home-made yoke, into the hollow eggshell, which I then stuck back together with rice glue. The egg was now complete enough, I hoped, to look like a proper egg when I broke it in the trick. All set up, we quietly settled down to our fifty-egg omelette.

That night I went to Osato's hut and performed for him and his visiting general. The trick usually involved a silk handkerchief, a glass and two eggs. In this case, Osato came up with a handkerchief of sorts and a glass and I, of course, had the eggs. The trick began with me holding the handkerchief with both hands held close together and cupped while at the same time shaking my hands up and down, waving the handkerchief whilst drawing it up into my cupped hands with my fingers until it had fully disappeared and was apparently secreted in my cupped hands. At this point I opened my hands to reveal an egg so that it looked as though the handkerchief had disappeared and become an egg. Then, supposedly as if to meet their need to know how the trick was done, I turned the egg around to let them see that there was a hole in the back of the egg and the handkerchief was simply stuffed into the egg through the hole. I then took the handkerchief out and did the trick again as if to make sure they could see how it was done. I finished once again with the handkerchief clearly inside the egg, but then just when they were thinking they'd got it, I took the egg and cracked it into the glass so that they saw it really was an egg. There was an eruption of Jap happiness.

Next morning I was summoned once again to the hut and, as it had gone so well the night before, I thought it was going to be a call for more magic, or perhaps a compliment even. When I went in, Osato was sitting at his table just glowering with his head down and sword on the table. I stood in front of him. Nothing was said. No gestures were made. Suddenly my legs began to tremble and my knees actually did knock together. I thought he must know what I'd done and I knew only too well that if you displeased him, it was treated as an insult to their beloved emperor. Off would come my head, no bother about that, no questions asked. On the table in front of him was the chitty I'd taken to the cookhouse. So that was it. 'I'm dead,' I thought.

In their code, any thieving was very, very serious – even amongst their own. You'd be killed for stealing a potato. Fifty eggs, worth several month's wages? You'd more than deserve to die, and I began to think, 'What a way to go, just for eggs.' To myself I was saying over and over again, 'You fool ... just for some eggs ... you fool!'

When you think you're about to die, you become suddenly very conscious of your surroundings – as if you need to hold onto something real, moment by moment, to confirm to yourself that you're still alive. In the silence, I looked at the wall of the hut behind Osato and saw how it was made of rice sacking, not hessian, and I studied the pattern of it, thinking this was the last thing I was ever going to see.

He opened his mouth and drew breath, still looking down. He said, 'You do trick. One egg. Why you take fifty egg?'

Heaven only knows where the words came from but I heard myself saying, 'Your show, so important, I practice all day long.'

The silence returned. His head remained down. I was in eternity. Then he slowly raised his head, jerked a nod and dismissed me.

Outside, I could scarcely walk and virtually collapsed behind a tree. I had no idea whether he'd fallen for it or knew damn well what I'd done with the eggs but nevertheless, he accepted what I'd said because it saved his face and meant I could still be his magic man. I didn't care. I was alive!

It was a relief the next day to get out once more on a *maki* party. The monsoon season had ended but still everywhere was drenched, dripping and soggy. *Maki* parties went out nevertheless, such was the need for wood, and as usual I did my foraging and, after burying it, went off to explore the jungle for as long as I dared.

On coming back out of the jungle, I suddenly realised my gold ring was missing off my finger. It had been covered by a bandage to avoid detection and, with my hands covered in mud from scrabbling around in the jungle undergrowth, it wasn't noticeable that the whole lot had gone, bandage and ring. Of course, there was no time now to go back and look for it and anyway, the chances of finding it this time were nil as I had fallen over several times in different places in the slithery undergrowth. No, this time the ring was surely gone.

Three days later, I got on another *maki* party and, after collecting and burying the firewood, I tried to retrace my steps from the earlier outing, noting the broken-off branches, trodden-down undergrowth and a particular hibiscus plant that I had seen along my way. Gradually, I navigated myself back to the railway embankment where I had climbed up to see if there were any locals around on the other side whom I might magic some food from. Then I remembered that I'd tripped on one of the railway lines and had fallen down the other side in the mud. Arriving at what I thought was the very spot, I looked down and saw the marks my fall had made in the muddy bank and I saw four holes in the mud where my fingers had gone in as I tried to stop the fall. Carefully, I went down and slid my fingers back into those same holes, displacing the water within and hey presto – out came my hand with the ring back on my finger! This was incredible and it lifted my spirits sky high. There was definitely something about this ring – twice lost and now twice found. Perhaps it was a talisman and I too would never be lost. The ring would be going home one day and me with it.

With the end of the monsoon season, life in the camp became more tolerable and the *maki* parties even more of a lift for me. I had become more and more adventurous in exploring the jungle and had developed a confidence in being able to sense the time of day so that I would always know when to set off back to camp. I had also learned how to indelibly mark my way so as to be sure of being able to retrace my steps and find my way back. What's more, I had Lucille with me, too! Strangely, on one of the *maki* parties, I had found the casing of a silver wristwatch lying in the undergrowth of the virgin jungle and thought it might just be the right shape and size to frame the Polyfoto of Lucille and me that I had kept secreted in my bed space. It fitted perfectly and so I made a strap for it out of the collar of an army shirt and made a fastening with a button. I could wear it like a wristwatch and it became a comfort to me on every *maki* party after that.

One day I came upon a sort of lush green flat area that looked almost like a lawn but in fact, it was a kind of moss on the jungle floor. It was perfect for a lie down. While I was lying there, I began to hear voices, very faintly. Listening intently, not moving a muscle, it seemed to me these were English voices. My thoughts raced. Perhaps they were an approaching British unit ... perhaps war's over! I listened even more intently and moved carefully in the direction the sound was coming from until I came upon a cave with an arched opening no more than 5 feet high where the sound appeared to be coming from. Stealthily, I crawled in, moving very slowly in order not to attract attention and, after my eyes adjusted to the darkness, I could see a golden Buddha, set in a huge cavernous space with a group of seven or eight men sitting in front of it while another stood and appeared to be lecturing them. I listened and couldn't believe what I was hearing. This man was giving a ball by ball commentary on a cricket test match between India and Australia as if it were actually taking place! It was like listening to the wireless. But it was not entertaining to me. This was a bunch of our officers passing the time of day, listening to an account of a cricket match while their men were being worked, starved or beaten to death on the railway. The experience did nothing to improve my regard for our officers in this war. The man relating the test match was, I believe, E.W. Swanton – well known before and after the war for his cricket commentaries.

Senior officers in the camp sometimes held talks in their hut after dark and they invited people they thought were knowledgeable about something to go along. I was invited one night. They wanted a talk on

146

magic but I chose to speak about the great Houdini. When I'd finished, they all asked questions and one of them asked me if I had ever performed in London. I told him I had and added that I lived only a couple of hours or so from the city.

'Do you know Sevenoaks?' he said.

'Yes, that's near where I live,' I replied.

'Do you know Dunton Green?' he said.

'That's where I was born!' I responded again whilst thinking this was all getting really odd, having a conversation like this in the middle of the jungle, starved and half-naked, cut off from the world.

He went on, 'Do you know Barretts Road?'

'That's *the road* I was born in,' I said, now somewhat incredulous.

Finally, he asked, 'Do you know Donnington Hall?' to which I proudly responded, 'That was built with funds that my father helped raise.'

'Well,' he now declared, 'the very first function they had there was my son's wedding.'

His son had married one of the pretty daughters of a neighbour of ours, who lived in Barretts Road. I was about six at the time and I had a particular recollection of the goings on for that wedding, which led me to recount how I had seen a Scots piper walking up and down our road ready to escort the bride and how impressive it was until some old drunk came out of one of the houses and poured beer into the bagpipe. The officer looked taken aback for a moment and then said assertively, 'I wasn't drunk!'

That officer was 'Pop' Hort. He was an RAMC (Royal Army Medical Corps) man and probably the oldest of us out there. His fellow officers and the men called him 'Pop' because he was old enough to be their granddad, being fifty-eight when war was declared. He was in 196 Field Ambulance as a captain quartermaster and had volunteered to come out with the regiment. None of us thought he would make it but, sure enough, he did. It was this 'Pop' Hort who had taught some of us the massage treatment for beriberi sufferers.

During my time at Chungkai I had generally sought to take up camp duties where I could observe and learn something about medical practice in those extreme conditions. Hospital work helped me keep Lucille in mind and that strengthened my determination to survive. I had certainly seen enough of those who had not survived when doing the job of sewing them up in rice sacks, ready for burial, during the monsoon period and when dealing with those who had been taken by cholera. Often I had seen, however, that it was simply a matter of willpower as to whether a person lived or died.

The thin line between living or dying and the need for the will to live was nowhere more evident than in what was called the 'moribund hut'.

This was where my friend Cliff Swann might have finished up, if he had stayed long enough. Working in there was often a salutary lesson and always, human nature – good and bad – was on display. We had one fellow in there who was all but dead. When our CO did his rounds, he asked me what his chances were and I said he was already just about gone. As things were in the camps, whenever someone died, any kit they had would instantly be 'claimed' by others – such was our general state of desperation. In this case as soon as I had said the man was as good as gone, the able bodied around us blurted out which of his meagre possessions they were claiming. At which point, the 'dying' man opened his eyes and said in a broad Norfolk accent, 'You'll have nothing of mine 'cos I'm not dead!' Suddenly he'd found a reason to live and he made it back on his feet eventually, if only to defy the rogues who wanted his stuff.

Another fellow in there was sadly more typical. He was visited by a captain from his regiment at the time the rice rations were being dished out. The captain had brought some peas to add to his ration and, having carefully put the peas into the rice, he offered the plate to the man. The man at first held the plate but then went into cardiac arrest, which finished him off. The moment of death, however, produced impulsive behaviour from those around him desperate to live. As he arrested, he dropped the plate of food but before it hit the ground someone lunged for it and caught it. Not an ounce was lost.

One of the afflictions that many of us got that was not life threatening, but very painful, was tinea of the feet. The condition makes the skin of the feet dry out and crack so that every step becomes excruciatingly painful. I got it but, being determined not to be confined with it, I finished up going about the place very, very slowly. Our medical staff found that it could be treated, strangely, by taking blood from your arm and re-injecting it in your backside. This produced a raging temperature, which had the effect of seemingly driving it away. In fact, the tinea just lay dormant and it would re-emerge as soon as your foot was scratched badly again. This turned out to be quite useful when we knew the Japs were looking for the able bodied to be sent to Japan. I would run my fingernails up and down the soles of my feet and bring back the tinea, painful though it was. Some men were more resourceful in making sure they were not taken to Japan. The artist Will Wilder, who was with me in Chungkai – in the next bed space, in fact – used his artistic skills to good effect. He successfully painted his foot to look as though he had an ulcerated toe which had turned the whole foot gangrenous making it impossible to walk. After the war it was evident how right we were to avoid being taken. Many of the ships were sunk in passage and those that made it delivered their cargoes only to be worked to death in the coal and copper mines.

Fortunately, when I had tinea, my Dutch friend Frans would sometimes come and carry me where I needed to go and often to *tenko*. He and I had, by this time, gone into business together. His laundry business had thrived so well that I suggested going in with him – the idea being that all the clothes he was washing could also do with some repair and I would do the sewing. So he would offer to do the washing for five cents and for another five cents they would get their things washed, dried, pressed and mended. The idea worked well and after we'd been 'in business' for a while like that we took it further. Frans would say to his customers that if they had a bit of material, we'd patch any worn out or shredded clothes and then wash and press them. After a while we had collected a lot of spare bits of material, which meant we were then able to offer, for a further five cents, that they could even have clothes patched up in the right coloured material – and there was a bonus in this for me. All the material we gathered eventually became enough to fill a small sack and this, of course, became a pillow for a good night's sleep!

It was during the time I was working the laundry business with Frans that I managed to lose my gold ring yet again, only this time there really was no hope.

I had been down at the river washing a pair of shorts and, in the process of bashing them on a rock, the ring must have flown off my finger. Worse still, it seemed to have flown out into the deep water of the river because there was no sign of it in the shallows around me at the riverbank. There was nothing I could do about it then as there were guards around, so I had to return to the huts without it. That night, I must have looked pretty glum because one of my Dutch friends asked me what was up and I explained. It was a no-hoper as far as I was concerned. The ring would be in deep water and so there was no point in going out looking for it. 'Well, I'll go,' he said. 'Tell me where you were on the riverbank and I'll go and dive for it tonight!' Well, apart from anything else, going down to the riverbank at night would get you shot if you were seen and it was a full moon that night too. I said, 'Look, you can't get shot for me like that. If you go I'll have to come too.'

I was in no mood for it and the whole thing seemed foolish to me from the moment we crept out. We couldn't go directly to the spot for fear of being seen so we reached the river by another route and then walked along the bank. I was getting more and more jumpy. My friend whispered to me, 'Where was it?' We were nowhere near the spot as far as I could tell and I just flung my arm out, truculently, pointing roughly ahead saying, 'Over there'. He stopped and looked out into the river for a moment and then quietly waded in and disappeared under the water, leaving me nervous on the riverbank. A few moments later he surfaced – holding up the ring in his fingers! This was impossible and at first I just thought he was messing about and it wasn't the ring at all but unbelievably, it was. Not only had it flown off my finger into deep water further up the river but it had also somehow carried with the river flow until it had landed here – perhaps the bandage that had covered it on my finger had acted as a float. In any event, how on earth he had chanced to find it, I'll never know.

Not long after that, the camp had a visit from Colonel Toosey. He had walked down from Tamarkan, which was not many kilometres away to the north-east of us. It created a big stir in the camp as most of us had already experienced something of the 'Toosey effect', which usually meant good news of some sort, or at the very least, a feeling that things would be alright. Well, he had brought with him official Imperial Japanese Army pre-formatted postcards that we could use to get word out to our families that we were still alive.

The cards were very basic with the pre-printed words to be crossed out as required and there was one space where we could enter some appropriate words of our own. When I'd finished mine it read:

IMPERIAL JAPANESE ARMY

I am interned in   *Thailand*

My health is excellent

~~I am ill in hospital~~

I am working for pay

~~I am not working~~

Please see that   *All of you*   is taken care.

My love to you *Fergus*

We were told we could only say 'Thailand' as our location, and not the actual camp. So the card was pretty useless but at least it was a communication of some sort. After Colonel Toosey had left that night with the cards, it occurred to me that my mother would probably question whether mine had come from me at all – if she ever received it.

About a month later, Colonel Toosey made another trip to Chungkai, coming this time by *sampan* with more post and more Red Cross cards. At long last there were letters for me – this being only the second time since landing in Singapore, twenty-one months earlier, that I had received anything. There was a batch of five letters and one was from Lucille.

It is indescribable what the words 'My Darling', in Lucille's hand-writing meant to me. Not knowing if I should ever get her letter, she was telling me how she had passed her nursing exams with distinction and was now a Blue Belt and how baby Stuart was nearly walking and how things were much the same at home – Pop, happy in his garden and Mum with her knitting. Lucille was writing the letter from my bed at home while visiting my parents. 'All's well,' she said, 'but only one person missing!' and then her words of reassurance, 'Don't forget, I seem to love you more than ever these days so don't worry.' The date on the envelope to Lucille's letter was 29 December 1942 – just about a year earlier, I guessed. How might she be feeling now?

The other letters in the batch were three from Mum and one from my eldest sister, Bing. All were written in September or October 1942. There was still no sign that they knew what had become of me. My mother wrote, 'Hoping to hear any day now that you're ok,' and Bing wrote wistfully, it seemed, 'You ought to be home soon.' Could the war be coming to an end; is that what they were trying to say? There was surely a message in my mother's last paragraph, 'Russia is through 4 places and winning,' and she had written in shorthand as part of her signature, 'V for victory!' I looked again at the dates on the letters. All were written after the Dieppe Raid that we had heard about while at Changi – that was late in August 1942. Thousands of Allied troops had landed and attacked German-held Dieppe, but we also heard that it had failed. Perhaps ... but these thoughts quickly dissolved as I realised how much time had passed since these letters were written and whatever had happened to raise these hopes then must surely have come to nothing by now.

Along with the censored post, Colonel Toosey had brought more official Imperial Japanese Army postcards for us and again we could have only one each. By this time, I had worked out how to get a proper message home using these cards and also how to authenticate myself as the sender. This was the moment when all my trials and tribulations with shorthand after leaving school and my eventual conquering of it, proved invaluable.

My idea was to convey my messages in shorthand concealed in the crossings out on the card and in my signature as well as in any flourishes in my handwriting when entering the few words we were allowed.

151

This is how my card looked when I'd finished:

IMPERIAL JAPANESE ARMY

I am interned in   *No1 POW camp Thailand*

My health is excellent

~~I am ill in hospital~~   (*strikethrough says in shorthand **Kanburi Camp***)

I am working for pay

~~I am not working~~   (*strikethrough says in shorthand **Don't worry***)

Please see that   ***your health and Luce***   is taken care.

My love to you ***Ferg***   (*flourishes say in shorthand*
                              still smiling)

I had crossed out 'I am ill in hospital' with a squiggly line that contained shorthand symbol's saying 'Kanburi Camp'. This was the main camp that the Red Cross delivered to and I thought they would easily be able to find it on a map. Then I crossed out 'I am not working' with another squiggly line that contained the shorthand symbols for 'Don't worry'. Then in the part where we could write our own words, I completed the sentence 'Please see that ...' with the words 'your health and Luce' so that it read, 'Please see that your health and Luce is taken care of', and then I came to the signature. As a child, I had been called 'Smiler' affectionately by my mother as I always had a smile on my face. When she was saying her goodbyes to me at embarkation, she had said, 'Whatever happens, keep smiling.' So, I signed the card with a flourish that contained the shorthand for 'still smiling'. If she ever got this card, she would know for sure that it was me writing it and that I must be well.

Then I turned the card over and filled in the address. There was one more message I wanted to send. It had occurred to me that my parents may have been informed by now that I had been injured so I wanted somehow to tell them not to worry. My idea was to embellish the word ENGLAND a little, with two flourishes on either side of the word – looking as if to highlight this destination for the card. The flourishes said in shorthand 'Wounds better'.

Before handing the card in, I made a point of showing it to Colonel Toosey to check whether it would pass censorship.

'Do you see anything in that card?' I asked him.

'No, why?' he said, and I told him that it contained code.

He examined it carefully and assured me that he couldn't see anything there at all. So into the bag it went along with my hope that it would find its way home. Heaven knows when it might be delivered, I thought, seeing that mail was taking more than a year to get to us.

Meanwhile, our situation there in Chungkai was changing rapidly. The railway had been finally completed and opened at the end of October and many of the men who had endured and survived '*Supido*' to build it, were being brought back down-country. Hospital treatment was needed for hundreds and hundreds of them. This meant that Chungkai was getting bigger and bigger, with more huts being added by the week. The camp was to grow eventually to hold around 8,000 POWs.

The increasing numbers in the camp meant that our Red Caps had a lot on their hands in keeping order. Colonel Owtram had been appalled when he had first arrived at Chungkai, finding almost complete lawlessness and an 'every man for himself' attitude, within which thieving was rife. Even the colonel himself had clothes, a blanket and other things stolen. So, with the agreement of the Japs, he had organised the policing of the men with our own Red Caps, who were then allowed to wear their full uniforms. Anyone found stealing or receiving stolen goods would be sent to the 'no-good house' and kept in cells there for days – usually on half-rations. The cells were made out of bamboo and just about big enough to stand or lie down in. Other than time in the 'no-good house', no other methods of punishment were allowed by the Japs, so the Red Caps made up a few of their own. They were given their own guard hut, which meant they had somewhere to take any supposed offender for 'questioning'. On many nights there would be the sound of beatings coming from that hut – as bad as anything the Japs could mete out. I developed a loathing of these Red Caps with their spick and span uniforms and healthy physiques – looking as good as if they were in England. To my mind, they must either have been running rackets of their own or they were very 'Jap happy', as we called it – friendly and cosy with the Japs so that they could get extra food.

One day, I went with another fellow out near the padi fields next to the camp in order to watch out for him while he met with locals to try and exchange some of his clothes for food. No sooner had he disappeared into a clump of trees to do business than two Red Caps emerged from nowhere. I had just enough time to say loudly, 'I think I'll be going back now,' when they collared me. The other fellow got away but the Red Caps had hold of me and were saying, 'Right, we know what you were up to. We want you in the guard hut tonight!' Well, knowing what went on in the guard hut, I faced them with it.

'Are you sure you'll manage beating me up – there's only two of you and you're only about 15 stone each, whereas look at me – skin and bone and probably half your weight!'

That night I did not go to the hut and they didn't come looking for me. Perhaps I'd shamed them – these Chungkai policemen.

As a means to improving morale in the camp and giving men some distraction, Lieutenant-Colonel Owtram and others set about the task of providing entertainment. He was himself a good singer and a willing impresario and he found that there was a huge resource of talent in the camp that could be engaged in producing shows. Using the engineering and enterprising skills of the Dutch, he had an amphitheatre built into the side of the hill that Frans Bakker and I had sat on that night to warn of rising floodwater. In addition, he had a rehearsal stage built separately in a jungle clearing and he and other producers set about putting on ambitious productions as well as ordinary everyday shows. They were attended daily by the guards as well as prisoners. I went along to the early ones but didn't take part as the people I knew were all dispersed.

Above all else, however, the camp was still preoccupied with sickness, disease and disablement. Medical supplies had been getting in thanks to the bravery and cunning of a mysterious figure. This was Boon Pong, a Thai trader based in Kanchanaburi who was revealed after the war to have been part of what was known as the 'V' Organisation, set up by a retired British businessman in Bangkok shortly after prisoners started to be sent 'up-country'. The organisation's purpose was at first to get intelligence on Japanese troop movements and on the progress of the railway but it also became a conduit for money and medical supplies, smuggled into the camps all the way up the railway. Items were concealed amongst food delivered by river in the *sampans* or by lorry along the jungle roadway that had followed the track as it extended further and further northwards. Medical staff could never have done what they did without the 'V' Organisation – especially those up at the jungle camps in Burma.

In the new year of 1944, our medical staff were joined by Lieutenant-Colonel 'Weary' Dunlop, who'd come down from those camps. Stories began to circulate about what he'd done for his men – preventing guards from taking those who were desperately sick out on working parties and how he'd taken bashings, humiliation and torturous treatment from the Japanese in defending them. A true account of the persecutions that he and his men had suffered appeared after the war in the diary he had managed to keep throughout. One entry alone reveals the plight of these men and how, for me, the Wampo incident had been nothing less than a merciful deliverance:

7 June 1943. Today notable for the beginning of severe, acute dermatitis of the feet. The feet become red raw with tinea, injury and secondary infection; they swell grossly with redness, weeping and loss of skin. The poor wretches stand either in mud or water or on rocks all day and the feet never get dry. Those suffering the ever present diarrhoea and dysentery, of course, are forever getting up in the mud and slush at night and that makes things worse. The plight of these men is pitiful. They take hours to walk four to five kilometres in from work and just about cry with the pain of walking and standing on raw, bleeding feet. The Nipponese, of course, just bash them for being late to work or too slow.

Now, as part of the team at Chungkai, 'Weary' Dunlop was dealing with the aftermath of it all.

Also, in the new year, more letters arrived. This time, three from Lucille, one from my mother and one from my elder sister again – all written in December and January the year earlier.

Eagerly I opened the ones from Lucille and put them in the date order that they had been written before reading any of them. The first was written on 3 December 1942 and opened with her saying how she was losing heart because 'almost every letter that I have ever written to you has been returned.' But then she went on with, 'My heart is just the same. Half of it is with another little boy somewhere. Perhaps he'll bring it back with him some day!' In the next from her, written on 21 December, shortly after my birthday on the 10th, she said how she thought of me on that day. I was twenty-four years old that year. Then, in the last from her, written in early January 1943, she was reminiscing on our first Christmas and new year together, two years earlier, when she had come and stayed with my family. I remembered it too as I read and thought how long ago and far away that now seemed.

My mother also seemed down at heart in her letter written at the end of December, saying forlornly, 'I wonder if you've received any of my dozens of letters. I'm writing every week.' She told how everyone was still trying to find out what had happened to me and that names were appearing daily in the newspapers of those who had been captured but mine was not amongst them.

There was also the chit-chat, of course, and news of who was doing what. Lucille had passed more examinations and was now a State Registered Nurse. Everyone was meeting up at home – baby Stuart being a grand little boy and my elder sister's boys, Graham and Clive, being boisterous. The feeling of being utterly alone and apart came over me.

I felt desperate for my attempts to get messages home to succeed. I had now sent three cards home – one from Changi before coming up

155

to the railway and now two more from here in Chungkai. But the time lapses made it all seem pointless. We were all trapped in this nowhere place with messages coming in from time to time and our almost meaningless cards going out. Neither our families at home nor we knew whether our messages were being received. It was as if we were the living dead.

Chapter 13

'WHERE ARE YOU GOING, ANCKORN?'

At some point in that early part of 1944, some of us were transferred up to Kanchanaburi camp – the camp we called Kanburi. This was the 'arrival' camp I had come to after being sent up from Changi. It was only 7 or so kilometres back down the railway from Chung Kai and close to Tamarkan, where Colonel Toosey had been in command. I recalled the display of humanity in the welcoming that Colonel Toosey had organised for us on that occasion. Nothing like that was expected this time and anyway, he had been moved to another camp before Christmas.

I was very apprehensive of what we might find in Kanburi because of the horrors that had gone on there some months earlier when I'd passed through with a working party on our way to the soap factory. We had been stood outside the camp fence that surrounded the parade ground, waiting for transport. The parade ground was filled with lines of men and beatings were going on. Well, we had seen plenty of beatings on parade grounds by now but nothing on the scale of this. It seemed the whole camp was being beaten up. When the guards got tired of doing the beating, they were telling men to turn and face each other and beat each other up. Where only half-hearted punches were thrown, the guards would shout and demonstrate, 'Not like that. Like this,' and bam! ... they would smack a man in the face as hard as they could. In the end they had everyone facing one another, knocking the hell out of each other. Black eyes, broken noses, lost teeth. All in silence. The men just took it. No complaints. Not a whimper.

We had learned later on the 'bore hole' that two men had been found with a radio, Officers Hawley and Armitage. In true Jap style, the whole camp took a punishment beating. Hawley and Armitage were beaten to death.

157

The 'bore hole' was our term for the latrines, or 'lats', in normal army parlance. They were the only place in a camp where you could be sure there were no Japs around. It was also the place where dysentery sufferers would have to sit often and for some time. The bore hole became the source of camp rumours and the means of passing on anything that had been heard about the progress of the war. It had been on the bore hole back in Changi that we had heard about the Dieppe Raid, raising our hopes that the war was turning our way and we'd all be home by that Christmas. Here in these camps at the railway, I had never heard anything more about the progress of the war. For all we knew the Japs were everywhere victorious. Their railway was built and they were moving their war supplies north with apparent ease. But a story I did hear on the bore hole about goings-on at Kanburi during this time, when men were coming back down from the camps, showed that our spirits were not subdued.

The rumour was that one of our lads had 'qualified' during his working party and later, during the night, he found the guard who'd done it and set about him with a shovel and killed him. He had dragged the body over to one of our officers' huts and got hold of someone there to tell him he'd killed one of the guards. The officer apparently listened to the story and realised that nobody at that point knew about it. He immediately said that they should drag the body to the latrine trenches and tip him in. As soon as the body submerged, it would be gone forever. This done, no one later ever said a word. The disappearance of the guard was probably put down to the fact that by this stage, Korean guards were known to simply clear off and there had been stories of Japs going missing when locals had set upon them for taking their girls.

So it was with some trepidation that we took up our places in the huts of Kanburi camp. Fortunately, it was to be only a few weeks before we were moved on again, but even in that short time, more Jap brutality was on display.

There were a couple of monkeys around the camp at Kanburi. One was the child of the other. I called them Nipper and Satan. They used to play around the camp and especially in a water well we had there. Monkeys, of course, are very good at picking the lice out of each other's coat and so I got Nipper and Satan to delouse my bed space every day. They were quite a feature of the camp until one day, Nipper took a banana from the guard room. The Japs had taken against Nipper because they thought his name was a mockery of them – the Nipponese, as they called themselves, and 'Nips', as we called them. So they took the opportunity to do to him what they would do to us for punishment. They tied him up outside the guardroom in the full glare of the sun and every time they changed guard they beat him with a stick or punched

Nipper and Satan. (*Sketch by fellow POW, Will Wilder*)

him. He died in the end. They beat him to death. It seemed to be a special feature of Kanburi – gratuitous beating to death.

As it happened, a few days later, the Japs saw me with the other monkey in my arms and shouted to me. I was near the perimeter fence of the camp, on the other side of which was a road and some Thai boys walking along. Having seen what happened to Nipper, I was not going to let Satan go the same way so I quickly threw him over the fence. The boys caught him and ran off with him. It must have been almost a month later, when I was on another working party at the soap factory, that I saw him again – or rather he saw me. We had finished for the day and were waiting outside for a lorry to pick us up. While waiting, I noticed some boys about 100 yards away playing with a monkey. This monkey suddenly detached itself and came tearing over to me and jumped on my shoulder, tears in his eyes and squealing away. It was Satan! After a minute the lorry came and Satan instinctively darted off again, back to the boys.

Having been at Kanburi less than a couple of months we were moved on again to work in the big marshalling yards at the very start of the railway in Nong Pladuk. This was where supplies brought up through Malaya and Bangkok were sorted and sent onwards to Burma via the now completed railway. The yards were enormous and were collectively known as 'Hashimotos'.

Nong Pladuk had two camps. One was occupied mainly by the Dutch. The other one, which we were assigned to, was right up against the railway marshalling yards. It was a well ordered camp and probably the most humane on the railway. There had been engineers at the camp and they had rigged up running water, pumped up from a well and delivered round the camp along bamboo pipes.

Amongst the Japanese authorities in the camp was Sergeant-Major Saito. He had been at Tamarkan with Colonel Toosey and when he had been moved to Nong Pladuk, he had put in a request for Toosey to be moved there too. This was done and early in 1944, before we had arrived, Toosey had taken over as the Allied CO.

It hadn't been long, apparently, before 'the Toosey effect' was felt in various ways and in one particular way that would mean everything to me. Back at Tamarkan, he had said to the Japs that instead of mail being held up for so long while they got round to censoring it, he would organise censoring to be done by our own people too. Toosey had been able to create a degree of trust between him and the Japs during his time at Tamarkan and that was why mail had finally come to us at Chungkai and the reason we got the opportunity to send postcards home. By the time I arrived in Nong Pladuk, sometime in March 1944, Toosey had once again got whatever mail there was quickly processed and there were two more letters waiting for me – one from Lucille and the other from my mother.

These letters predated the ones I'd received in Chungkai, both being written in the summer of 1942 – nearly two years previously. I didn't know, of course, that the only official news that my family had received about me up until that time was a formatted letter from the Royal Artillery Record Office, which said:

> According to our records ... your son ... was serving in Malaya when the garrison of Singapore capitulated ... Every endeavour is being made ... to obtain information concerning him ... and it is hoped that he is safe, although he may be a Prisoner of War. Immediately any information is obtained it will be sent to you, but in the meantime it is regretted that it will be necessary to post him as 'missing'.

This might have been the first time they were made aware of our being in the Far East. All expectations were that we had gone to Egypt and, even if they had received my letter from Bombay, it still said nothing about where we were finally going.

In her letter, Lucille was telling me that they had only just been told that it was possible to get letters to us and that my mother had immediately sent off two in quick succession and my elder sister had written as well. Lucille told of how lonely she was feeling and of how worried Mum was, not knowing if I was alive or not. They were desperate to hear something from me. How must they be feeling by now, almost two years later, I thought. The chit-chat in the letters once again carried me back into the life I was missing – Mum had been playing tennis, which she was so good at, and Pop had found his sense of humour again ... baby Stuart was 'the sweetest little boy and always laughing' and Gordon, my scallywagging brother, was 'fitter than ever'.

But it was a letter I received a month later in April 1944 from my mother that refreshed my hope and belief that there would be an end to all this. She had written excitedly in November 1942 with things to tell me that she wanted to get past the censors:

> Do you remember old Mr Argent, who used to have a certain job when you were a good little choir boy? Well of course you remember that particular job was taken from him and all others doing the same kind of work until a certain thing happened? Well, he's doing his old job again today and all the others too.

And she continued:

> I suppose you don't get the new songs over there? But there's a very appropriate one you can sing for all you're worth about a rabbit, remember?

She was telling me that something big had happened and her mention of Mr Argent was to tell me that church bells were ringing again, having been silent since the day war broke out in September 1939. I read her words over and over as possibilities sprang into my mind. Too much time had elapsed since then, so it can't have been the end of the war at home – but perhaps a turning point in which the words of the song *Run Rabbit Run* were appropriate!

But even more intriguingly, she went on in her next paragraph about what my old school friend, Robin, was doing now, having been studying architecture since the September of 1941.

> He's very busy at the office doing post war planning and everywhere there's great activity.

And also about Alan, my twin sister Beryl's husband who was an officer in the army.

> Beb was worried for a few days last week as Alan had to go somewhere and do something important in connection with his work and we were all very relieved when he rang up to say he's been and come back. Where or when we don't know.

I tried re-reading the previous letters I had received – some written in the December of 1942 and others in January 1943. Still none the wiser it nevertheless gave me the feeling that things were, at least at that time, on the move and perhaps on the turn.

Now, of course, it is possible to see what it was that so excited my mother. It was on Sunday, 15 November 1942 that the church bells of St Paul's and every cathedral across the country rang out to mark the victory that General Montgomery had achieved at El Alamein. This had been the first and, as things turned out, the only major battle of the war that Britain had won without direct aid from America on the battlefield. 'Monty', as he was called, had defeated Rommel's *Panzerarmee* with his Eighth Army and turned the tide in the fight for control of the North African peninsula. It really was a moment to rejoice in Britain; so much so that the BBC Overseas Service made a broadcast of the sound of the bells ringing with the commentator saying provocatively, 'Do you hear them in occupied Europe? Do you hear them in Germany?'

They must have also been playing the Flannagan and Alan version of *Run Rabbit Run* on the radio after that, hence my mother's message to me. My mother had been very clever in choosing her words to convey the news of a turning point, because it was indeed at that time, on 10 November, in fact, that Winston Churchill had spoken those now immortal words:

This is not the end. It is not even the beginning of the end. But it is, perhaps, the end of the beginning.

I put the letters carefully away, feeling once again the intense frustration of not being able to communicate back in any proper manner. The Red Cross Imperial Japanese Army postcards weren't available at Nong Pladuk and so we were once again completely silenced. It was hard to put those letters away and get on with the day to day business of staying alive. But now that we were in a 'Toosey' camp, at least we all felt a lot safer and there was an increasing sense of optimism around the place. This was the essence of the 'Toosey effect'.

Once Lieutenant-Colonel Toosey had become the Allied commander of the camp, he had demanded changes that would improve living conditions. As a result, the camp was extended and soon it had a football ground and a couple of basketball pitches. As the camp already had a small theatre, Colonel Toosey gave his encouragement to the production of concert party shows.

At that time, I had still not come across any of my old divisional concert party friends. The last time I had seen any of them was at Changi. It was only after the war that I found out what became of them.

They had, in fact, all been sent up-country after me as part of the ill-fated 'F' Force that went to the railhead at Hellfire Pass and beyond. I had heard stories that were circulating about 'F' Force when I was at Kanburi because many of the survivors were brought there after the railway was finished. The full story, however, was something I only learned about bit by bit over the years since the war. My friends had been brought up-country in April 1943, about four weeks after me. 'F' Force was the largest group to leave Changi, consisting of 7,000 men. This massive exodus coincided with the new imperative, handed down by the Japanese high command, that the railway should be completed by the end of the monsoon period, months ahead of the previous schedule. It was, of course, the beginning of '*Supido*' and the Japanese Command wanted every available POW up there on the railway, including, if necessary, those who were unfit. Of course, the Japs continued to pretend that the reason for the move up-country was the food shortages in Singapore and this time they also proposed that medical care could be better provided for those who were unfit. As an additional ruse, they insisted it was not a working party and that men could take musical instruments if they wished as well as all their personal effects and they could leave blankets, clothing and mosquito nets behind as these would be provided.

I'm sure nobody believed these pretences any more than we did. Nevertheless, they gathered all their kit and left Changi in that April of 1943. The first sign of what the Japs were really up to would have come, as it did for us, when they were being packed liked sardines into the steel rice trucks and sent on the long journey up to Ban Pong, with few stops and very little food. But for them, the situation would have worsened on arrival at Ban Pong because their journey was to continue on foot up to Kanburi, which was about another 50 kilometres, where they were ordered to leave all their kit behind 'to be sent up later'. The full nightmare of the journey would have begun to unfold, however, after they reached Kanburi, where they were told that they would be continuing onwards in what turned out to be a forced march for 300 kilometres, lasting eighteen days – or rather nights, as they would march in the night along a rough jungle track and get what rest they could by day. Men became ill and exhausted but, at each of the fifteen staging camps along the way, there were no arrangements for treating them or for leaving the seriously unfit to recover. Every man had to continue, brutally driven mile after mile, camp to camp through the monsoon rains, regardless of increasing dysentery, malaria and ulcerated feet. Then at one of the staging camps, cholera broke out, which the men then carried onwards to infect each of the five camps they were finally destined for. On arrival at their designated camps, the nightmare got even worse. Their huts were without roofs for weeks so that, on top of everything else, men began dying of pneumonia. Regardless of their plight, they were all put to work on the railway – fit or unfit, driven by the engineers who by that time were fully aware of the deadline they now faced for completing the railway. With poor access to the camps due to the monsoon rains, food and medicines were scarce and in addition, the Japs imposed their half-ration policy on anyone who was sick, believing as they did that, if men were given less food, they would be forced to get out of their sickbeds.

The situation rapidly became desperate in every possible way for the men of 'F' Force, as was described in a report made by Colonel F.J. Dillon MC – Royal Indian Army Service Corps:

As the health of the men grew worse, the demands of the engineers were more and more difficult to meet and their treatment of our weak men whilst at work became more and more brutal. The work was often beyond what reasonably could be expected of fit men, and it was certainly beyond the strength of our weak men. This especially relates to the carriage of heavy logs. It was noticed that with Thai or Burmese labour, two or three times the number of men were used. It became common for our men to be literally driven with wire whips and bamboo sticks throughout the whole day. Hitting with the fist and kicking also frequently occurred through-out the day. The beating was not for disciplinary purposes, but was intended to drive unfit men to efforts beyond their strength. Hours of work were excessive, fourteen hours a day was a common occur-rence and work went on day after day without a break for months. Many men never saw their camp in daylight for weeks on end, and never had a chance to wash themselves or their clothes. In some camps where the numbers of fit men fell below the engineers' demands, the engineers came into the camps themselves and forced the prisoners out of the hospital beds to work.

The colonel's report went on to say that during this time:

Several men, sometimes alone, sometimes in groups, disappeared into the jungle. Some probably had the idea of escaping, some undoubtedly left so as to die in freedom rather than in captivity from disease, illness and ill-treatment. The men on the whole were in despair. The choice in front of them seemed to be death from disease or death from never-ending toil and brutal treatment at the hands of the engineers. Their officers were unable to protect them in spite of all their efforts. One party of officers, seeing their men dying and ill-treated around them, and in despair of getting any redress from the Imperial Japanese Army, attempted to escape so as to let the world know what was happening to the prisoners and to obtain help from the International Red Cross. This party failed as was inevitable. Five perished from privation in the jungle and the remaining four were recaptured.

Of the 7,000 that left Changi in April 1943, it was reported that by December, 3,000 had died already and 3,000 more were in hospital either in Burma or back down the railway in Chungkai or Kanburi, and many of these were expected to die in the months that followed.

All of my concert party friends died except for Denis East, our exceptionally talented Philharmonic Orchestra-playing violinist. But he had suffered a tropical ulcer in his wrist and like me, nearly had his hand amputated. Fortunately, he had recovered by the time we met up again at Nong Pladuk.

I have often thought since that if it were not for the row I had with the regimental sergeant-major in Changi, which resulted in my being sent up-country at the earliest opportunity out of spite, I would have gone later with the rest of my concert party friends, as part of 'F' Force and probably gone to a miserable death. It is so awful to reflect on the horror that must have befallen them and so many others in 'F' Force. Talented men of artistic temperament, whose lives before the war could not have prepared them in any way for their ordeals.

So, at Nong Pladuk, with only one of the original cast of our divisional concert party still around, and with strong encouragement from Colonel Toosey, I began working in earnest with lots of new people to create shows. As always, there was plenty of talent in the camp and it had already made its mark by the time I arrived. We were able to build up a group that could put on a new show every week, often making up the story and putting together the acts 'on the hoof' as we worked and usually having no time at all to rehearse together.

An officer, Lieutenant Allum, produced our shows as well as Sergeant Ray Fairclough – the man I'd worked the 'fly farm' business with at Changi. We also had Lance-Bombardier Norman Pritchard, who had been a calligrapher before the war, making the concert programmes. He marked all his programmes ostentatiously 'Pritchard Publicity'. Later he worked with a Dutchman, Van Holthe, to produce the stage sets as well.

We got together some musical instruments too – all made out of this and that. The double bass was made out of a couple of tea chests and the strings came from the innards of a cow. Drums used real animal skins, and my friend Denis East made up a violin from heaven knows what. We had a musical director, 'Ace' Connolly, who led his 'Kings of Swing' orchestra, as he called it, and we had a prolific songwriter called Bob Gale.

There were female impersonators, too. Basil Ferron, who was Anglo-Indian, made himself thoroughly beautiful and we had Bobby Spong, who was so good the Japs checked his 'equipment' more than once. Bobby Spong was eventually taken away to Japan and we learned after the war that he had been put on one of the 'hell ships' – so called because men were battened down below decks with no hope of getting out while the ship would run the gauntlet of US submarines as it crossed the South China Sea on their way up to Japan.

The female impersonators had wonderful dresses made for them by a sergeant, Phil Hutt, using old mosquito nets and parachute material that officers came up with and they would dye the materials using pigments from the local flora and fauna. Their offstage personas were almost as funny as their stage characters – scrapping with each other over who had the better dresses. 'I wouldn't be seen dead in the scruffy stuff she wears,' was typical of Bobby.

And we had comedians. Les Cox did a sort of Ted Ray act with regular appearances entitled 'Fiddling & Fooling', in which he would always be about to play his violin when he'd think of something more he wanted to say or some story he wanted to tell. Then there were the 'Two Black Crows' – they blacked up and told daft anecdotes to each other. This was one of their classics, picking up on a skin infection that was common in the camps and that we all knew about – erysipelas:

'How are you today?'
'I'm not very well, actually, but I don't think I'll go to the doctor.'
'Oh, why ever not?'
'Well, a friend of mine said he went to the doctor with *ear*rysipelas and he had his ear cut off.'
'Oh dear. Now you mention it, I know a bloke who went to the doctor with *pnee*monia and he had is leg cut off.'
'Well, I'm definitely not going then. I've got prickly heat!'

Then, there was 'Hank & Frank', stand-up comedians – like Morecambe and Wise – and our very own Crazy Gang, who were imitating the Marx Brothers. They called themselves 'The Woodwork Family', with the catchphrase 'Would work but won't!'

Generally, at concert parties we were not allowed to laugh because the Japs thought we were laughing at them. So these comedians would be busting a gut to make us laugh while the audience were doing their damndest not to. Their humour had even more impact, of course, because of the comedy of the situation. Our tendency had always been to find the funny side of things in any situation and here in captivity it was essential to our very survival. It seemed to me in fact that throughout it all, I had rarely seen anyone constantly downhearted. Perhaps we all knew instinctively that to lose heart would be the end of us. One real character amongst us that kept our spirits up was 'Pinky' Kerswell – called 'Pinky' because he was as plump as a pig before captivity. He was a West Country lad and something of an imitator. He did voices and sound effects to a tee. Sometimes I was with him on working parties and we'd be going along carrying a load on a stretcher when suddenly there'd be the sound of air emitting from a burst tyre and the sound of a deflated wheel rubbing along a road. 'Hold on a mo. Better pull in. Got a flat tyre here,' he'd say. Another time we'd suddenly hear the sound of Red Indians and galloping horses followed by the sound of a flying tomahawk embedding itself in a tree and he'd say, 'Circle the wagons!' There were times when we would almost drop our load because he had us so much in stitches. At night, in the hut, he used to make up cops and robbers stories and tell them with all the voices and sound effects – New York cop accents, gangsters and their molls, screeching tyres, phones ringing, gunfights and bullets flying, the lot. It was just like listening to a radio play and there in the darkness, he had our imaginations, at least, running free. Unbelievably, there were times, despite the horror, pain, isolation and degradation of our lives, when we were scarcely able to stand for laughing.

Our concert party was called 'The Harboured Lights', which came from the fact that Lieutenant Allum had started his first concert party in Singapore at a camp near Keppel Harbour and the name was, of course, a pun. In his new shows at Nong Pladuk, I was the conjuror using my stage name Wizardus as always. Apart from the usual tricks of misdirection that I did, there was one in particular that went down well. There were cats roaming about the camp that had survived long enough to produce kittens. Having come across the kittens by chance, I hid them from my fellows while I worked out a trick with them. It would be a version of the 'rabbits out of the hat' trick. The culmination would be these tiny kittens emerging from a supposedly empty hat. To do it, I needed to get the kittens to be still and quiet until the moment of being pulled from the hat. So, for an hour or so before the show, I would play with the kittens until they were so exhausted they fell asleep all together in a little ball. Perfect. The trick worked well and I did it a number of times before the kittens were found by somebody and eaten.

Apart from my regular conjuring acts within each production, there were other contributions I could make. We created short plays and dramas as well as variety shows and, because the ideas and scripts were put together while on working parties, with no time to rehearse before the shows went on, there would sometimes be lapses in the flow with cast members forgetting their parts. When this happened, I would come on and interrupt the proceedings with a 'Have you seen this trick ... never before performed ... etc.,' and hold the audience's attention until everyone got sorted out and the play could continue. I used to do this even when I was part of the cast! One of our best musical comedy shows, billed as *Stardust* and in which I did my usual conjuring, we later reprised as *Sawdust*, in which I played a nightclub manager as well, and I would sometimes have to make an impromptu switch of character to keep the show moving along.

Away from the distractions of concert parties, football games and basketball, the nastiness of our existence remained. The working parties continued every day and in Nong Pladuk this would be in the rail sidings shifting supplies from place to place or loading trains to go up to Burma. There were also working parties sent into Hashimoto's workshops.

These engineering workshops were notorious for rough treatment of the working parties. The Japs insisted that an officer went with every working party, which meant they would bash the officer as well as the men if the men weren't working hard enough. It also meant of course, that our officers were very reluctant to go. There was one heroic officer, however, who put himself up for it virtually every day – Lieutenant Harold Payne. He got terrible bashings because each time that men were getting bashed he would go and stand between them and tell the Jap to hit him instead. Which they did. With pleasure. They used to bark at him, *'Bakiru'*, which sounded like the English swear word, and Harold used to shout back, 'and b***** you too!' The word in Japanese wasn't, of course, complimentary. *'Baka'* meant 'fool' and *'bakiro'* meant 'unwitting fool'. In our book, Harold Payne should have been decorated after the war for what he'd done for the men, but I don't believe he was recognised for it in any way.

As 1944 progressed, there was a growing threat of Allied bombers targeting the railway and, in particular, the workshops and sidings of Nong Pladuk. Our camp was positioned right next to it all, with our huts almost adjacent to workshops and Jap encampments. When aircraft had first made an appearance, the reaction in the huts was a defiant cry of 'Come on lads, give it to 'em!' My reaction was a hardly controllable urge to creep into a hole, fearful of another bombing. Singapore had created in me a dread of the sound of anything overhead.

Here in Nong Pladuk, there was no protection for any of us. Word was that Colonel Toosey had made it his priority to persuade the camp authorities that slit trenches should be dug. Clearly, the Japs did not accept that there was a threat to their supreme existence and so nothing was done. The result was that we all came to dread the possibility of bombers arriving and, by the middle of the year, we were on tenterhooks having increasingly seen reconnaissance aircraft coming over. The Japs used to look up at them and say, 'He no bang bang ... he come looksee go back tell plane.' I looked up at them too as they cut their engines and circled over us in almost leisurely style and I thought how the crew would soon be back at base, with probably a nice dinner waiting for them and bacon and eggs for breakfast before another day's work. Had they any idea what they were looking down upon and how our existence contrasted with theirs? We began to watch the phases of the moon, day by day, knowing that an air raid was most likely when the moon was full.

That consciousness of the sky used to haunt me all my waking hours during that year. One afternoon, during a full moon phase, I was making my purposeful way across camp, as was my habit, when suddenly a great feeling of foreboding came over me. Something nasty was about to happen. Just then I was passing a puddle on the ground and there in the still water was a reflection of what appeared to be a very bright crescent moon. This was odd in itself because it was so bright but also because the moon should have been full anyway. The sky began to darken and it was as if there was going to be one hell of a storm. Yet, there were no clouds in the sky at all. As the darkness increased it also became cooler. Then everything went quiet too – the raucous jungle noise desisted. There was dead silence. It was an almost total eclipse of the sun and the crescent was not of the moon but of the sun. After just a few minutes, lightness returned as well as the jungle sounds and the familiar heat. Nobody commented on the event – perhaps that showed how dulled our senses had become or how used we had become to just accepting anything extraordinary, or perhaps it was just that a momentary darkness didn't seem that strange in the middle of the monsoon season. But for me, witnessing the eerie event in full, it left a sense of unease, which added to my apprehension about bombing.

There was another 'celestial' aspect of camp life that was a great source of amusement rather than dread. Sundials. Being almost civilised in this camp and having activities going on such as the games of football and concert parties, we needed to keep some sort of track of the time of day. We did it with sundials made out of a piece of bamboo stuck in the ground and a circle drawn around it with marks so that the shadow would tell the time of day. The Japs had seen these and thought they were a good idea so they had us make more of them to put all around the camp in order that wherever they were, they could see what the time was. They were so very pleased with them, in fact, that they had us put little roofs over them to keep the monsoon rain off! Someone even saw a sentry at night coming along with his lantern to see what time of night it was. They had no comprehension whatsoever of how they worked and we were not going to explain it to them either. Their enthusiasm was boundless – even wanting one put up on the inside wall of their guardroom. We played along with it all, making as if this was all perfectly fine – concerned as we were for Jap happiness!

In early August that year, our lives were brightened by the arrival of another batch of mail and for me it was tremendous – one from Lucille and three from my mother. I looked at the postmarked dates of sending – March, April, May and July of 1943, and I opened them in date order. The first from Lucille.

TODODAY IS A DAY AND DATE WHICH I SHALL REMEMBER
ALL MY LIFE ...

were her opening words in a letter written completely in block capitals,
as if she wanted to shout the words out.

THIS MORNING POP PHONED THE HOSPITAL TO TELL ME
WHERE YOU WERE, THE FIRST NEWS OF YOU FOR THIRTEEN
LONG WEARY MONTHS!! THREE HUNDRED AND NINETY
FOUR DAYS!!

I looked again at the date – 10 March 1943. She couldn't be referring to
my cards sent from Changi or Chungkai. Perhaps the War Office had
told them something. Whatever it was they'd been told, it had created a
real stir.

She continued:

I WONDER IF YOU CAN IMAGINE EVERYONE'S DELIGHT AT
THE GOOD NEWS OF YOU? ... IF ONLY YOU COULD SEE
MOTHER NOW, SHE'S TRIPPING ROUND THE HOUSE SING-
ING AND WHISTLING JUST LIKE SHE USED TO DO ... POP
LOOKS TEN YEARS YOUNGER.

Then in her closing words it was evident they had also been told about
my injuries.

LOOK AFTER YOURSELF AND BECOME WELL AGAIN.

If my cards from Chungkai ever did get home, she would at least get an
answer to that from my message *wounds better* written in shorthand.

Looking for more clues about whatever news they had received at
home in March 1943, I quickly read my mother's letters:

I hope darling that your wrist wound was not terribly serious. I
heard about it from Mrs Christian.

... she wrote in one letter, and in another:

Heard that letters from Malayan POW camps should be here in
June.

What had actually happened, I found out after the war, was that the
War Office had sent three communications – the first in January 1943,
being worrisome:

Dear madam,

I am directed to inform you, with regret, that an unconfirmed report
has been received that your son ... was wounded on 13 February
1942. No further information is available at present but endeavours
are being made etc....

170

Tel. No.—Liverpool Wavertree 4000

Any further communication on this
subject should be addressed to :—
The Under-Secretary of State,
The War Office,
Casualty Branch,
Blue Coat School,
Church Road, Wavertree,
Liverpool 15,
and the following number quoted :

Our Ref./ MB/OR/71318 (Casualties)

Your Ref./

THE WAR OFFICE,

CASUALTY BRANCH,

BLUE COAT SCHOOL,

CHURCH ROAD,

WAVERTREE,

LIVERPOOL 15.

30 January, 1943.

Madam,

I am directed to inform you, with regret,
that an unconfirmed report has been received
that your son No. 947556, Gunner F.G. Anckorn,
Royal Artillery, was wounded on the 13th
February, 1942. No further information is
available at present, but endeavours are being
made to obtain confirmation of the report and
to ascertain the nature of your son's wounds.
In the meantime Gunner Anckorn will remain
posted as missing.

I am to convey to you an expression of
sympathy in your anxiety and to assure you that
you will be notified without delay of any
further developments.

I am, Madam,
Your obedient Servant,

W. Gamble

Mrs. Anckorn,
3, Corner Mead,
Dunton Green,
Sevenoaks,
Kent.

A copy of the original typed letter from the War Office sent to Beatrice Anckorn in
January 1943.

My father had queried the War Office on the source of the unconfirmed report and received a reply in February:

> Sir, I am directed to inform you that the unconfirmed report ... was furnished by an officer of his unit who escaped from Singapore.

That officer was Lieutenant Mickey Burrows, who led the escape party that included Lance Bombardier Porter, the man who relieved me of my dog tags after the bombing.

Then, in early March 1943, they had received the good news from the Royal Artillery Record and Pay office:

> Sir, I have to inform you that a report has been received from the War Office to the effect that Anckorn, Fergus Gordon ... is a prisoner of war in Japanese hands interned in Malaya camp.

So yes, as Lucille put it, thirteen long weary months had passed by at home before they knew anything definite about me, yet they had still been writing – my mother saying in her letter that she had written a weekly letter ever since I left home, just hoping some would get to me, wherever I might be. Now she was saying how much she longed for some words from me, given that they had been told that we were first able to write home in January of that year and post was expected in July. How 'normal' that must have seemed and yet how far it was from reality. My mother went on in another letter saying that she had heard that letters from Malayan POWs should be in Britain by June and she went on to express further 'normal' ideas about my likely situation:

> I am so thankful to know you are actually a prisoner. God grant that you may be well and get plenty of food ... I do hope your wrist wound was not terribly serious and that you are still practicing conjuring ... don't let your fingers lose their cunning as it will be much help when you come back to get lots of engagements.

Only in her last letter written in July did my mother indicate that she may suspect something wasn't 'normal':

> Letters and cards are beginning to come in from Japanese camps. We are still keeping our thumbs up, though your plight is perhaps not so good.

My mother ended philosophically:

> There's always an end to the longest of lanes and we sometimes come upon it unawares.

But it was some of Lucille's words that lifted me the most, and which stayed in my mind:

172

THERE ARE MANY THINGS WHICH I MUST DO ONCE AGAIN. I STOPPED GETTING THINGS FOR OUR HOME BUT I'LL START AGAIN.

All my hopes were revived.

I think now that the Japs must have been aware the war was not going their way by this time. The Jap Command would certainly have known that, earlier in the year, their armies had started to suffer major defeats way up in the north, where British and Japanese forces fought tooth and nail and where one particular battle had taken place at Kohima.

In any event, around this time we were getting visits from Jap generals. The camp commandant came up to me one day and told me he wanted me to go down the road to a hut where he was to have some important guests that night. He was going to put on a bit of entertainment and he'd been aware of my doing magic tricks around the camp as well as my performances in one or two of the concert parties that he'd seen.

I went to Colonel Toosey to see if he knew anything about these visiting generals and to ask what he thought of the idea of entertaining the Japs privately like this. Colonel Toosey gave me an enigmatic reply: 'Anything you can do to keep things calm between us and them is a good thing, particularly at this time.'

Well, of course, I didn't catch the hidden meaning in this but Colonel Toosey must have been getting his own information as to the progress of the war and the defeats inflicted on the Japanese.

I duly attended the hut down the road and put my ability to perform in Japanese to good use – or so I thought. I was doing magic for them for nearly an hour using anything edible that they had in the room, and cigarettes, of course. It was still the case that anything a prisoner touched was immediately contaminated and they would tell me to take it away with me.

There was much Jap happiness throughout the show and at the end they all clapped. The commandant presented me with a rice ball – manna from heaven! Then one of the generals came up to speak to me and cheerfully carried on as if I would understand every word he said. I had to stop him, saying apologetically, in Japanese, that I didn't understand. Instantly his mood changed. He became transfixed with anger and I got a punch in the face and a body blow that knocked me to the floor. He then kicked me half way round the room, accompanied by yelling, before I was finally thrown out of the hut.

I guessed that it had all gone wrong because he had taken my attempt to say 'I don't understand' as arrogance in the extreme. Perhaps he thought that whilst I was perfectly willing to perform in Japanese and to thank the host for his rice ball gift in Japanese, I was not willing to speak to him.

I dragged myself back to the camp with an aching rib cage, bloodied face, eyes that could only half see and lips that felt like balloons. Colonel Toosey was there apparently waiting for me.

'My God, Anckorn!' he said. 'What's happened to you?'

'They didn't like the show, Sir!' I said with an air of professional detachment and we both laughed.

'Bloody critics – you just can't win!' he said.

From then on, Colonel Toosey made sure I carried a card that said that I could only speak some Japanese parrot fashion and that I could not understand Japanese when spoken to me.

Being in a bit of a mess after that incident, I managed to keep off the working parties for a few days and stay in camp. It was during this time that an incident occurred involving my friend, Lieutenant Primrose – a tall, no messing Argyll & Sutherland Highlander. He had gone to do some running around the parade ground to get fit for the next football match. As he passed the Jap guardhouse the first time he made the obligatory salute but when he came around again he made no salute. On the third lap, the Jap guard stopped him and began laying into him for not saluting. An enormous row developed and Toosey was called. He explained that in the British Army, in this kind of situation, a salute would only be given on the first occasion of meeting a senior rank and no insult was intended. But of course, the Imperial Japanese Army would have none of it and feelings began to run high on both sides. By this time in the war – late in 1944, the mood in the camp had become fragile – the Japs probably being aware of their increasing defeats and on our side, an increasing apprehension over what could happen when our bombers turned up. Later, Toosey called a camp meeting in which he referred to the 'incident'. His closing words were portentous:

> I know this incident made many of you want to take things into your own hands and retaliate. The time for that is not now. There will come a time and when that time comes, I will let you know.

We didn't have to wait long for further developments.

At the beginning of September, the two camps at Nong Pladuk were amalgamated into one, which meant that our camp was inundated with Dutch and we were bursting at the seams. For me it was good news because my old friend, Frans Bakker, had been in the other camp and we were reunited.

The Japs still had not allowed us to dig slit trenches, saying we were to stay in our huts in event of an air raid and 'die like soldiers'. The other camp at Nong Pladuk that the Dutch had occupied was further away from the railway workshops than ours was and it looked like the Japs were thinking that the more POWs they could bring close to the workshops, the less likely a bombing raid would be.

On the moonlit night of 6 September, only days after the move, the bombers came.

During that evening, before the raid, there was talk in our hut about how we all thought the war was going and how much longer it would go on. The mood was not good and someone spoke for us all when he spoke his mind, 'We'll never get out of this. The Japs will slaughter the lot of us as soon as our forces get anywhere near.'

A sergeant in our hut, a Brummie, tried to lift spirits with a rousing counter-thought. 'Look ... within six months I bet you I'll be buying you all a drink back home in the Horseshoe!' He quickly rekindled memories of good times they'd all had in the pubs at home and worries gave way to humour.

The bombers came in without warning that night, as we always thought they would. Whilst they successfully hit the workshops and railway yards they also devastated the camp. Huts were ablaze and bodies were everywhere. Amongst them – our Brummie sergeant lay dead, with the top of his head blown off.

The official record shows that the raid had killed 76 and injured 250, of whom 20 died later. On top of everything else we had endured, we were now facing death delivered by our own side!

In the mayhem of the raid, many men simply ran for it, into the nearby jungle. When it was all over the Japs prepared to set off in pursuit, fully armed, with the intention of shooting whomever they could find. Toosey stepped in and persuaded them that if they would leave it to him, all the men would be brought back. He spent the rest of the night scouring the likely boltholes with our own Military Police. By morning he was hoarse and all the men were back in time for *tenko*.

That following day, all our dead were laid out near the camp gate. A dreadful sight. It was too much for me to take and for once I made a decision. I would get myself out of the camp on a working party for the day and not then have to take part in their burial. But we were returned early and were met by Colonel Toosey. He quietly asked us to lend a hand with transporting our dead for burial – promising us an extra rice cake at the end of it. My loathing of the task ahead was no less and I thought, 'Well, it's come to this. An extra rice cake for burying our dead!'

The situation in the camp was dreadful and to make feelings worse, there was an almighty storm brewing too. The sky was a boiling mass of thick black and green monstrous clouds. The bodies had been laid out ready for collection and the commandant had allowed a large Union Jack that had come from somewhere to be placed in the middle of them so as to be visible to any more reconnaissance planes. The Japs must have thought it would send a message that would stop any future bombing.

We made a long procession in single file, carrying the dead on rice sack stretchers. The sky was darkening by every footfall. The boiling mass of green and black clouds suddenly erupted in streak after streak of lightening with terrifying cracks of thunder. Then the rain started. It might as well have been the apocalypse! As we went along an arm from the body I was carrying fell off the stretcher and we stopped so that I could pick it up out of the mud. It was warm. At first I thought the body must be alive, but no, it was simply that the corpse had been in the sun all day. Meanwhile, the Japs hurried us along, fearful themselves of the storm.

We arrived at a burial pit that had been dug, and took our corpses down into it. A Dutch Catholic priest was there to carry out the last ceremonies and he stood at the edge of the pit while we lay our dead to rest.

'Just a minute,' said the priest.

'Are these Roman Catholics? I'm only dealing with the Roman Catholics here.'

This touched very raw nerves.

'Look 'ere, Vicar,' came the response from the pit. 'You're bloody doing this lot or you're bloody well coming in with 'em.'

It was unbelievable that this priest was actually ready to turn his back on the non-Catholics. He had no idea how close he came to having a shovel round the back of his neck.

When I was returning to the huts my friend Frans came towards me carrying a mugful of something. He must have noticed how shaken I was and he handed the mug to me, directing me to drink it as if it was a life-saver. It was a mug of tea, full of sugar. I hadn't said I was troubled in any way, it was just another job. After all, I'd buried many dead over the last two years. But he must have noticed that I was shocked to the core. I didn't know that I was shocked. I was very glad to have the cup of tea though, I know that, and for the first time in captivity, I reflected, in those quiet moments, with the mug of tea in my hands.

It seemed to me that I had drifted along up until this time, in limbo. I hadn't known or wanted to know what day it was. I was taking everything like an animal would. Living moment by moment, no feelings – nothing meant anything. I had got myself to the point where I didn't think about anything – never worried or complained about anything and never questioned why all this was happening. I had been existing, that is all, day by day, in limited consciousness. But now, suddenly, this event roused all my senses. It was personal and it touched me deeply.

What had really got to me was the death of that sergeant. Such a decent fellow. There he had been, encouraging others to look forward to the day when he'd be buying them a pint in the local pub back home.

176

Then almost the next minute, he was lying dead with the top of his head blown off and pipes and bits of brain all over the place. Gripping the mug of tea tightly, I said to myself, 'I can't put up with much more of this!'

It was after that first bombing raid that the Japs had us digging manholes for their protection and allowed us to start digging slit trenches for ours. The Japs preferred manholes to slit trenches for themselves in order to avoid blast and it wasn't long before the camp became 'pot-holed' with these. Only after the manholes were dug were we allowed to start digging the slit trenches for ourselves.

We were all assigned to particular slit trenches and the ones that my hut were assigned to were right up next to the Jap camp. We couldn't have been nearer to a bomb target. Bombs would only have to miss by a yard and we'd be dead. There was much grumbling about how unfair it was – those at the top end of the camp could damn nearly watch a bombing at their ease, but us lot – we'd cop it! Anyway, I had at least worked out a routine for myself to get out of my bed space and into the trench with all my meagre possessions in thirty-five seconds flat, whenever the next night raid came.

We started to think of other ways of protecting ourselves from our own bombers. One of the things we did was to set about re-marking out the football and basketball pitches with lime. We made this seem routine but in fact, what we were doing was putting extra lime on some of the line markings and less on others so that when we'd finished, the pitches would spell out 'POW' when seen from the air.

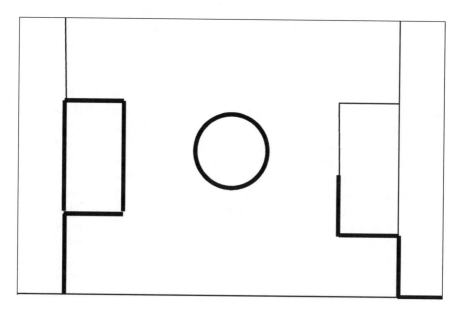

Once all these things were done and camp repairs had been completed, things settled down again as much as they might and our precarious existence continued. But aspects of it were becoming utterly surreal by this time.

We had an unfortunate Dutchman now in the camp who had lost his mind and because of this, he was left alone to wander about. The Japanese hated anyone like that and would simply keep away from them. So this Dutchman had the run of the camp and did no work. His constant companions as he wandered around were a duck, a chicken and a mynah bird. The mynah bird would talk to the Dutchman, the duck and the chicken. It would repeat Dutch words to the Dutchman, go 'quaack, quaaak, quaaak' to the duck and make a cockle-doodle do sounds to the chicken! The most amazing thing was the fact that here were two walking meals, a duck and a chicken, yet no one touched them because everybody knew they were his pets. They all had complete freedom of the camp and it became commonplace to see him with the animals walking around, the mynah bird walking along with them. It became even more comical when the Dutchman took to listening to the Japs on their telephone in the guardhouse and mimicking their voices – which the mynah bird then repeated too. This little troupe would be going around making all this noise, talking to each other, and mimicking the Jap voices, with no one batting an eyelid.

There were, in fact, two mynah birds that flew around the camp. They obviously enjoyed the goings on because they never seemed to leave us. They'd been around so long that the one that learned Dutch and befriended the Dutchman had also learned English and Thai words too. We called him 'Oscar' because of his startling performances! But they were capable of putting on a show together as well.

When the trumpet call sounded for *tenko*, both of the birds would immediately fly down to the parade ground and sit in a tree to watch the proceedings. On one occasion, we were drawn up to parade formation by Sergeant-Major McTavish and dressed off ready for his reporting to the CO, Colonel Toosey, in all proper fashion – except that we were in rags and tatters or half naked, but it didn't make the slightest difference. We all stood as the colonel made his way onto the parade ground. The colonel and McTavish, of course, had uniforms of sorts, albeit faded, patched and tattered by this time, and they also had their dress caps. Just as the sergeant-major brought us to attention, one of the mynah birds flew down and sat on his hat. McTavish took absolutely no notice and proceeded to about turn to face the colonel in order to make the salute and present us. The bird fluttered a bit and rebalanced itself on his head, at which point the other mynah bird flew down and sat on Colonel Toosey's head. The two men faced each other, each with a mynah bird perched on his head, the salute was taken and the formality 'All present and correct, Sir!' was delivered, together with the response 'Carry on, Sergeant-Major', and McTavish swung round again, the bird still on his head, to dismiss us. Not one of us made a sound during all this. It was surreal in the extreme but actually just another episode in the entertaining lives of these birds.

But it couldn't last.

The Japs were gradually getting tired of the birds. Oscar had too often mimicked the oversensitive Jap guards and too often made the sound of the ringing telephone in the Jap office, causing the guard to go rushing in to answer it! But that wasn't the worst of it.

We all feared more air raids after the first one in September and we now knew that there would be no warning. Almost as soon as anyone might hear the bombers, they would be upon us. It meant that whatever call went out, the response would have to be immediate and drastic to take whatever cover we could. We had a bugle call to raise the alarm if the bombers could be heard early enough and we all lived in dread of hearing it – especially the Japs. Well, Oscar had learned the bugle call when it was being practiced and inevitably, in the middle of the night, more than once, Oscar made that call. All the Japs would come running out of their huts in their pyjamas, carrying their swords and everything. Humiliated on each occasion, the Japs eventually had enough and they did him in.

The jumpiness that now prevailed in the camp was alleviated in October with the arrival of post – three separate times. The first batch brought me a letter and a card from Lucille written in January 1944, from which it looked like the cards I'd sent from Chungkai might have got through. 'How wonderful to have news of you, also to know that you are well,' she wrote. Then in the second batch there were two cards from my mother that said it all and gave me such a boost:

Delighted to receive your 3 cards Xmas. All well here. Lucille passing all exams. Pray your health keeps good. Also still smiling. All our love.

The words 'also still smiling' told me that she had read my shorthand message. I found out after the war what had happened at home when my cards from Chungkai arrived. On reading them, my mother had looked at the signatures carefully and immediately distrusted the whole thing, believing the cards to be fake because there was something about my signature that wasn't right. She had gone to bed that night disturbed and depressed. During the night, her mind's eye continued to roam over the cards until suddenly, she realised what was odd about them. She got up to re-read them and looked again at the signatures. Then she saw it . . . 'still smiling!' in shorthand. With that she went on to see the rest of the messages. I had come alive to her again after over two years of anxious waiting.

When I got my mother's card, I went to Colonel Toosey and told him all about my shorthand messaging and the fact that my card had got through. I suggested that I could send messages for him if he could get more cards, pointing out that my father had the opportunity every week to pass on messages when attending the War Office for briefings. But Toosey said he couldn't allow me to put my family in the firing line and added that he had contacts of his own that we could try sending messages to instead. He managed to get some cards from the guard room over the next few days and we set about writing one that contained details of Nong Pladuk ... how many British, how many Dutch and all the rest of it. The card went off, but I do not know to this day whether it got through or whether anyone was able to decipher it.

At the beginning of November there were more raids on the railway yards. The first one we all survived with no casualties and we wondered if our football pitch 'POW' sign had worked. Word came to the camp sometime later that our bombers had hit the bridges at Tamarkan too. But I was beginning to be aware of paranoia coming over me towards the very thought of bombing. There was just nothing you could do in an air raid but take it as it came and hope your number wasn't up. It can't have been many days later that the bombers returned. This time in broad daylight.

The camp was quiet with just about everyone in their huts. I was wandering along on my own, returning to mine. Suddenly, the planes were there – a sky full of them – coming in at very low level. I dashed to my trench, which fortunately I was just near to, and dived in. There was just me and one other fellow – everyone else from our hut had just stayed put. I looked up and saw the bombs descending straight for us but then they seemed to swerve to the left and every one of them fell on the railway yards, not on us. But it was still too close for me. I was gripped with paranoia. During a brief respite while the bombers circled to come in for a second run, I took my chance and got out of the trench to make a dash for a safer one further up the camp.

I had just emerged from the trench and started to run for it when Colonel Toosey appeared and grabbed me by the arm.

'Where are you going, Anckorn?' he said.

'I'm going somewhere away from here!' I replied.

'Where's your trench?' Toosey asked, and of course I had to say it was right there. 'Well,' he says, 'that's where you have to be.'

I, of course, couldn't hold my lip.

'No it isn't, Sir. I'm going up there because I'm going to be dead if I stay in that trench!'

He drew his face closer to mine. 'Anckorn, look. It's people like you that I rely on. The men all look up to you. What will they think if they see you clearing off?'

I shrank. I felt really small and, in that instance, remembered why I had not put myself forward for a commission at the outset. I had always feared how I might behave under fire and just look at this! I crept back into the trench, still full of fear and dread, and now with recriminations too. I was going to get killed, for sure, I thought. I just knew it. If he hadn't spotted me I'd have been off up the other end of the camp somewhere and to hell with it.

When the bombers came in again they were lower than before and I found myself literally staring the bomb aimer of one of the air-craft in the eye! His bombs were loose and flying just as before onto Hashimoto's yards but then some of them didn't. They came on to us. Bombs started exploding all around us and one of his bombs hit just near my trench. We were buried alive. It felt like the epicentre of an earthquake.

When it was all over and we had clawed our way out, we saw the real damage. Two of our huts were completely destroyed and the hospital was on fire. Official reports after the war stated that five bombs had strayed and fallen directly on the camp. This time nine were killed and thirteen injured. The workshops and rail yards, however, had been completely destroyed.

The rest of December had passed without incident and without any further mail from home. I passed my 26th birthday. On 1 January, however, mail arrived and this time, there was a letter written in June 1943 by my mother and one in December 1943 by Lucille. My mother's made me laugh to begin with:

> So glad to read that in some camps the food is excellent and plentiful.

And then she settled my fears:

> Lucille is coming here for 3 weeks' holidays. I think she wants me to teach her housekeeping, so that's significant isn't it dear.

Lucille had written me just a short note wishing me a happy birthday '... if ever you should get this.'

At the end of January there was more post and this time it was very intriguing even though, once again, they had all been written in 1943 – one of them in February 1943, nearly two years earlier. Reading the earliest ones first, my mother wrote on 28 February 1943:

> The twins, Beryl and Gus, may be able to spend their birthday together as the work Gus was sent to do is on the way to being

finished. But of course it would take some time for him to come home so I expect they may have to celebrate the occasion a bit late.

She had clearly been thinking the war would be over before December 1943. We know now that it was Montgomery's taking of Tripoli on 23 January 1943 that deprived Mussolini of his last stronghold in North Africa and the German surrender at Stalingrad on 31 January 1943 that had created this optimism. On 1st June 1943, my mother had written again:

Old Argent has now got his old Sunday job back again, regularly every week. You will remember why he had to give it up, but the reason is non-existent now ... By the time you get this it will be Christmas. Lots of things will happen before then and soon after.

This was giving me the strong impression that big events were shaping a potential Allied victory. The reference to 'old Argent' once again in her letters was to say that the church bells were allowed to ring again – only now it was every week – indicating a sort of normality at home. That was about all I could take from it as well as some relief that it probably meant the family was out of danger. History now tells us that what got the bells ringing again was the continued success of Montgomery in North Africa with his Eighth Army throughout March and April, ending with the surrender of 190,000 German and Italian troops in Tunis. It might also have been Churchill's speech to the US Congress, which was broadcast in Britain on 19 May:

We will wage war at your side against Japan while there is breath in our bodies and while blood flows in our veins.

It was probably also the news on 23 May 1943 that Germany had ended its U-boat operations in the Atlantic. This we now know had been aided by the release of Royal Navy ships and aircraft carriers from the Mediterranean after Montgomery's success in North Africa, as well as the development of more sensitive radar and Asdic sonar, which combined with the continuing successes of Alan Turing and his team at Bletchley Park deciphering the German Enigma codes, meant that the German U-boats had no hiding place.

I could only reflect on the fact that it was now 30 January 1945 and we were still in captivity. Never mind. In one of the letters from home my mother had included a photo of herself with my father and I had actually received it. Instantly, I felt they were here with me and as I looked for the moon that night, as I did every night in fear of bombing, I thought that it was the same moon that my parents would gaze upon. The same moon so many eyes gazed upon with so many different thoughts and ours, perhaps, the darkest, as an officer friend of mine in the camp, Louise Baume, wrote in his diary:

The moon
cold, hard, impersonal
punctual and relentless
in its wanderings round the earth
Subject of many a discussion
Companion in our troubles
Comforter in our secret sorrows
How often have we stood
in the early hours of morning
watching the setting moon
wondering that as it shone on us
so too it shone on those at home
Constant friend, now chilling foe.
The bomber's moon

Chapter 14

'PULL THE OTHER ONE!'

Despite our fears of bombing, there was an increasing sense of optimism at the start of the year 1945. We knew that the bridges at Tamarkan had been struck by our bombers on four separate raids by that time and the damage done to the marshalling yards at Nong Pladuk must have seriously limited the usefulness of the railway to the Japanese.

We knew nothing definite about what was going on but the Japs were getting increasingly nervous and some were actually trying to get friendly. Our morale was high whilst theirs appeared to be failing. Perhaps for that reason, the Jap command decided to break up the camp by moving all officers to Kanburi. We lost Colonel Toosey and no doubt the Japs thought this would leave us in disarray. But they didn't reckon on our regimental sergeant-major, McTavish. He became our CO and immediately pulled the camp together so that nothing much really changed.

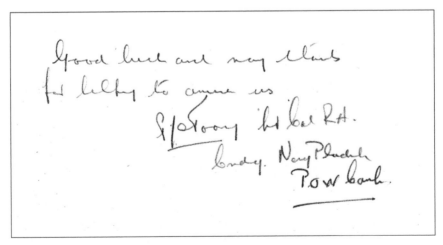

A personal note from Lieutenant-Colonel Toosey saying goodbye when he was removed from Nong Pladuk along with all officers in an attempt to break morale

But then the Japs decided to move more of us.

We were taken in groups on a long journey, which turned out eventually to be to another camp far to the east of Bangkok. In our optimism about how the war might be going, we imagined they were taking us away from what could be an Allied counter-attack down through Burma. We knew through the 'bore hole' that our Fourteenth Army was winning some battles and, for all we knew, they might not be far away.

The move was done in several stages, the first being to Bangkok on the railway, late at night. There, we were taken down to the river and crammed into waiting *sampans*. It must have been midnight by that time. Ours set off with hardly an inch of gunnel above the water, as did all the others. But our *sampan* was also old and leaking and the further we went, the lower it got in the water until finally the Japs shouted that we should be ready to jump into the other boats, as we steered towards them. This was a disaster in the making mid-river, because the other boats looked as precarious as ours. Nevertheless, as we came alongside other boats we jumped. Everyone in the boat I jumped into looked fast asleep. I landed without warning in someone's lap with a crash and he awoke, startled. It turned out to be my friend, Frans Bakker!

Somehow the boats remained afloat and our journey continued downriver, taking us past the Grand Palace on one side and later the enormous spire of a temple on the other. This was Wat Arun, also known as the 'Temple of Dawn'. The moon was three quarter full and in the tranquillity of the river at night, the whole scene was beautiful to see – the moonlight reflecting off the surface of the water and the backdrop of Wat Arun, and the Grand Palace spires looking mystical as we passed.

This scenic interlude ended as we came to our destination on the opposite bank of the river not long after we passed the temple. From here we were marched into the town and arrived shortly afterwards at what looked like the main railway station. For the next three days and nights we were quartered in warehouses that locals called '*go-downs*' beside the railway yards, sleeping on the floor at night and batting off mosquitoes as big as your fist – so big, in fact, they looked as if they were wearing black and white striped rugby jerseys!

Each night as we waited, our anxiety grew about bombing again. The moon was in its final phase and almost full. By the fourth day, we still had not been moved and the moon was full. During the day, the Japs got us out of the *go-downs* and put us into trucks on the railway – the old familiar metal rice trucks that had transported us from Singapore. We were not so packed this time but the trucks were then shunted into the middle of the vast conjunction of railway lines that made up this main station. We just knew that this huge railway station was going to get it that night and there we were, right in the middle of it!

Evening came and then nightfall. Still we hadn't moved. I could feel my dread of bombing mounting. Suddenly there was movement. A steam engine was moving towards us. It connected itself to our trucks and after an excruciating further wait, we began moving with a determined chug from the engine and clouds of smoke billowing into the moonlit sky. It seemed an age before the train was well clear of the station and before my fears subsided. We found out eventually that the station, marshalling yards and *go-downs* of that main station of Bangkok did, in fact, get blown to smithereens the night after we left.

Meanwhile, our journey continued into the night and for many hours before we arrived at a place called Korat, where the train could go no further because of a bridge being down. In the dead of night we were marched over the bridge and at one part we walked along a series of broad planks before reaching the other side, where there was a station platform, but no train. We spent the rest of the night sleeping on the platform, which was surfaced with loose granite chippings, and when I woke up in the morning, I had a face full of them, which had to be picked out one by one.

In the light of the day, we could see back to the bridge that we'd walked across during the night and I had an immediate attack of vertigo! The bridge spanned a river and at the part where we walked along the series of planks, the drop was a good 40 feet. If I'd been aware of it when we crossed in the night, I would have needed my friend Frans to carry me!

The train that finally arrived to collect us had normal carriages and so the rest of the journey was luxury after the metal rice trucks. It took us to a place called Ubon, where once again we were marched off and over a river – but this time over a solid bridge – and by continuing along the riverbank on the other side, we came to our new camp.

Our journey had taken us right across Thailand so that we were now near the border with French Indochina, as it was called then. The purpose of the camp was to provide labour for a big airfield they were constructing outside Ubon – a major project that was going to mean long days of breaking rocks, digging, transporting and laying turf.

It was February 1945. Almost as soon as we arrived, there was a distribution of post. We wondered where this batch had been until now because one of the letters for me had been written by my mother in February 1943 – two years earlier. She was saying that they had just been notified by the War Office that they had received an 'unofficial report' that I had been wounded on 13 February 1942, but she wasn't banking on it being accurate. Of course, her subsequent letters that I'd received back in Nong Pladuk confirmed that she got to know more after that date. The other post I received was in the form of postcards in which my mother said they were only allowed to say twenty-five words. This was quite a test if anything useful was to be said. Many of us got these postcards and some were pretty hopeless. A fellow in our hut read out one that he received:

So worried about you. Just drop us a line and put it in the post. We'll pay the postage.

It was always good to receive any mail but, by this stage, it was torture to receive postage written so long ago. Most of us were acutely worried about how things would be at home – especially those of us with wives or girlfriends who might by now have given up hope. In this remote camp, seemingly further now from anywhere, our feelings of being lost to the world resurfaced. Our imaginings of being set free by a resurgent British Army driving its way across Burma and into Thailand were becoming replaced by a certain trepidation about how all this could finish up.

It was apparent that the Japs were also beginning to worry about their situation as they seemed to be getting more and more edgy as time went on. They must have known they were losing the war and it had the effect of some guards becoming more brutal than ever, whilst others would suck up to us and try to be friendly. Mostly they were just jumpy.

At the airfield we had no sooner built the runways, than they had us dig trenches across them – to render the airfield useless to the enemy. There were constant searches of the camp and during one, the notebook I had been keeping was found. I had kept this notebook since the early days in Changi, where I had made it out of bits and pieces that someone had got from a crashed aeroplane. By the time it was found, it was full of all the things that had happened, with little drawings to help me remember them easily. All my writings were in shorthand so that it would be illegible to anyone but me. Well, of course, keeping a notebook was a big offence. Pencil and paper were forbidden in the camps and severe punishments followed if found. My magic saved me again though. I persuaded them that it was all about my magic tricks and how I did them – written so that no one could read how they were done. They just confiscated it and sent me off. Perhaps they thought they might learn some magic from it if they could find someone to read it!

Amidst all these jitters, the important thing for us was simply to settle into a routine and take each day as it came. But at the same time we began to be wary and to make certain provisions. When we were transferred from Nong Pladuk, we had come more or less as a complete camp – including many of the Dutch and so it was easy to re-establish our concert parties. The Japs allowed us to build a stage out of earth and when it was finished, it appeared to be just a heap of earth with a proscenium made out of bamboo and covered with rice sacking. What the Japs didn't know was that we had built secret compartments into the mound that would give at least some of us a hiding place in the event that the Japs turned on us, as we suspected they might. It seemed to us that the best place to be if the Japs thought you might have escaped was actually in the camp!

We got very ambitious with concert party productions at Ubon given all the experienced talent we had around. In one show we even had a revolving stage with three different scenes built onto it. It was built by a fellow who had worked at Waddingtons, the games and playing cards company. It worked by setting the stage on casters, which then ran on a sort of rail, and it was cranked round by a handle applied to a wheel and cog mechanism. Ingenious!

In another production we actually had a mock-up of a four-engine bomber, with people in it and propellers turning as it hung above the stage. Most evocative for all of us, however, were the songs that in some cases, through constant repetition, had become well known by everyone, word for word. One was *Out of the Blue Came Sunshine*, which was a song about peace. Another, which had followed us from Chungkai, where it was performed throughout 1943, was Home.

> *When shadows fall and dreams whisper days ending*
> *My thoughts are ever wending*
> *Home.*
>
> *And when love birds call my heart is ever yearning*
> *Once more to be returning*
> *Home.*
>
> *When hills conceal the setting sun*
> *and stars begin appearing one by one*
> *and night covers all*
> *Though fortune may forsake me*
> *Sweet dreams will ever take me*
> *Home.*

Towards the end of July 1945 we received more mail. The irony of it was beginning to hurt. In one of the letters my mother was saying how they had just received the card I had sent from Changi a month before going up to the railway. There were, however, a couple of postcards from her too, written in May and June 1944 – only about a year past. The one dated 21 June 1944 said something significant:

Alan is somewhere near Helene's home.

This was her way of saying that British forces were in France because Alan was my twin sister's husband and a captain in the army whilst Helene was the name of our French governess when we were both

188

children. She was trying to tell me about D-Day of course – the biggest combined land, sea and air operation of all time and that by 21 June, it had progressed successfully into the French hinterland.

The other card promised an eventual homecoming, with the words: 'Keep smiling a little longer.'

Work on and to do with the airfield was regular and normal hours were kept with regular rest days. On one of our rest days, a Thai, whom we took at first to be from the cookhouse or somewhere on the camp, strolled into our hut. He was unexceptional but for the fact that he was dangling a gun in his right hand – a long barrel .45 hand gun. We all deliberately took no notice of him as he came in and just stood there, looking at us. This could have meant anything. For all we knew, we were all about to be slaughtered. We just didn't know what to think, the place had got so jumpy. Over the years on the railway we had got used to keeping ourselves to ourselves when we needed to. Eye contact was never a good idea.

Then the Thai spoke.

'Five men,' he demanded in a hushed tone. I think everyone thought like I did that they would be going before a firing squad, but that thought faded as he went on to say in hushed tone that he wanted to instruct five of us on Bren guns.

'Oh yeah?' someone said, believing none of it and reflecting the fact that we'd had years of tricks, traps and lies from the Japs. No one budged and he then just cleared off out pretty quickly.

As things were, the Japs had got us not only digging trenches in the airfield but also around the camp. This had started in the manner of being another latrine ditch and when the Japs said they wanted it extended round the camp, they described it as a boundary to prevent escape. To us, it was beginning to look like a mass grave. As we dug this deep pit all around the camp, it occurred to me that if anyone ever found our bodies after the war, they would have no way of knowing my identity as I had no dog tags. So I got a Dutch friend of mine, Jack Biet, who had run a jewellery business until the war, to make me a tag. He used the top of a mess tin and inscribed it with all my details meticulously. Fortunately, I still have it today.

During this time, it had become a preoccupation in the camp to try and find out what was happening in the war. Colonel Toosey had made a farewell speech when he was leaving us at Nong Pladuk back in January in which he said, 'It won't be long now.' Well, more than half the year had gone by since then.

I belonged to a French speaking circle in the camp – we were a group of five Dutch and myself and we used to have a get-together every fortnight to disseminate any news we'd gathered. We'd arranged with the French speaking locals that when any of us could get out of camp at night we would go to a certain hillside. They agreed that for money, they would keep watch on the hillside and if they saw any of us they would come out and meet with us and tell us any war news. Whilst it's one thing to break out of a prison camp like Ubon, it's quite another when you want to break back in. We were very seriously risking our necks doing this. So when the locals gave us news that a 'bombe atomique' had been dropped on Hiroshima and flattened it, I'd had enough of it. Once back in the camp I remonstrated with the others.

'I'm not risking my life again for that kind of news,' I said. 'We pay them money and they just come up with any old cock and bull story – anything they think we'd want to hear that's different from the last time. This time they really are talking complete rubbish. Hiroshima flattened with a single bomb?!' I said, disgusted. 'If they call it a bomb atomique, that can only be something atom-like so they must mean a damn small bomb! And anyway, I happen to know Hiroshima is about the size of London so if you're going to tell me that one tiny bomb has landed there and wiped it out … it's plainly rubbish,' I asserted flatly.

We never spoke of it again and I didn't go out again to the hillside.

The following day the camp guards became extremely jittery and some of them were getting belligerent. One little Korean, Guard Commander Takamini, who was well known to us at Nong Pladuk for his brutality, decided he'd see if he could knock me out for some reason. Whether he'd seen me coming and going from the camp or not, I don't know. Anyway, I was told to stand in front of him while he took a swing at my face, rather like a golfer addressing the ball. He placed his clenched fist against my mouth and then drew his arm right back before swinging his fist straight into my teeth. He didn't knock me out but he did knock my front teeth out and gave me a very bloody face and thick lip.

Three or four days later things took a turn for the worse. It felt like something was about to happen and it could have been the end of the war or it could have been something beastly. There was definitely something afoot. A couple of Japs came to our hut and mustered five of us. I was one of them and they marched us off into the jungle where they had a machine-gun mounted. They lined us up against the trees and aimed the gun at us. We stood there, horror-struck. No blindfolds or anything, we just waited for the bullets. The Japs hesitated, then talked to each other and then argued with each other. We muttered desperately between ourselves, 'What are they doing? … Let's go for them … we could make a run for it …' Then suddenly, the Japs stopped arguing and started packing the gun up. Still shaking, we were marched back to the camp.

For the next couple of days, there were no working parties and the camp was alive with rumour. Then working parties resumed. I went out with a group to complete some pillboxes we were building on the airport but no sooner had we got started than we heard voices coming towards us and a couple of Japs appeared shouting, 'All men stop. War finish. All men back to camp!' None of us really took it in or believed it.

We looked at each other and just saw doubt and distrust in each other's faces. Like automatons we started walking back to the lorries that had brought us out of camp. For all we knew, it was a ploy and they were about to shoot the lot of us this time. But on our return, there was a great hubbub of chatter coming from the huts and we noticed that most of the guards were missing. When I got to my hut I found them drinking Dutch rice coffee with my friend Frans, who had come over to find me and celebrate. But it was a muted celebration. As yet, you could tell, none had fully accepted the idea of 'war finish!'

Then we were called to parade – the whole camp. In front of us was McTavish and the Jap camp commandant, Major Chida. There was also our interpreter. We watched as the commandant talked quietly to McTavish then there was a pause while the interpreter did his bit. Then McTavish spoke.

'The great East Asia war is ended,' he began.

I don't think many of us heard much after that. There was no sudden cheer, no throwing of hats – just complete silence and stillness as the meaning of this for every man really did begin to sink in.

For me, unexpectedly and strangely, it was the worst moment of the war. It was terrible. My mind began racing and racing over all that had happened. Everything flashed by, all jumbled up ... the hunger ... the bombings ... the beatings ... the isolation ... the moments sensing imminent death ... All that time, trying to survive, keeping control ... I found myself short of breath and my heart pounded with the sudden surge of memory and feelings. I almost couldn't take the strain of it. My heart was thumping so much it seemed I was going to burst. All those days now gone when I didn't know if I would live through each one ... all those nights when I didn't know if I would wake up. I had taught myself never to think of tomorrow. I had been like an animal ... living moment by moment taking whatever came along without emotion ... trying never to feel. Now, a tomorrow and a tomorrow and a tomorrow stretched before me!

Even when the big speech had ended, we all just stood there, grizzling. Then we were brought to attention and dismissed but I could hardly find my voice. When I did the words came out slowly, quietly, as I spoke to myself.

'At last, I can say no again.'

The camp had been taken without a fight. We learned later that the war had actually ended three days earlier, but on this day our regimental sergeant-major, McTavish, had assumed command, while the working

191

parties were out and all the guards were ordered by the commandant to leave their rifles in a pile by the guardhouse and surrender their swords – the worst humiliation for a Jap is to be parted from his sword.

After the speech, McTavish had the Jap flag pulled down and replaced with a Union Jack.

The cheers finally came when we were visited by Colonel Toosey and his entourage the next morning. When I saw him, the men were swarming all around him and cheering him into the camp. It was like the biblical arrival of the Messiah.

Eventually, a parade was organised and the salute was taken by the leader of a group that we were told had liberated us. His name was Colonel Smiley. It had been he who had sent in six of his men and medical orderlies while we had been out on working parties that day and it turned out that the Thai who had wandered into our hut dangling a .45 by his side a few weeks earlier was part of a Special Operations force led by Colonel Smiley. He and others had been in the jungle nearby preparing for the liberation of the camp. If there had been any resistance by the Japs or any attempt to kill us all, they had men ready to fight and they had wanted some of us on the inside to be ready to fight too. Colonel Smiley had been commanding a group named Force 136, which was large enough to have men in position not just there at Ubon, but also at Nong Pladuk, Kanburi, Tamarkan, Chungkai and many other camps. They were aware of the Japanese High Command order that every POW was to be liquidated in event of Japan losing the war.

Colonel Smiley stood on a box and gave a speech and then walked down the ranks inspecting and at times talking to the men. By the time he passed me, he must have seen and heard enough because he looked pretty torn up – almost with tears in his eyes. Later we heard that, in every camp he and his medical orderlies had been to, they'd found people lying around dead or dying, but it was different when they came to us. Despite it all, there we were in our rags and tatters or near nakedness, lined up, counted off in threes and delivered 'All present and correct' to the colonel by McTavish. We could have told him it was the Toosey effect that had brought us through!

Command was then handed over to Colonel Toosey who likewise spoke and told us that food was on its way and arrangements to get us home were being made.

How the war had finally come to an end mattered little to any of us at that time. Hearsay during the weeks and months that followed gave us some idea but it was a slow awakening. Our interests were simply food, freedom and going home. News of Germany's defeat and of victory celebrations having taken place months before only heightened our need to see the end to our isolation. It took years, in fact, to get anything like a true picture of the sequence of events that ended it all for us out there in the Far East and to understand the awful meaning of the words *'bombe atomique'*.

On 6 August 1945, the first atomic bomb the world had ever seen was dropped on Hiroshima, vaporising the entire city. Three days later, on 9 August, a second atomic bomb was dropped on Nagasaki. These extreme acts had been decided upon as shock tactics to persuade the Japanese emperor to declare a surrender in the manner that only he could and in effect call for an end to *'bushido'* – the imperative that every man should be willing to die for the honour of the Emperor – a deep-rooted Japanese concept that would inevitably mean a very long war of attrition across all of the Southeast Asian territories that the Japanese had occupied. These bombs, together with a new declaration of war on Japan by the Soviet Union and their invasion of Japanese-occupied land in Manchuria on 9 August, did the trick, so that on 15 August, Emperor Hirohito broadcast a surrender message to his people. Up until this point, preparations had been made by our forces for an invasion of the west coast of Malaya by General Slim's Fourteenth Army, and the Special Operations Executive had been training local Thais and positioning them around the main prison camps in order that they might overrun them when the time came, to prevent the Japanese from exterminating all of us POWs. Colonel Smiley had over 1,000 men under his command in Force 136 ready to take Ubon. His men told us that the Japanese High Command had given orders to liquidate all of us in every camp without trace in the event of the enemy setting foot on the Japanese mainland. Camp commandants had even been given directions on how to do it, such as herding us into caves and incinerating us with flame-throwers or, as in our case, digging deep ditches around the camp and machine-gunning us into them. The trench we had dug really had been intended for this.

With the war ended and the tables turned on our Japanese and Korean guards, some normalities of life returned. Those of us that had kept any sort of diaries or notes could now bring them out in the open for example, and for my part, although I had lost my diary and scrap-book when the Japs had confiscated it, I still had my autograph book, as I called it. I'd started it in Changi when I was being sent 'up-country' to the railway, and on that occasion collected messages of good wishes from friends in the 18th Division as well as the surgeons that had saved my hand and others. Later, when we were all being dispersed from Nong Pladuk, Colonel Toosey added a good luck message, and now with the liberation of Ubon camp by the SOE under Colonel Smiley, I was pleased to get his autograph as well and those of all nine of the others that took part. One of them was a Thai, who was also a lecturer at the University in Ubon, and he had volunteered, like so many other

Thais, for this insurgence against the Japanese, at great risk to themselves and families.

Camp life generally continued for the time being but with more food and, of course, no working parties. We were also getting into proper clothes again. The clothing was being dropped in by air and much of it was American. When it was dished out you just got what you were given and I gained a pair of shorts but I gave them to a fellow who needed them more than me because I had made my own out of bits and pieces of cloth. When a second planeload of US Army uniforms came in the sergeant-major said, 'Anckorn can have first pickings as he gave away his shorts last time,' and this time I got shorts and shirt to match made out of the much in demand gabardine material that keeps you cool. I was still wearing them years later at home in England.

The biggest change, of course, was our freedom to go outside the camp. Colonel Toosey had warned us, however, not to eat and drink just because we could. Some of those with the money to do so ignored that advice and had no restraint. Some died as a result.

In the immediate aftermath of the liberation of the camp, some in my hut went off and got hold of the Korean guard, Takamini – the one that had tried to smash my face in a few days earlier. They brought him to the hut and said to me, 'Right, come on, kill him now.' But I said I didn't want to kill him and that I just wanted to go home and forget the whole thing. They said, 'Look what he's done to your face.' I had no idea what my face looked like as I had determined ever since seeing my skull-like image in a cracked mirror at Changi that I would avoid seeing my own face at all costs. I knew what my face was feeling like though. Someone then gave me a spade saying, 'Go on, knock his head off and we'll bury him under the bedshelf. No one is ever going to know or care anyway.' I told them that if we did, we'd be the same as they were.

'The war is over!' I said. 'Let's just get home!'

They released him and Guard Commander Takamini walked out of the hut laughing his head off. They always thought we were soft, now he had proof of it.

In those last days at Ubon, we were also provided with pens and paper for letter writing and I settled down to write my first freehand letter for three and a half years. My writing was slow and, even to me, unrecognisable. So bad, in fact, that I found when I got home that my big sister had re-written it so that the rest of the family could read it. The letter was a fitting epilogue to that dreadful period.

Dear Folks,

I don't know whether you will be able to recognise this writing because it is the first time I have had the chance to write and it will take a bit of time to get it back. Anyhow <u>it is</u> my writing, strange though it may seem and I am free – free – free! After three and a half years.

You poor things! You must have worried. All through these horrible years we have known that you were safe and we have had only ourselves to worry about but you have known nothing except bad rumours I expect. Anyhow I know you would keep smiling the same as I have done and I have had two photos from you proving it.

It is so difficult to write for the first time, so much to say I don't know where to begin. I'll just give you a rough outline of everything and let you have the full details when I get home. By the way, I am still in the prison camp but we know the war is over! It had been rumoured for a long time but we could see by the behaviour of the Nips what was in the air. Working parties were stopped; in fact, I was put out on the last one! We went out to build pillboxes and had just arrived and were about to start when the Nips started shouting through the jungle at the top of their voices 'All men stop. Senso (war) finish!' We were put on lorries and taken back! My friend Bill Wilder from Wallingford Oxfordshire quite near Bing's and Frans, were on my bed drinking coffee to celebrate and saying what a pity I was not there and in I came so we celebrated! Oh the excitement but of course you know the feeling as well as I so why try and explain.

The next day one of our bombers dropped leaflets, what a wonderful sight. The first time we haven't felt sick with fear and had to grovel in trenches at the sound! We have had a hell of a time, torture, starved, beaten, sweated, in fact we've been slaves! All my friends but one have died foul deaths. I have seen the worst deaths possible, 15 a day for months, each time wondering if I could last.

However, more of that when I come back if you want it. Now for the good. I think the percentage of people who have had malaria is 99.99%. I have not! Dysentry 50%. I have not. In fact Mum darling I have had nothing worse than sore feet since I left home!!!! Of course we all had vitaminosis but that is nothing if it doesn't get bad. I have had beriberi. Luce will . . . (page lost) . . . in one leg but it is due to my wounds. You said you hoped I would fall on my feet. I have had nothing but good luck. I have escaped death by inches several times. My conjuring has saved me from starvation. I have had to do command performances to Nip commandants who have given me food in return! In action I would have 'snuffed it' but there again it helped. They were going to take my hand off, however an orderly in the operating theatre recognised me from England as a conjuror and he told the doctors so they said they would do what they could. Now all that is wrong is the little finger will not lift up properly! However it is very little inconvenience and I am used to working it now! (Right wrist by the way). My left leg is dead in patches and I have a slight limp when I have a heavy shoe if I walk long. I drove through a herd of about 200 bombs and 2 hit me with shrapnel! One through the wrist, one in the kneecap from behind, one on the left thumb, right 3rd finger and one under the right eye. The last three scarcely show at all now! It was a 'blighty one' and I was marked X Malaya. I was too weak to go – lucky again 'cos the boat was sunk with all hands. However I am ok now Mum darling and as fit as ever. I have looked after myself with scrupulous detail and am as good as new. I will give you all details later. I think I have developed my body well too, unfortunately not my mind. We have not been allowed to have any books or anything, paper, pencils, lectures, at times no talking, whistling, singing or laughing but we could still smile. The only thing is that I have been told that I have aged.

However, no need worrying Mum, I will soon be back and raring to go. You can imagine how happy I am at the prospect of seeing you soon after all this.

Love to all

Ferg.

Autograph book entries after liberation at Ubon camp

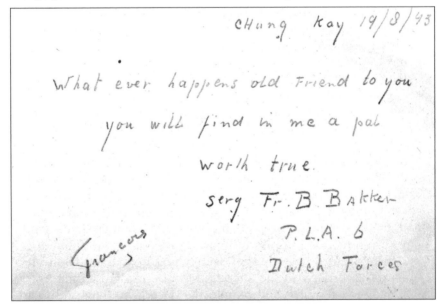

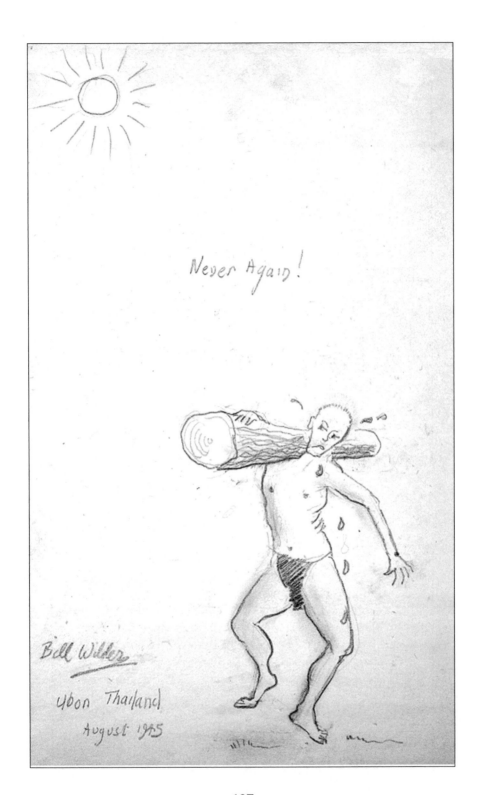

Never Again!

Bill Wilder

Ubon Thailand
August 1945

We've missed many things
when you've been around,
But well miss you more
then any
Best Wishes
Les Cox.

41, CRANLEIGH DRIVE
CHEADLE, CHESHIRE

"You're a mystery to me"

Good Luck and
Keep fooling 'em!
Bob Gale

Thanks Gus for your great
co-operation and friendship; which
I hope will continue.
Best of Luck and good days ahead!
Raymond G. Fairclothe

FAIRHOLME
STATION ROAD
REEPHAM
NORFOLK

198

Chapter 15

FATTENING UP

The 118th Field Regiment of the British Army's 18th Division had been nearly 700 strong on arrival in Singapore. The records show that 287 of us died, some in the fighting but mostly 'in Jap hands' as slaves in prison camps in Thailand or in transit by sea elsewhere. The rest of us were going home with tortured memories.

From Ubon, the journey would first be to Bangkok by rail and then by aircraft to Rangoon, in Burma, where we would stay for a while before making the final trip home.

But not everyone in the camp would be going home. My friend Frans and his Dutch fellow countrymen had no 'home' to go to because the Dutch East Indies, where they had been living, declared independence as the war ended and Java, where Frans had been, along with all the other islands that were part of the East Indies, became Indonesia under their new leader, Sukarno, and the Dutch were their enemy. The repatriation of the Dutch colonialists to the Netherlands was not a straightforward matter and would take some time so the Dutch contingent in our camp had to remain.

Once transport had been organised, the rest of us began leaving the camp in batches by lorry. As we passed through the camp gates, the Jap guards had lined up and they actually bowed in their traditional manner to us and some of them waved as we sped through! The lorries took us to a place where we were going to make a crossing of the river to get to the railway. The river was very wide at this point and the crossing was to be made in small boats that were no more than dug-out canoes – six to a boat.

There had been a bit of a row between the authorities before we finally left in this way. One of the SOE people that had arrived at the camp was in touch with the RAF to have us all flown out. But the RAF said they wouldn't come because they believed the runway at Ubon was mined. The SOE man sent back a message accusing the RAF of being 'chicken' and stating that he would personally come and fly in the first plane if they were so frightened. Nothing was happening so he suggested they send in a reconnaissance plane to watch him drive a lorry up and down the runway and around the aerodrome and he would prove there were no mines. When the plane arrived, the SOE man set off in the lorry – with a Jap guard tied onto the front – as an 'equaliser' if things went wrong!

The RAF still wouldn't come. The SOE man sent a final message saying something to the effect of, 'We'll make our own way but don't you realise what it means to these boys to see you. Can't you at least fly over and let them have a good look at you?'

They finally came and flew over us at something like 100 feet – huge Liberator bombers. With their doors open, they waved and dropped canisters of bully beef and magazines.

The SOE man wasn't satisfied. He sent a further message. 'Is that as low as you can fly?' In response, one plane circled and came in very low across the camp and we saw that his line would take him straight into a couple of trees that were not wide apart enough for him to get through. He put on full throttle as we watched and we felt the thunderous vibrations of the engines passing overhead. Right at the last split second he lifted one wing and cleared the trees! The pilot sent back, 'Low enough for you?'

The next day when we were crossing the river, the Liberators came again – this time straight down the river and no higher than the river bank. As they flew over, some of our boats lost their balance and tipped over, ours included, so we all ended up in the river!

When we finally arrived in Bangkok by train and got ourselves to the aerodrome there, the place was a hive of activity. We saw aeroplanes, one after the other, coming in to land while others were taking off. They were planes we'd never seen before – Dakotas – and they were picking troops up and flying them away by the planeload every few minutes.

It didn't seem that long before it was our turn and we strode out to a waiting plane. It was about one in the afternoon and roasting hot. When we got on board we found no seats or anything, just a bare fuselage and we were to just sit on the floor. Once we were full up, a crewman came to the door and said there would be a delay – probably not take off for an hour. He threw in a bundle of newspapers saying, 'Here, you can catch up on the news,' and then he slammed the door shut. I was reminded suddenly of the doors to the rice trucks that were also slammed shut on us as we left Changi to go 'up-country', where 'things would be a lot better'.

We were in high spirits, enjoying our freedom and the prospect of getting out of there at last – even if it was only to Rangoon. We grabbed the newspapers and someone read out the headlines:

GOVERNMENT CONCERN OVER GROWING NUMBER OF
DEATHS IN RAF TRANSPORT COMMAND ACCIDENTS.

Whatever we each thought, it was masked by the guffaw that followed.

Waiting there, cooped up in a fuselage that was beginning to feel like an oven under the heat of the sun, it was not surprising that at least one person went off the whole idea of taking to the air in that 'crate', as he saw it. This was 'Swill' Meadows, nicknamed as such because he had been a cookhouse assistant in the camps. He'd never flown before. None of the others had flown either but they kept up their high spirits. Privately for me, this was going to be a new experience too – flying in such a big aeroplane – twin-engined and spacious enough to walk around in – but it wasn't my first experience of flying.

When I was fourteen and starting to learn proper conjuring from the wonderful Lionel Cardac, alias Major Branson, Vice President of the Magic Circle, there was great celebration going on for Britain's achievements in flying. This was marked by National Aviation Days that had been instigated by Alan Cobham, who had made a name for himself making long-distance flights all over the place when such things were unheard of. These Aviation Days involved big flying displays of all sorts of aircraft and more than that, the public were encouraged to have a go as passengers in the smaller craft. These events went on all over the country. My daredevil elder brother had a go when one came to Kent and he was smitten with it from the word go, which meant I grew up in a household where talk of aeroplanes was commonplace. Besides Cobham's big shows, there were also pilots who set up their own commercial 'flying circuses', which visited localities and offered short flights for five shillings or longer ones with aerobatics for ten shillings. Where we lived, near Sevenoaks, there was a field that they often used and so when I was a little older, I got the chance to fly each time they visited. I flew on one occasion with Flight Lieutenant Stainforth. He had been in the RAF team that won the Schneider Trophy in 1929. The plane we went up in was an Avro 4C, which had great long wings and struts everywhere. Its big open cockpit could accommodate two passengers and I went up with a friend of mine. We danced around the sky in this thing and my friend hadn't strapped himself in properly so he was hanging on for dear life. Then when Stainforth banked sharply to come in for a landing, he almost fell out! But my best experience was flying with Pauline Gower just before the war. She, of course, became famous during the war for her part in Air Transport Command, flying newly built fighters and bombers to their designated squadrons all over Britain, ready for service. She took me up in a Tiger Moth. Wonderful! And her landing showed real skill. That field near our house was not very large and was bordered by hedges and tall trees. She came in low and dropped the plane over a hedge onto the grass and the plane ran across the field towards the trees, which seemed to race at us. Just at the last minute, she flipped the plane around and drove it calmly back into the middle of the field.

Now, there in Bangkok, the prospect of a long flight in a Dakota was truly exciting for me and I did my best to encourage 'Swill' Meadows to feel the same. He almost became paralytic with the fear when the engines started up and, as the plane started moving, fear seemed unconquerable. He shivered and shut his eyes, even pressing his clenched fists into his eye sockets to hide himself from it. Once we were up, I began describing the view through the window, trying to persuade him to look out by saying how much he would like it if he just opened his eyes. Finally, he did and once he did, he was struck with the wonder of it all and his fear vanished.

Our pilot took us to Rangoon, flying over the railway. This was breathtaking for us all. We flew low over Kanburi and Tamarkan and recognised Chungkai as we flew onwards to the Wampo Viaduct, where I had come a cropper. Mile after mile, bridge after bridge, the whole thing laid out below us was amazing to see but also a horror, thinking how it was that our slave labour had built it. We gazed down, just as those crews of the Mosquito reconnaissance planes had done, but we knew what it had been like down there, lost to the world and trying to survive each day amidst brutality, starvation, disease and horrible death. For a time, we were all silent, looking down as if at a vast graveyard.

As we travelled on, monsoon weather forced us to fly low beneath the clouds – so low that we were scattering herds of buffalo as we passed overhead. Finally we arrived at Rangoon without mishap but a plane ahead of us had crashed on landing and we had to fly around until it was cleared. We saw that one of its undercarriages had collapsed and the plane lay, lopsided, as everyone scrambled out.

There was a cheer from all of us when our pilot put us down safely, and when we had come to a standstill there was a real treat in store. The door was opened and we were met by a group of women who were, to us, the most beautiful girls we'd ever seen – all dressed in white – they could have been angels. We learned they were actually 'WAS bees' – members of the Womens Auxilliary Service in Burma, W.A.S.(B) and part of General Slim's Fourteenth Army that had pushed the Japs out of Burma. They had been in support of the troops throughout the retaking of Burma – with tea, cake, and sandwiches! Now they were here to make a fuss of us, helping us down the steps to their canteen truck, where they served us mugs of tea. I think they had been warned about us though, because I noticed they were very careful to get their mugs back after we'd finished with them! Then we were escorted to a big marquee, where we were served peaches and cream in an atmosphere of cleanliness and good manners. No one shouting at us. We thought we'd died and gone to heaven.

We were there in Rangoon to be fattened up, so this was a good start. However, most of us couldn't eat solids and our diet was to be only milky substances like Horlicks, Bovril, soups and soft fruit with cream.

Our camp was just outside Rangoon at Insein Road – which seemed very appropriate in the way we pronounced it. We were by now a completely mixed bunch and I knew nobody. We were just eight bods to a Bell tent – feet round the middle pole. But everything was specially organised for us because we had a special status – we were classified as RAPWI (Recovered Allied Prisoners of War and Internees). After we had been there a month we decided the initials stood for 'Retain All Prisoners of War Indefinitely'. We just wanted to get home and not be 'fattened up'.

We were looked after mostly by nurses and doctors – which was a bit of a danger for some fellers, as they gradually became restored to health! Lord and Lady Mountbatten were there too for a short while.

They issued us with special green uniforms made out of a sort of denim that made us visibly different from everyone else. It meant that other troops could spot us and because of this, we found people were pretty decent to us. We became very much aware of being 'RAPWIs'. We were never counted or required to parade. We could just wander off as we liked, which I did, eagerly but also tentatively, looking over my shoulder and all around in front of me, expecting trouble and unable to fully trust this freedom.

Out and about, the town was buzzing with people and no one took a blind bit of notice of me. Gradually I relaxed and acclimatised to it, enjoying the people around me, the colour and bounty of the street markets and the most glorious women! I stopped looking for Japanese soldiers about to recapture me.

English was spoken beautifully by many of the locals and so directions were easily obtained. I took myself off to look at the big landmark in Rangoon, the Shwedagon Pagoda. Magnificent! The biggest temple in the Far East, in fact, with a single golden spire that they call a 'stupa', rising to over 300 feet. I climbed the wide steps to the entrance, very slowly, feeling how weak and unfit I had become, and once inside I couldn't help but stand there and just gawp, trying to take it all in – the many Buddhas, some of them golden and all the intricate walls and ceilings and vast golden pillars that surrounded them.

In the days and weeks that followed, I went on to do a lot of sight-seeing, revelling in the complete freedom we now had. I found I could also wander around the aerodrome at Mingaladon where we had flown in. When we had landed, I noticed how the place was littered with

203

crashed planes, both ours and Japanese. The Americans were there in force doing a lot of the clearing up, servicing aircraft and flying around. They were all very friendly and I found that I could easily hitch a ride on a plane when it was getting ready for take-off – all I had to do was ask the pilot where they were going and they'd take me along with them. Sometimes I ran alongside them while they were moving away and when I thumbed a lift, they would open the hatch door and gesture or shout, 'Hop in!' These were often test flights after the engineers had done some servicing. It was a rule that the same engineers that did the work should test the plane and they would just fly around for a while and land again.

One day when I was down there, I hopped into a plane that turned out to be going to Calcutta. When we got there, the monsoon closed in and we were stuck there for three days. I thought this would be stretching my freedom a bit far and that there might be trouble when I finally got back. However, I just walked into my tent and nobody said a word.

I was having a wonderful time with all this flying until on another day, the crew of a plane that was going up after some servicing decided to play tricks. As we flew, the starboard engine stopped and the engineer cast a worried look out of the cockpit window saying, 'Uh oh! Here we go.' At which point the pilot added, 'Hey, this one's gone out too!' as he stared out the port side with serious concern. I looked from side to side. Sure enough, no engines. The plane began to fall. I must have turned white thinking we'd had it but after what seemed an age, the engines restarted one after the other and the crew howled with laughter. I laughed too but the experience had dented my enthusiasm for flying and my next visit to the aerodrome finished me off completely!

I was there watching the flying going on and a Dakota came in just above me. As he landed a tyre must have burst because it lurched onto one side and swung its tail around so that it careered down the side of the runway, crablike, churning up the soft ground and knocking out guy ropes on a line of tents with its wing so that many collapsed as it passed. It came to a halt in a cloud of red dust at the far end of the runway after finally spinning round a couple of times. To my astonishment, the crew just walked away from it as if it was the most normal thing in the world! It was enough for me, what with all the wreckage around, pilots playing tricks and those newspaper headlines we'd read in Bangkok while waiting for take-off. I decided there and then that if I was given the option, I would go home by ship from Rangoon, not by air!

The routine for going home was that someone would come round the tents with a list and if your name was on it, you'd be told, 'Right ... you're on your way!' One day a feller came in to my tent dressed in shorts and short-sleeve order and he had tattoos all over his arms.

I was told the boat that had been taking men home was back in again and I was to be on it.

'You're going home tomorrow,' he said. 'You've just got to fill in these forms first.'

I said, 'I'm not filling in anything.'

Since being freed from the camps I had found myself only too ready to say no to anything I didn't like and I certainly had no time for officialdom, after all that we'd been through. He insisted that I had to fill in his forms but I just said, 'No. I'm not. The war's over, I'm going home. What are they anyway?'

'They're about war crimes and you have to name at least three Japanese you knew by real name or the names you called them by. Then they will be brought up and tried.'

That seemed unlikely to me, although I had actually seen many of the guards I had known, all behind bars in Rangoon – including Takamini, the one that had tried knocking me out. Troops were not allowed to go anywhere near them, for fear of reprisals. There had been incidents up at the camps after liberation when the Australians had got hold of a few and sorted them out. Anyway, it turned out that an old school mate of mine had become an officer and was in command of the jail. He had taken me down there one day and I'd had the pleasure of seeing them all locked up. I had gestured to Takamini when I saw him, that he was for the chop or so I hoped. The facts that came out after the war justified my gesture.

After the Japanese surrender, over 1,000 were eventually rounded up, arrested as war criminals and imprisoned in chains in that Rangoon jail. They were kept there for a year on starvation rations. Amongst them were seven officers from the railway regiments and eight of their men as well as Major General Sasa Akira, who had commanded the construction of the infamous railway. He, along with one of his platoon leaders, Captain Hirota, was later hanged.

In addition, seventy-one officers and guards from the prison camps were prosecuted and twenty-five of them were hanged as well. Guard Commander Takamini got ten years.

The man with the forms persisted.

'Well look,' I said, 'I'm not filling in anything. I can see all this turning into a load of form filling and questionnaires. Why don't you just clear off.'

'Right. You're on a charge!' came the reply. I didn't realise he was an officer!

He took me to another tent and started the proceedings. The charge was 'Insubordination to an officer'. In my defence I pointed out that there was no rank on him and, because he had his arms covered in tattoos, I didn't think he could possibly be an officer. Well, I didn't make

205

any friends, but at least that was the end of it. Except that I was still faced with the forms. If I didn't fill them in, I simply would not get on the boat. So I filled them in and Takamini was on my list.

Our ship for the journey home was the SS *Orbita*. It was its last trip carrying troops from Rangoon. It was nothing like the SS *America* that I had convoyed out on from Nova Scotia, but here I was, finally sailing out across the Bay of Bengal on my way home.

We seemed to have nurses looking after us on board the whole time and they did everything they could possibly do for us. Their attentiveness did, however, get a bit much and on one occasion I thought I would pull their leg. I had watched a 'Yogi' show in Bombay in which the Yogi would pierce himself with needles in impossible places without showing any signs of pain. Well I did the same for the amusement of my fellows, while the nurses looked on. Their faces were a picture as I put a large safety pin apparently through the skin of my wrist and then a needle through both my cheeks – in one side and out the other!

But on another occasion, I was taken aback by a comment of one of the nurses. Referring to our being ex-POWs she had said, 'Doesn't it bother you that you didn't get to do your bit in the war?' I don't think I even answered her, feeling as we all did that we had done more than 'our bit', thank you, in the war.

Returning by ship was definitely the right choice. No duties, just resting for weeks. We stopped along the way, first at Colombo and then a longer stop at Port Tewfik on the southern end of the Suez Canal.

At Port Tewfik, we were taken off and led to a library in the British Army garrison there, where we could write and send messages home. They sat us down at tables on which notepads and pencils had been put. The pads were sets of preformatted telegrams on which you just had to select an appropriate message and write your name and the address of the person you were sending it to. Ingenious! So quickly done. Nothing was ever said but after each group had been in, they had to replace the pencils and pads every time. We couldn't help it. It was still a reflex action of ours to pick up whatever we could, wherever we found it – in case it might be useful later.

We were then taken to a big army supply warehouse, the biggest any of us had ever seen. The idea was to kit us out for the cold weather we would be sailing into as we got nearer to home. It was coming on November and of course, we had no notion of what cold weather was like any more. The quartermaster gave each of us an empty kit bag and directed us to piles of clothing laid out for each of us that we could take. Then we were allowed to go and fill the rest of the bag with whatever we wanted from the stores in the space of a couple of minutes. No records were kept of what we took as we each departed with our kitbags topped up with all sorts of stuff – some of it quite ridiculous. Amongst the bits I grabbed was a potato peeler. That must have been instinctive as I had spent so much time on fatigues peeling spuds thanks to my big mouth!

We also received mail from home while we were there and I had one from Lucille. 'Don't worry,' she wrote, 'I don't care what's happened to you, I've got a good job and I can look after you.' I suspected she thought I was coming home very badly injured, with loss of limbs, which made me hope that my letter from Ubon would get home before I did.

As we passed through the Suez Canal, it was amazing to see roads and cars right next to us and to have ships passing each other so close. All the eastward-bound ships had to pull in to passing places to allow the westward-bound ships through. It felt good to have priority! At one point we passed the young King of Egypt, King Farouk, on his royal yacht. Many of our lot jeered at him but I didn't know why until later. He had made himself very unpopular at the outbreak of war because he had delayed in declaring war on Germany. It was not until 1942, when British forces surrounded his palace, that he decided whose side he was on. We didn't know those details then, of course. He had been written off as a traitor and there he was now, on the deck of his yacht – more or less the same age as me. 'Get out of it you **** bastard!' went the cries. He went below quietly.

In what seemed no time at all, we were at Gibraltar, where we called in briefly while we all stayed on board. The next leg of the journey would be the home strait. We would be saying goodbye to the hot weather that had become so natural to us and gradually the weather would get colder and colder as we progressed up through the Bay of Biscay. By tradition in the Navy, a rum ration was issued from Gibraltar onwards – one serving every day. Real proof stuff that we had to drink on the spot so that fellows didn't hoard it. Wonderful!

On this last leg, the effect of the colder weather was to make me want to sleep a lot and so I spent a lot of the time in my bunk, which was against the side of the ship. One night I woke to hear a bang ... bang ... bang against the ship's side. In my drowsiness, the thought of it being a concert party going on came into my head. It turned out that it was a mine! Heaven knows how we weren't sent to kingdom come.

As we sailed on, the skies became overcast and uniformly grey. Mist came up as evening turned into night and on deck you'd be chilled to the bone. We were nearly home, just over four years since we sailed out on the SS *Orcades* from Liverpool, knowing nothing about where we were going or what we were to do. I was twenty-two years old then and now almost twenty-seven. Had I *'done my bit'*?

Chapter 16

MISFIT

Our arrival in Liverpool wasn't what we expected.

After sailing up the Mersey during mid-afternoon with ships' horns going off in all directions, it seemed that everything was then done in secret once we were allowed to disembark. The winter evening had drawn in and we came down the gangplank in the dark with hardly anybody around. Visitors had not been allowed to the dockside. There were just a few dockyard women, saying thank you for what we'd done as we passed through. We were split up and taken rather hurriedly to various reception centres. Quite a number of us were packed into a local community hall, where the only welcome was from a general. He announced that nobody should leave the premises and we were to be there for the night. First thing in the morning, we would have fresh uniforms issued with campaign medals attached and thereafter, we would be put on a train. The good news was that we would receive back pay for the whole period since we left in October 1941. Finally, we were to be given a meal that night – and by the way, the cutlery we'd be using would be the only cutlery we were going to get so we should make sure we bring it back for breakfast! He had clearly dealt with many returning POWs.

The train we were put on the next morning had all its blinds pulled down in the carriages that were reserved for us. Once we had boarded, all the doors were locked and they stayed that way all the way to London. We believed they didn't want anyone to see us and that in effect, we were in disgrace. We were returning soldiers, but we also knew that we had been part of the biggest capitulation in British military history and suffered humiliation for it at the hands of the Japanese. We didn't expect the disgrace to continue at home.

Reminiscent of the journey from Singapore to Ban Pong in rice trucks, we were peering out of our carriage through whatever gaps we could find as we left the station. Our eyes, eager for the familiar and friendly, glimpsed only bombed-out buildings in all states of collapse and some

208

just a pile of rubble. Throughout the long journey, at each conurbation we saw just chimney breasts and staircases where once houses had been, and in stations there was broken architecture propped up all over the place and parts completely flattened.

In my compartment, eight of us spent the journey somewhat subdued. Some just slept. Perhaps we all still felt like prisoners, doing as we were told, bearing up in the situation, not needing to make up our minds about anything. Thoughts and ideas flew around my head like a whirlwind. I wondered if the same applied to the others. We were only hours away from whatever may be the situation for each of us at home. It was easy to conjure up in the mind's eye all the things we were longing for but the reality could turn out to be very different. Some might find their homes had been bombed, like the ones we were seeing. Others may find that parents, brothers or sisters had been killed or badly injured and those who had wives, fiancées or girlfriends just four years ago, may find others had taken their place. Whatever the situation, it was hard to believe that we were going to be free and that we would be able to do whatever we jolly-well liked in only a few hours time.

We arrived by some circuitous route in Paddington. Our doors were only unlocked after ordinary passengers from the rest of the train had disembarked and were well clear. Once off the train, we were not allowed out of the station area but guided to lines of cars and lorries that were waiting for us, each with a destination plastered on their windscreen. We each had to choose the one that would do for us and then we'd be away. I chose a lorry that had those wonderfully familiar words 'Charing Cross' emblazoned on its windscreen and jumped on board. Despite the devastation, the town was recognisable and I noted we were going by a peculiar route, which I put down to the fact that some roads may be closed off. But after a while I banged on the driver's cabin window and shouted to him, 'You're going the wrong way!'

The driver hunched his shoulders and shouted back. 'Don't know London mate ... never been here in m'life! ... drafted in, see.'

So I directed him there.

Charing Cross was an absolute bustle of people and yet, as I jumped down from the lorry, there was my brother, his wife and daughter – and Lucille. Whether it was because of my state of mind after all those years of being controlled or because they were in a state of shock at seeing me, I'll never know, but the fact was our greeting was not an emotional one. It was very formal and I didn't like it. We were almost like strangers saying 'Good afternoon!' to each other before dissolving into the crowds and silently shuffling our way to the train that would finally take me home to Dunton Green.

I found myself just wanting to be alone with Lucille – thinking that only with her might there be some release from this constancy of deadness.

Our conversation was typically reserved as always when in a public place and in this instance, a crowded train carriage. I spoke more with my brother than with Lucille. He gave a running commentary on what we were seeing as we came down from London but later we relaxed enough for us to start joking about how Japs spoke and I made quiet impersonations. The girls talked between themselves while, from time to time, Lucille's eyes met mine. None of us broached the subject of what had happened to me these last four years. I might just as well have been away at army camp somewhere. I was quite happy though, keeping it within myself, not knowing where to begin. I only wanted to be alone with Lucille.

The train plunged into the long Polhill Tunnel and we sat in the dim light, unspeaking, each of us waiting expectantly for the exit. I had a deep feeling of apprehension at what we might see when we emerged. On the journey out of Liverpool, we'd seen houses with their rooms blown open to the winds and odd looking staircases rising to nowhere. Now, on this journey out of London, everything had seemed even more smashed. It was as though the whole country had been devastated by this war and it had been awful to see.

We came out of the cutting on the south side of Polhill and the countryside lay before us. There it was! Everything that was so familiar to me – just as I was used to seeing it. I realised with joy that, while whole towns and cities could be obliterated by war, the lay of the land and the skyline it made would always remain. I knew those trees ... those woods ... that hill ... those fields ... that skyline. I must have gazed like an enraptured child as the feelings rose inside me. I'm home!

Everything here was untouched yet, before the tunnel, everything was laid to waste. It was uncanny, like passing from one world to another ... from one time to another ... from the past nightmares into a new present. It seemed that everything that had been so awful was behind me now and all that I loved and felt for was here in front of me and around me.

When we finally arrived at Dunton Green Station there was my mother with the car. But once again, it was a formal greeting, devoid of expected emotion. My mother was more concerned about how we were all going to fit into the car – there wasn't enough room for everyone.

'Don't worry,' I said spontaneously, 'I'll walk home. It'll be wonderful to do it. I'll see you there.' And I was gone. No hugs, nothing. As I walked, I imagined what a mood my mother was probably in because she hadn't even touched me or anything. She told me afterwards that she could have killed the lot of them. She dumped them at home and turned the car straight round to come back and find me.

I had walked through the woods that I knew so well and came back onto the main road in the gathering darkness of evening. My mother was coming along the road in the car and when she saw me, she stopped the car, jumped out and we hugged, there on the pavement.

'Oh you haven't changed a bit!' she said with great thankfulness in her voice, but I was conscious of being a bag of bones in her warm embrace.

'Yes, it's the same old me,' I said, 'still smiling, Mother!'

We drove home in a sort of glow of togetherness, without speaking of anything important.

Lucille was there when I got home, of course, but there was still no opportunity to be close with her. It must have been because I'd forced myself, during the three and a half years of captivity, to take each moment as it came without question or demand, that I just accepted this. Whatever it was, I did not break out of the formality of it all and no one sought to break in to my stifled existence. My mother, in her usual commanding way, had set the scene and the proceedings. She had prepared dinner and we all sat down at the table, just as we had so many times in the past. It was as if this were just another weekend. Lucille was shy in company and she didn't speak much one way or another. The conversation was mostly about the goings on at home but there was awkwardness around the table. It occurred to me that they might all be so pleased to see how I hadn't lost any limbs and hadn't been badly disfigured, that anything less was not worth talking about. Finally, the dinner ended, my brother and his family went home and my mother and father went about their business in the house. Lucille and I could finally be together.

Just touching hands was the most incredible experience you could possibly imagine. I had known only harsh, sun-parched and calloused skin for so long and now; suddenly, the softness and wholesomeness of Lucille was like an electric shock, awakening me.

We talked about lots of things but not about what had happened to me.

In the days that followed I really didn't think about things much, I just floated along and took everything in like a sponge. It took me such a long time to feel that it really was all over. All those years when, at any moment, they could kill you and all that time, feeling constantly that something awful was about to happen. All those nights when, in accepting sleep, I had also accepted that I may not wake up again. Now, here in my own home and in my home surroundings, no one was going to kill me. I would see tomorrow.

The everyday things of life for everyone else now seemed extra-ordinary to me. People hurrying about their business and saying hello to each other; trains running at set times; buses coming and going with no one visibly directing them. But unfortunately, just being amongst other ordinary people again was a trial for me. I just couldn't identify with them and their busy lives or with all this orderliness – tables with place settings of knives and forks and everything so clean and cared for. It was all so strange to me. I felt so out of it that I didn't want to actually meet anybody and so at first I only went out in the dark or out in the nearby woods for a walk in the daytime. If I saw someone coming, I'd turn round and go back the other way. When I did venture out to the local village, it seemed that wherever I went, people knew about me. Perhaps the whole village knew. They were certainly looking at me and on occasion I sensed whispering about me too: 'He's been a prisoner of war.'

It was impossible to put it all behind me and blend in. I really couldn't accept that it was all over and there never seemed to be a way of telling people what it was that I and so many others had been through. Everybody at home was full of their own stories of hardship that they felt deeply – how could they ever understand what it was like for us? My mother told of having only 2.5oz of bacon a week on rations. Well – bacon! My elder sister was saying things like, 'I suppose you had plenty of fruit out there – we haven't seen a banana for years!' I didn't really respond. How could I explain the depths to which we'd been plunged? How men would fight over the smallest scrap of food that might have been dropped on the dusty or muddy floor. We had been worse than wild animals. I couldn't even begin to tell them, so I just sympathised with their plight and said little about my own. An overwhelming thought occurred to me. They didn't know me. When I left home, I was naïve and unworldly in every way. Since then, I'd been through so much and seen so many unspeakable things, I was returning as a different person. They could look at me but they couldn't see inside of me. They were simply glad to see me return home with all my limbs and still looking like the person they knew.

I don't think I was in touch with reality during that time. I was withdrawn, as if stunned by all the goings on around me. I would simply wander around, go into the woods that I loved and look at the trees. I would listen to the wind blow and once again gaze at the cloudscapes, recalling the words written by George Borrow that I'd read as a youngster amongst my father's collection of his works:

> There's night and day, brother, both sweet things;
> sun, moon and stars, brother, all sweet things;
> There's likewise a wind on the heath.
> Life is very sweet, brother.
> Who would wish to die?

That was it, I just felt so lucky to be alive.

It was sufficient and I needed for nothing more. But it made me feel out of place and that I wasn't one of them any more as if I shouldn't be there. I was existing somewhere between the living and the dead. I didn't realise it then but these were typical of the feelings of all of us who had returned, while others had not.

My saviour was Lucille. Whilst I found people in general difficult to come to terms with, being with her was just absolutely right. She knew exactly how to deal with me right from the word go and she would show sympathy with anything – especially when I would lose my temper, which I did quite a lot. She would instinctively know how best to react and quietly tell me I was just being silly. It was a wonderful relationship. I wouldn't have got anywhere if it wasn't for her – and let it be known that everything good that happened to me after the war was because of her. We were as one.

Gradually my limited outlook in being happy just to be at home and alive gave way to thoughts of venturing forth properly amongst people and of even taking the train up to London, like I used to.

Hitler may have nearly demolished the Houses of Parliament in the Blitz, but his *Luftwaffe* completely missed the wonderful Lyons' Corner Houses. Before the war, I had gone to one of these near the commercial college I was attending whenever I could. They were huge cafés on three floors, serving food on all three in different styles. There was a brasserie on one floor, a formal restaurant on another and a sort of 'help yourself' arrangement that they called 'The Salad Bowl' on another. It was the Salad Bowl that I used to frequent – a place where you could eat as much as you wanted for two shillings and sixpence. Their waitresses were called 'Nippies', because they were so nippy in serving customers and they were dressed in black with white aprons and frilly bodices and caps. They would often have a quartet playing too in the background. I remembered the one near the college as a place of utmost opulence and I wanted to go there again and enjoy it. So I took myself off there one early evening, meaning to meet up with Lucille after she had finished her shift at the hospital. Well, that did it for me.

I went in and sat down. There was the quartet, all in white tie and tails – all superb musicians. There were the tables, all beautifully laid out with white tablecloths. There was the glistening silver cutlery and the sparkling clean crockery. I just sat there taking it all in – dumb-struck, like a child again, filled with wonder at this unbelievable sight. Then, gently, the orchestra struck up with Jerome Kern's *Long Ago and Far Away*, and that was it.

My head went down into my hands and I began to sob. It just wouldn't stop. I just sobbed and sobbed. It was all too much. Everything was so fine and so clean and the music so beautiful. Somehow, at that moment, all of the past four years seemed to explode out of me. Things

I had kept within myself now impinged themselves upon my mind and tore at my feelings with a vengeance. I realised, on seeing that orchestra perform, how much I had taken it upon myself to entertain my fellows in the camps and keep spirits up. I had been the smiler, the positive one encouraging others, ignoring my own feelings and saying how things weren't that bad or how they would get better. Now, it seemed, the grief of it all had hit me, all at once, here in a Lyons' Corner House. Not the best place to fall apart, but that's what happened.

A waiter came over to see if I was alright. I said I was fine but felt I just had to get out. I didn't have a meal or anything; I just left and walked around London thinking how lucky I was to have survived.

But that wasn't the end of it.

On another day, I had tried taking myself up to London again and arrived at Charing Cross Station. Suddenly, I didn't know who I was or what I was doing there. The funny thing was – it didn't bother me, not in the slightest. I seemed to be possessed with a private euphoria at being alive and free. After all, why should I worry; I knew I had arrived at my destination and that I was in England. That's all that really mattered.

There was a policeman nearby whom I could have gone to but I considered it best to reserve that for later … if I couldn't sort myself out. So instead, I went to a phone box and started to casually look through the phone books to see if I could recognise any names, hoping to jog my memory. Nothing registered. But still I wasn't bothered … there were many phone books to go through and the phone box was nice and quiet and comfy! Fortunately, after a while, I came across an advertisement for the company that my father worked for – DC Thomson – and that I did recognise. So I phoned the number and asked to speak to 'my father, Wilfred' – at least I remembered that, and I was grateful they didn't ask for the surname. A few moments later, he came on the phone saying, 'Where are you? I've been waiting for you.'

I had obviously arranged to meet him and have lunch or something and there was a pause while I took this in, trying to remember.

'What's up?' he continued 'I've been waiting over an hour.'

'I'm not very well,' I replied. 'I'm on the station here in London.'

'Charing Cross?' he asked usefully, reminding me what my destination had been.

'Yes' I said.

'Wait there, then. I'll come and collect you,' he said, sympathetically.

When he arrived, we simply got on the next train and he took me home. I didn't go into any details as to what had happened, which he seemed to accept, and we duly arrived home as though nothing much had happened.

But going into the house, I found I didn't even know where my bedroom was anymore. So I tried, without drawing attention to myself, going purposefully into each of the likely rooms, hoping it would be mine and that I would be able to recognise it. Eventually, I found it, and for the rest of that day, I went about the house pretending nothing was wrong and believing my memory would come back, surrounded as I was by familiar things. But it went on like that for days. It really didn't worry me though and I said nothing about it. The odd thing was that nobody else in the family noticed anything or thought anything was wrong. Life went on as normal. Once again, I was dealing with something privately. Only I should know about it.

I set my mind to work on how I might get my memory back and the idea came to me that I should write down four or five things in my room that I did recognise and see if I could recite them back again after a minute or two, without looking. I kept doing it with different objects until I not only recited them back but also got them in the right order. Then I gradually increased the number of objects in the list so that after a day or two I found I could write down ten objects and recall all of them in the right order. It wasn't long before I could write down twenty objects – numbering them one to twenty – and not only recite them back again, but also choose any number and name the item that corresponded with it. I gained in confidence and believed I had developed my memory to be better than it had ever been before – all thanks to my sudden memory loss on Charing Cross Station. Once again, something bad had turned out to be good for me. I had taught myself a new memory technique and I have used it ever since in my magic act!

On my return from the war, I had no enthusiasm for doing magic but this whole episode got me thinking about starting again. It was winter, however, and needed a proper coat if I was going to be out and about in my white tie and tails, so that was the first thing to sort out. I thought I might get myself something pretty decent with my army back pay sitting in the bank and I started scouring the classified advertising section of the newspapers to see what was going. It wasn't long before I came across exactly what I was looking for in *The Times*: '*Dress overcoat for sale. Montague Burton. Second-hand*'. The address was Queen's Gate in London, and when I phoned the number, I found it was actually Montague Burton himself selling the coat. I arranged to go up and see him.

As I was crossing a road near to Queen's Gate, I suddenly heard the familiar sound of bombs coming down – that deadly, portentous whistle. Instinctively, I flung myself down into the gutter, pressing myself against the high kerb, waiting for the inevitable and, once again, was gripped with fear. People came over to me and asked if I was alright. I couldn't understand it – why weren't they taking cover –

they would all be killed! I said, 'The bombs!' but all I got in reply was, 'What bombs? ... that's a jet aeroplane flying over.' Well, I'd never heard a jet before. My brother told me later that I'd probably heard a Vampire as these were just coming into service for the RAF at that time. He explained that it would have been slowing down as it went over London. Well, to me, that descending whistle sounded just like a bomb and that meant only one thing ... dive for cover!

'It's alright mate. War's over,' I heard someone say. I felt such a fool.

Dusting myself down, I went on to the address in Queen's Gate, where I tried on the overcoat and decided to take it. Mr Burton said he'd had someone else interested and they had promised to come back but he thought for a moment and then said, 'Since you've made up your mind like that, I'll let you have it.' So now I could be every inch the professional magician and what's more, I had a dress coat that was to last me the next fifty-odd years, it was such good quality.

But I really wasn't ready yet to take to the floor and perform again. In any case, there was a much more important event still to be arranged.

It was because of my awkwardness with other people and my difficulty in coming to terms with everyday life again that Lucille and I decided to get married by special licence to avoid any ceremony. A special licence would cost seven shillings and sixpence and needed a canon to officiate – which seemed entirely appropriate, me being an Artillery man! We found we had one in Sevenoaks so I called him up and told him I wanted to get married by special licence. He told me to go along and speak to him about it the very next day, which was a Saturday morning.

'Come in,' he said. 'Have a glass of sherry.'

'Thank you very much,' I responded politely.

'Now what can I do for you?'

'Well, as I said on the phone, I just want a special licence to get married.'

'When were you thinking of getting married?'

'January 26.'

'Oh well, there's plenty of time to read the banns ...' he began but before he got any further, I interrupted.

'I don't want the banns read. I just want to get married as quickly as possible.'

There was a moment's pause and a piercing look.

'Oh! I see ... I see,' he said in a knowing tone of voice, presumably thinking I'd got some poor girl into trouble. He then proceeded to more or less throw some papers at me and bring the meeting to an abrupt close, effectively kicking me out in short order.

In my still strange state of mind it didn't bother me. I'd got the papers. That's all I had gone for. But I left there, conscious yet again that I was different now after this war – different in every way from the happy, personable and cheeky young man that joined up in 1939.

Lucille and I were married on 26 January 1946 – six years almost to the day that she had walked onto that ward in the Joyce Green Hospital in Dartford and I'd impulsively said to the fellow in the next bed that she would be the girl I'd marry. For more than three and a half of those years, I had clung to that possibility as a matter of survival and the letters I had finally received from her had allowed me to glimpse a future that kept hope alive.

The wedding certainly was without ceremony. At 2.00 pm we met the Canon and by 2.20 pm we were having dinner at Donnington Manor. Apart from family, the only guest was the editor of the local newspaper, who knew me through my brother, and whom I'd bumped into that same morning in Sevenoaks. He'd heard I was getting married and asked casually when it was to be. 'Today, at 2.00 pm,' I said. Rather awkwardly he said he would like to come along to it, which I accepted. Our little party sat down to not much food at the Donnington Manor, but a very decent wedding cake, created jointly by my mother and our gardener's son, who was a confectioner and dab hand at icing cakes. When he was doing the icing at our house, I came into the kitchen just as he was spitting vigorously into the icing bag before applying the topping. 'Trick of the trade!' he said, 'spreads better and doesn't crack later.' Least said, I thought ...

That night, Lucille and I spent our first night in the luxury of the Strand Palace Hotel in London before taking the train the following morning, up to Scotland. Our honeymoon was to be in Melrose, where my idea was that we would walk every day in the Eildon Hills and on the banks of the river Tweed. Melrose was the location of our divisional headquarters while I was in the concert party and, despite some hard times there, I had good memories and friends whom I wanted Lucille to meet. I had always said to myself that one day I would come back and enjoy their beautiful landscape.

Unfortunately, Lucille got chilblains due to the cold weather and that put paid to any idea of walking anywhere. It rather pointed out that, although we were soul mates, we were very much physical opposites in one way. She never knew what it was to be warm and I never knew what it was to be cold. Regardless of that, we were as one together and it seemed as though our long separation had never happened. We just picked up from where we left off – quietly at peace and enjoying each other's company, never mentioning the horrors or trials of the 'missing' years. She never pressed me on anything and I felt no need to talk about what had happened to me. While I was with her, everything was alright and she knew just how to handle the moods I might find myself in. She would simply take over when there were details to be dealt with –

details that to me always seemed so unnecessary and that could easily make me fly off the handle. After everything that had happened to me, I was just happy to be alive and to know that nobody was going to kill me today! The sound of the wind in the trees and birdsong was enough for me. I preferred to walk away from anything at all troubling if I could and detested getting tangled up with arrangements and peoples' questions.

We were able to spend a whole month on honeymoon, during which time we went to the New Victoria theatre in Edinburgh where we'd put on our concert party for the public and we visited my uncle and his family, still living in Arbroath. My back pay had amounted to a king's ransom – over £400 and not only that, it had been paid to me in £5 notes. Never before and never since has my wallet been so bulging or have I ever felt such a sense of ease with money! We could go and do as we pleased. The discipline of living each day as it came that I'd mastered while in captivity was now a wonderful thing because it meant that I savoured each of these honeymoon days all the more and had no worries about how our future would be. When we were married, my notion, if I had been conscious of it, was that Lucille would stop working because it was not the done thing in those days to have your wife working – at least, that was how it was before the war. But the world had changed a lot in just six years and it seemed that many women now worked, married or not. Lucille loved her job and there was actually never any question in her mind about stopping work just because we were married. So, once we were home again, our married life was much the same as before we were married. We lived very happily at my parent's house and I simply awaited demobilisation.

Chapter 17

HOSPITAL CASE

It was July 1946 when I was finally sent for demobilisation, or 'demob', as it was known. I was to report to Hobbs Barracks just outside East Grinstead, a big army camp designated as a War Office Selection Centre, where a lot of the demobilisations took place. It should have taken just a morning but it was the start of a long and testy relationship with the military and medical establishment that was to end with my eventual release, six and a half years later, in November 1952.

The problem was that, after a medical check, they suspected that I had all sorts of residual infections, including TB, and they'd also found liver complications, which I knew was thanks to a rifle butt bashing in one of the camps. So I was given eight weeks 'release leave' while further medical tests could be done.

The testy relationship started right there with the signing of the Release Leave Certificate. My assumption was that any form of discharge papers issued by the army would be an essential part of my applying for a job and the words used would be critical to the kind of job I would be considered for. So when I read the officer's testimonial: 'Gnr Anckorn has been sober and trustworthy. A man of average intelligence and ability,' the 'Anckorn' in me wanted to take him to task. I asked to see the officer and once in front of him, I challenged his statement.

'Do you know me, Sir?' I said.

No, Gunner Anckorn, I don't,' he replied.

'Well, Sir, it's just that you've described me as having average intelligence, whereas in fact I speak three languages, which I suspect you do not and I doubt if you would describe yourself as below average intelligence.'

'It's just a routine classification, Anckorn,' was his only response and the statement had to remain.

It seemed to me that I had a battle on my hands if I was to be treated properly in being discharged from the army, and the antagonism that ensued later had its routes there.

So, for the next couple of months I was to be subject to further medical tests and treatments, which wasn't all bad, of course, because I would remain on full army pay. They issued me with a small container to take away and fill with a sample, which I was then to send back to them before attending the Military Hospital at Roehampton. When I arrived at Roehampton they told me that, apart from anything else, I had amoebic dysentery and it was serious. Well, I had no symptoms, so I suggested they had their samples mixed up. They sent me home again with a fresh sample container, which I duly filled and sent back. After a few days I was sent for urgently by telegram: 'Attend immediately.' This time I was met by staff, looking at me very worriedly and telling me again that I was full of amoebae. I insisted I wasn't or at the very least, the amoebae and I were getting on famously and they shouldn't worry. They took no notice and took me in straight away for treatment.

Part of the daily routine while I was there was to take Epsom salts every morning to 'clear out the system'. It was someone's job then to sort out what had passed through – looking for hookworm, amongst other things.

I didn't want to take any of that stuff and as it happened my bed was by a window in the ward, so when they came along with a mugful each day, I'd take a sip but wait until they'd gone and then chuck it out the window. This went on until one of the nurses became suspicious. However, my magic saved me! She came to me and said she was going to stand there whilst I drank it. I said, 'Yes nurse, that's no problem. I don't know what you think the matter is . . .' and while we were talking I managed to swap the mug she had given me for another that I had concealed under the bedclothes, full of water. I submissively drank from the mug right down to the bottom and proudly handed her the empty, which she took, triumphantly, and strode off very pleased with herself. With her back turned, I quietly chucked the Epsom salts out the window as before. That was all very well until the day came when there was a hospital inspection, which they would do from time to time without warning, and the ward sister and her retinue would go round, under the command of an inspector looking at everything. Well, it happened that the inspector stopped by my bed and glanced out of the window, where he spotted the white dust of the dried Epsom salts all over the flowerbed outside.

'Wrong time of the year for snow, isn't it?' he said, sardonically.

The nurse gave me a look and put two and two together. That was the end of that little ruse!

The doses of Epsom salts that did go through me revealed the presence of hookworm. Most POWs came back infested with hookworms. These little niceties sit in the intestines and suck blood, causing anaemia and gastric complications if left there. The procedure for removing them was known to us as the 'atom bomb treatment'. This involved swallow-ing a large capsule, the size of a cigarette lighter fuel capsule, filled with carbon tetrachloride – CTC, as it was known. More commonly this was used as an industrial cleaning agent! Anyway, once swallowed, the capsule would dissolve a little while later and what can only be described as an explosion of fumes would rise up from the stomach to seemingly envelope the brain. Somewhere in there the hookworm copped it. But of course, CTC could have serious side effects besides killing the hookworm and so it would have to be pumped out of you within a couple of hours. During that couple of hours, you'd be lying in bed shivering with an extreme temperature.

By the time they'd finished with me, my medical records ran to thirty-four pages and the war pension I was to receive in place of army pay was based on 'effects of malnutrition and privation; injury to right wrist; injury to left knee; ancylostomiasis and amoebic dysentery'. I was also told that I would be called to attend St Mary's Hospital, Roehampton, every year for the foreseeable future in order to monitor and treat these conditions as necessary. It turned out that this would be for the next ten years and on each occasion I would have to be an in-patient for up to a month, along with other returnees from the Far East. During this stay in hospital, we would also be required to discard our civilian clothes on entry and don army blues that designated us as wounded soldiers – blue jackets, blue trousers, white shirt, red tie. This had been something started after the First World War so that when people saw someone dressed like that they knew he was a wounded soldier. That was all very well but the result was that, for up to ten years after the war, we were required not only to dress in army togs, but also to comply with army discipline – stand by your beds for inspection; polish the floors into glasslike condition and eat in a mess hall. Year by year I became more and more resentful of it. It was disgraceful – we were civilians!

However, these annual stays in hospital became an occasion to meet up with other ex-POWs and the first thing we all did on arrival was to exchange 'credentials' as to which camps we had been in. At what turned out to be the last of these for me, ten years after the war, I attended as usual and, having got to my designated bed, I introduced myself to the fellow next to me and asked the usual question, 'Which camps?' The answer surprised me.

'I wasn't in any camps,' he said.

'What do you mean?' I asked, wondering what he was doing in 'our' ward.

'Well, I wasn't a prisoner of war but I was stationed in the Far East.'

I joked that he couldn't have been in the Far East without being a prisoner – everyone was a prisoner. Anyway, I told him, he should probably be in another ward if that was the case, because this ward was for ex-POWs.

He wanted to explain and told me he had been in India in the RAF. I responded impetuously.

'I hope you weren't one of those bastards that came and bombed us on the river Kwai.'

'I'm sorry to say that I was,' he replied, and he went on to explain.

'It was very difficult for us because we knew you were there in all our target areas but all we could do was to try and miss you. It was dreadful. We spent the four-hour trip outward thinking about it all and how it might be if it went badly and then we had four hours flying back again to dwell on what we thought we'd hit.' He paused for a moment and there was a silence between us. Then he continued, looking somewhat troubled by what he was about to declare.

'One day, in broad daylight, I did the best bit of bomb aiming I'd ever done, but somehow it all went wrong with the last stick. The POW camp was right next to the Japanese engineering works – only yards away from it – and I had to get all my bombs into the works and not into the camp. I got them all in but suddenly the last five went wild and fell right across the camp. I'll never know how many we killed.'

'Well I can help you there.' I said. 'You killed nine and buried two alive. I was one of them!'

'In that case,' he said, 'this belongs to you,' and he brought out from beneath his pillow a picture taken from the bomb aimer's camera showing the exploding bombs across the camp in deathly black and white. I looked at it in astonishment because there it was, a bird's eye view of the very devastation I had actually been in, and I could pick out the familiar trenches, including the one just visible under a blast that was the one I'd been buried alive in. I could also clearly see the dried-up old well next to the trenches, which was where Colonel Toosey had sheltered.

'What on earth are you doing with that picture under your pillow so long after the war?' I asked in astonishment. His answer was pitiable.

'It's been a thing with me. I've always worried about what I did to you chaps. I've brought it with me each time I've had to come here, just in case I should meet anyone who knew anything. Now at last I've met you and you've told me, so now you can have it, I'm done with it.' He handed me the picture as if relieved to be free of it. This man must have been thinking ever since the bombing that many more had been killed, so perhaps he was relieved to hear that it was relatively few.

That wasn't the only chance meeting I had in those post-war years when the past became suddenly part of the present again. Early in 1950, just over four years after returning home and about the time the Far East conflict was re-igniting with the Korean Emergency, I was walking down Gower Street to where the Magic Circle Club rooms were. As I was arriving there, I got a tap on the shoulder.

'How's that hand doing?' I was asked by a well-dressed stranger.

In the rather impersonal manner I had adopted since the war, I replied, 'Who are you?'

'Don't you know me?' he said as he looked at me intently. 'What about the operating table in the Singapore post office?'

'What about it?' I responded, coldly, still showing no recognition of this man.

'I was about to amputate your hand when my orderly stopped me, saying you were a conjuror. It would have come off otherwise.'

This was quite extraordinary. We hadn't seen each other since I was sent up-country from Changi to the railway and he had signed his best wishes in my scrapbook. I had been half starved and near naked then but somehow he'd recognised me from behind, walking up Gower Street, seven years later. I must have stared at him in searching astonishment for a whole minute before continuing the conversation. I genuinely did not recognise him.

'Well, it's like this,' I said, demonstrating the restricted movement I had become used to. 'Anyway, I get on alright using the left hand now.'

'Oh that's not very good, is it?' he said, looking concerned. We really ought to have another go at it. You must come into my hospital and we'll see what we can do with it.'

Apart from the surprise in finding myself talking to the man who had saved my life in the heat of battle, I was daunted by the idea of paying medical bills. Stunned, I responded apologetically, 'I'm afraid I can't do that because I don't really earn that much money.'

'You can be my guest,' he insisted. 'I'm at the University College Hospital here at the end of the road. Come along with me and we can make arrangements.' I followed his command and my attendance was arranged for the following week.

I was in there eleven days as he meticulously worked on the wrist and the hand. He did it all under local anaesthetic so that we could talk through the work he was doing and so that I could make movements of my hand when he needed me to. At the end of it, I had a virtually normal working hand again.

Julian Taylor wasn't a young man by the time we met again in London and it was perhaps the age barrier that meant our chats did not include our experiences of the war or our activities in its aftermath. I have read since then that he had served in both the First and Second World Wars and in the First he had been a Territorial and a driver, like me, only he drove a heavy-horsed ambulance. He had received an OBE after the First War and became CBE after the Second. When he treated me in Singapore, little did I know I was being treated by a consulting surgeon, Malaya Command, with the rank of Brigadier. He was taken prisoner like the rest of us but he remained in Changi throughout and lived through the continuing horrors there, long after I had gone 'up-country'. When he came back to England after the war, his malnutrition was so bad that he broke both his arms soon after returning – just trying to get back to normal activities. Perhaps it was just an affinity between us when we chanced to meet in Gower Street again, one prisoner to another – something on the radar! All I know is that, had it been three minutes later, we might never have met because I was just about to disappear into the Magic Circle offices a few yards further on. A bit like my turning up on his post office counter operating table in Singapore – a few minutes or so later and I'd have been dead.

Chapter 18

MAKING A LIVING

During the years immediately after the war, I did not really progress much in the way of earning a proper living. It seemed to me that it was enough just being alive and I did not worry about what I would do with the rest of my life. Besides, Lucille had qualified as a nursing sister and she had said in one of her letters to me, 'I don't care what may have happened to you, I will be able to look after you.'

It was difficult to get started again doing my magic shows too. Even though I had gone out and bought myself the second-hand Montague Burton coat, to complete my magician's attire, I couldn't actually bring myself to perform again. It was fear of people that stopped me getting on with it and the extreme discomfort I felt whenever there was a likelihood of engaging in conversation with those other than my own family or of becoming the centre of attention in any way.

However, the local village hall in Dunton Green hosted a very special variety show once a month on a Sunday afternoon. They called it *Brighter Sunday Afternoons*, and there would be just local people singing or reciting poetry or playing a musical instrument. They had a small orchestra and a fellow there who could play any music you liked in the style of any musician of your choice. He would play, for example, *Love is the Sweetest Thing* in the style of Benny Goodman if you wanted it. He had worked for the Ministry of Information during the war, broadcasting music in the Germanic style in order to attract listeners in Germany who were forbidden to listen to anything British on the radio. These programmes were, I believe, used to deliver propaganda as well as coded messages to resistance groups.

Brighter Sunday Afternoons was started by an inspector of buses who lived in the village, and it made Dunton Green possibly one of the first places in the country to break the mould created by religious observance, that had meant no entertainment on Sundays at all. I think the shows were intended as a bit of a morale booster because 1946 turned out to be a year of gloom all round. There seemed to be increasing worry and concern everywhere – not only due to so many of us servicemen returning home and having no jobs to go to on top of broken marriages, broken homes and broken lives, but also because of continuing food shortages that meant there was no end to rationing and people were queuing everywhere for everything. On the radio, there were also dire warnings from Winston Churchill, who, whilst no longer our Prime Minister, was nevertheless a voice to be listened to. He was warning now about Russia and the spread of communism, suggesting the very freedoms we had just been fighting for might be very shortlived:

> From Stettin in the Baltic to Trieste in the Adriatic, an iron curtain has descended across the Continent ... The dark ages may return on the gleaming wings of science. Beware I say, time may be short.

Well, anyway, the organisers of the *Brighter Sunday Afternoons* show had been asking if I would perform and it was my father who coaxed me into it in the end. My idea was that I would disguise myself as some kind of mystic from the East and I wouldn't have to speak a word, because the act would be done in silence, with just music playing throughout. Lucille encouraged me too, suggesting that she could be my assistant. So, we set about doing it together.

We got hold of a make-up artiste who worked for Leichner in London and he came and transformed me into an entirely believable Eastern mystic, just as I had envisaged. He did such a good job that I couldn't even recognise myself! He did just as good a job for Lucille, although not many would recognise her anyway, once she removed her glasses and had her eyebrows painted. Donning a beautiful sari, she became every inch the obedient Indian servant mistress, and I, in a splendid kaftan and slippers, was recreated as her mystic master. To complete the disguise, I decided my stage name would be 'Ali Bay' to avoid any possible connection with 'Wizardus'.

The only problem was that Lucille was very short-sighted and without her glasses, she wouldn't be able to find a cigarette in an ashtray if she'd placed it there. Nevertheless, we rehearsed all the moves without her glasses and eventually she could do it all blindfolded if necessary. So, on we went!

The act included much of the usual sorts of magic but the grand finale was to be my own version of an audience favourite. The trick involved asking a man in the audience to lend me his hat and I would proceed to break a couple of eggs into it and pour some flour, sugar and milk in as well, such as would make a cake. The cake would emerge and I would return the hat to the man in the audience, untouched. Well, usually the 'cake' is not a real cake and so the handling of it is relatively easy, but I wanted the cake to be real. So Lucille baked a cream

226

sandwich cake just before the act and my idea was that, in order to prove it really was a proper cake when it was produced from the hat, Lucille would cut a piece out and offer it to a member of the audience to eat. But we hadn't thought that the orchestra would be there immediately in front of us.

Well, to the applause and wonder of the audience, the cake was produced and sliced. Lucille went forward purposefully and, realising she couldn't reach the audience, attempted to offer the cake to the nearest member of the orchestra, thinking that would do the trick. As it happened, she approached the violinist, who continued playing oblivious to her presence, partly because he was intent on his music but also because he happened to have a glass eye on the side from which she approached. Lucille leaned forward with the cake, offering it as she thought to this person to take, but to the audience, she appeared to stuff it in his face! It brought the house down and that was how we closed on my first magic act.

It was all good fun and I thought I'd got away with it without being recognised. But the very next day, a local press reporter came up to me in the village.

'That was you last night, doing the magic show, wasn't it?' he said.

I thought for a moment about denying it and clinging to my imagined anonymity, but instead I replied, 'How did you know?'

'Those hands!' he said. 'I recognised your hands.'

That was the only act in disguise of that kind I ever did. It had got me back onto the stage and I carried on from there, as myself, in the white tie and tails of the typical magician in those days. I found I could earn at least double my army pay and with Lucille continuing with nursing, which she loved so much, it meant we had enough to get by on.

In the October of 1946, the army reclassified me as a Reservist and normally speaking, my army pay would have ceased. However, because of my health and need for continuing treatment, I was awarded a war pension that was 100 per cent of my normal army pay – to be reviewed annually.

So it seemed we could go on living, for the time being anyway, on my war pension, Lucille's nursing pay and the income from my magic shows. But Lucille and I had been living all the while at my parents' house in Dunton Green and we needed to find a place of our own. This meant I really needed to have a proper job. As with every other returning soldier, the business of finding a job was not easy. In the end I contacted Marley Tiles, where I had worked before the war. I remembered the meeting with the Managing Director, Mr Aisher, just after war was declared in 1939. He had promised us that, whatever happened, there would be a job at Marley for those of us who made it back. Well, that time had come.

227

When I went for the interview, the reception wasn't good, however. There was a new man in charge who had a very different and challenging attitude.

'So what have you been doing with yourself since you came back?' he enquired.

I made no attempt to hide my own attitude, which must have come across as somewhat detached from reality.

'I haven't been doing very much at all,' I replied.

'Have you read any books?' he went on.

'No, not particularly,' I said.

'Oh, I see. You've just been sitting around then, have you? Have you looked for any other work before you came here?'

'Yes,' I said, 'but I haven't found any.'

'So you've come back here. You can't find a job anywhere else – so you come back here expecting me to give you one.'

I was beginning not to like the way this was going so I responded brusquely, 'Yes, that's right. Because we were promised, before the war, by Mr Aisher, your predecessor, that whatever happened, we *could* come back – and here I am.'

We looked each other straight in the eye. He gave way.

'Well alright then, I'll give you a job,' he said.

So I started on £5 a week, and that's where I stayed for the next six years, with my pay rising eventually to the glorious height of £8 a week. I had thought at first that I was doing well on £5 per week because it was twice what I was paid in 1939. But then it became clear that £5 per week could only just about buy what two guineas a week bought before the war.

Even with the job at Marley, the only way we could have our own place was to rent and we found a flat in Sevenoaks that we could afford. It was on the top floor of a four-storey house perched on the top of the railway cutting, overlooking the trains coming in and out of Sevenoaks Station. It was a mountaineering exercise to get to our rooms. Apart from the walk up the hill to get to the house, there were then several flights of external iron steps to climb, followed by another flight of steps inside the flat, once we'd opened the front door! In normal circumstances, we could treat this as just good exercise, but the winter of 1946/47 turned out to be one of the worst in living memory, with snowfall ten feet deep in places. Needless to say, the iron staircase outside the flat became more like a toboggan run!

We became settled as best we could in that flat at the top of all those stairs, until a few years later, when we started looking for a house for my twin sister, Beb. She and her husband, who had become a major in the Army of Occupation in Germany, were due to return home and they needed a place for their little family too. Well, a place came up that was just right for them, a detached three-bedroomed house in Westerham, with lovely gardens front and back. The price was £3,500 but suddenly, it was reduced to £1,750 to get a quick sale. I said to my sister that it would probably be snapped up before they could do anything about it from Germany. So we agreed that Lucille and I should go for it instead and, with a deposit put up by my mother, we got it – as well as a mortgage!

Two years later, by 1952, money had become a pressing matter for us, partly because my war pension had been reduced on account of an improvement in my health but also because of my over-relaxed attitude to earning a living whilst having a mortgage to pay for. It meant that we'd run up an overdraft equivalent to a year's wages! Fortunately, a friend of mine, who had also worked at Marley before the war, was now managing a small timber yard nearby in Brasted and he asked me to join him as Office Manager and Bookkeeper. My pay went up from £8 a week to £10 a week and we were off the rocks. But there were more changes to come in 1952, which would mean, in the haunting words of Owen Aisher, that life would change again '... inexorably from what it is now'.

In October I was finally released from the army and shortly after that, Lucille became pregnant. This was wonderful news for both of us, but especially for me because, on arrival back in Liverpool after the war, we had all been told by the general in the reception centre that we were all probably sterile due to our privations. As time had gone on since then, I had almost believed it to be true.

The thing was that my magic shows were doing well by this time and with the mortgage to pay I was out most evenings. It meant of course that, with Lucille working away at the hospital in Dartford during the day, we were hardly seeing each other. So I suggested that I should reduce the number of shows and that I knew a good way of doing it without actually turning people down.

'I'll double the fee and then I'll be doing half the work,' I said to Lucille confidently.

Well as soon as I did that, even more work started coming in and instead of getting five guineas, I was getting ten guineas and going out *every* single night. We carried on with it for a while, putting up with the little time we had together on the basis that we would be getting the overdraft paid off and we could even start putting money aside for when our first child would be born.

It was during that time that I was stopped in the High Street in Sevenoaks by a man who announced himself as Principal of Night Classes for schools in our area. He asked me if I would like to teach shorthand and typing at night classes. I wondered why he had approached me out of the blue when I hadn't done any teaching that he would know about and he explained that my brother had mentioned me to him. My brother must have remembered me telling him how I had taught shorthand in Changi for a while, before being sent 'up-country'. Well, I did think I'd like to have a go at the evening classes – purely out of interest. I wasn't thinking of what I might earn. He invited me to meet him at a local school the following Monday night and I duly went, as arranged.

My expectation was that there would be an interview and some sort of assessment together with a discussion about what was required. But no! He took me along to a room and on opening the door said, 'There's your class, Mr Anckorn,' as he ushered me in and shut the door, leaving me alone in front of a classroom full of people, many older than myself, all waiting to learn about shorthand and typing.

Well, out of necessity came the instinctive style in which I would teach for the rest of my working life. I did what all the teachers I'd ever had at school never did. I spent the first hour simply asking the class what they thought shorthand was all about until I felt they really understood the value of what they were going to spend their time learning. It turned out that I very much enjoyed this evening class work, especially when I found it was something I could do well. I was overjoyed when, a month later, the Head of Department came up to me and handed me a payslip. I had thought, for some reason, that this was an unpaid position!

So now I had a day job in the timber yard as well as a teaching job on two nights a week *and* my magic shows on the other nights. All very well except for the little time that Lucille and I were having together. We accepted it though because the job in the timber yard was near to our house which would mean that, when Lucille stopped work to have the baby, I could easily be home at lunchtimes. It was into this happy setting that our first child, Deborah, was born and later, when she was just toddling, we would have many picnics together during my lunch hour.

But it was not to last. On Christmas Eve 1955, while I was getting on with the bookkeeping in the morning, looking forward to an early finish that day and doing some Christmas shopping on my Christmas wages, three men turned up wearing dark suits and bowler hats. One of them leaned over my desk and slammed a date stamp down on the page I was working on.

'What on earth are you doing?' I said in outrage.

'What do you do here?' he replied coldly.

'I'm the Office Manager,' I said.

'Not any longer,' he said. 'You're fired.'

He and his fellows then proceeded to go around the office and the yard putting labels on everything. The business was in liquidation.

Well, apart from a ruined Christmas, I didn't let it bother me too much, reckoning that with my experience of office systems by then and my shorthand and typing, it would be easy to find a job again. It wasn't. I was thirty-seven and a bit old to be doing just an office job. Months and months went by and my search for a job took me further and further afield until finally I got an office administrator job at Redland Brickworks, less than a mile from our house in Westerham.

It was sometime later, after settling down again with the new job, that I spotted an advert in the local newspaper for a part-time evening class teacher in French and shorthand at West Kent College of Further Education. This seemed perfect for me and was better money than my existing evening class work, teaching just shorthand. So I applied.

When I went for the interview it was by special permission of the manager at Redlands for an hour off. I was to make up the time lost at the weekend. The appointment was set for 10.00 am. When I arrived, the receptionist asked me to take a seat. Time passed and when it got to 10.30, I pointed out to the receptionist that the appointment was for 10 o'clock and that I only had an hour off from work. Eventually, as more time went by, I asked very abrasively if they really wanted to see me or not. She went into the Principal's office and came out saying, 'They'll see you now, Mr Anckorn.' So I went in and introduced myself, conscious of how little time was now left. The Principal introduced himself and then turned to introduce another person in the room whom, he said, was going to be my head of department. It seemed they'd decided the job was mine, but then the Principal went on, 'Look, Mr Anckhorn, we have no intention of offering you the job you've applied for and ...' Before he could finish his sentence I was ready to make for the door.

'Well thank you for wasting my time,' I said. 'I won't waste yours!' and I started to flounce out.

The Principal leapt up out of his chair to come after me.

'Just a minute, Mr Anckorn ... we're offering you a full-time lectureship.'

It didn't help much. By this time I'd become annoyed and I was still in the dark as to what they were really about.

'I didn't apply for a lectureship and, in any case, how do you know I can do it?' I said.

The Principal then explained that he had been the Head of Night School Classes for colleges in the whole South East area and in that capacity he had been well informed about my teaching capabilities.

Still sceptical, I asked what I would be teaching and he started to reel off a list of subjects including economics, commerce, English, short-hand, typing, bookkeeping – ten subjects in all. I protested that I knew nothing about most of those subjects but their response was simply that it wouldn't take long to read up on them.

Well, it was all a bit strange and sudden and that night, Lucille and I discussed it. It seemed impossible to me and my first inclination was that I shouldn't take it. I already had the Redland job plus the night class teaching and what if I gave up the Redland job to take the lectureship and then found I couldn't do it. Redlands wouldn't have me back. Yet, if it did work out, it might be the start of a proper career for me. I was in a real quandary.

While I sat ruminating over it, Lucille began reminding me of something we had seen years earlier when we were living in the top-floor flat overlooking the railway cutting. One morning at breakfast we had sat looking out of the window and seen a squirrel venturing out onto the end of a branch and it looked like it was going to make a leap for a branch on the other side of the cutting in Sevenoaks. It was a long drop down to the railway, so if it fell it would almost certainly be dead. It swung there on the end of the branch, apparently thinking about it as we watched. Minutes went by and then suddenly, the squirrel made an almighty leap ... and made it to the other side – just!

'I think *you* should jump!' she said.

I took the job.

Just as the Principal had said, it didn't take me long to read up and learn what I needed to learn in order to teach it to others and I found I could do the job and enjoy it. It was to set the course of the rest of my working life.

More than ten years had gone by since the end of the war and for the first time, I felt settled. Lucille had her career as a qualified nursing sister and we had started a family. The house we had bought and its garden were big enough for children to grow up in and within a few more years, Lucille was expecting our second child. I was finally and properly back in the land of the living.

And yet it nearly wasn't that way.

Back in 1950, at the time I had met the surgeon Julian Taylor in Gower Street, the Korean conflict had started – war in Southeast Asia all over again. He had already served in two wars and later on that year, it looked as though I was about to do so as well. People I knew who had been in Singapore or up on the railway with me we're being called up again and I, as a Reservist, was more than likely to be called up too.

But it didn't happen. The buff envelope that I dreaded did not give me new call-up instructions when it arrived. Instead it read:

Anckorn FG. Army No. 947556. Classed as of physical standard no longer fit for service.

What did happen at that time, however, was that we got a knock on the door one day. It was the local police sergeant who had been appointed recently to our area and who had been going around introducing himself and inviting people, if they needed anything, to come to him as their local bobby.

He'd knocked on our door because they were recruiting 'Specials' again, just as they had at the start of the last war. He asked me to think about becoming one and he'd come back the next day. Well, my father had been a Special in the First War and eventually he had become the Head Special in the Dunton Green area. It had occurred to me that if this war developed anything like the last one and I was not to be called up, then it was likely to be the Home Guard for me but that might mean duties some distance away. So, when the police sergeant returned the next day, I said yes, I would join. We shook hands and he said his name was Hort, Frank Hort.

'That's an unusual name,' I said. 'Did you have a relative out in the Far East?'

'Yes,' he said. 'That was my father. He was a POW on the river Kwai.' My recollections of that man at Chungkai, showing us how to treat fellow prisoners who had beriberi, came flooding back to me. Now his father was working at Fort Halstead, which had become a high security establishment where the development of our own atomic bomb was being carried out.

Once I had become a Special, it wasn't long before my responsibilities included Chartwell – the private residence of Winston Churchill and the place where perhaps many decisions that had shaped the course of the Second World War, including perhaps my own destiny, might have been made. I was to find myself involved in the personal protection of the man himself and sometimes other members of his cabinet too, after he became Prime Minister again, leading our country in a still very troubled world.

But that really is 'another story'.

EPILOGUE

When Fergus was a child, he wanted for nothing other than the wonders of nature and the countryside where he could go running with his dog and give free rein to his inquisitive mind. As he grew up, he developed an ability to see, like an artist does, rather than to just look around at the world, and in this idyll he sensed the difference between being alive and just living. It was an idyll that formed his inner self, creating a well of inspiration from which to draw in later life. It was an idyll never sullied by ambition.

In fact, it could be said that Fergus has spent most of his life not really knowing what he wanted to achieve or where he was going! He had not known what would become of him when he left school, having nothing to his credit academically and feeling that he wasn't good at anything. Then, just as he began to find himself and look upon the world as full of opportunity, it closed in on him with the outbreak of war. Having been called up, he soldiered all over Britain with the Royal Artillery, never knowing the whys and wherefores of the regiment's movements, and when his regiment was sent into action, none of them knew for sure where they were headed, as they endlessly traversed the oceans in convoy. Finally, when a destination was reached and the possibility of purposeful action presented itself, all was lost again in the humiliation of defeat in Singapore and the total and desperate isolation of being a prisoner of war in camps hidden deep in tropical jungle. Captivity forced him to live like a dog with no thoughts of the future or the past and to deal only with each present moment. That was his existence for three and a half years until liberation came as intrusively as the war had. So deadly had been that captivity that being alive was all that mattered to him after liberation. His only aim was to get home and his only ambition was to spend the rest of his days sitting in his father's summer house in the garden, listening to the birds.

Yet, this man, who has had so little idea of where he was going or what he would be, has become so much.

The war did not annihilate him. It defined him. He contributed to the war effort with a kind of heroism and leadership borne out of his unique ability to entertain, lift spirits and raise morale in the face of unimaginable suffering. He defied a brutal enemy not with a cunning military mind but with cunning hands that performed mesmeric magic. He did not emerge from captivity as a broken man but as an inspiring man, holding on steadfastly to life. Whilst the scars of battle, the habits of captivity and the damage from starvation and slavery have remained with him for life, hatred of his oppressors has not. Only hatred of the war itself. Today, over sixty-five years since his liberation from the prison camps in the jungle, Fergus will still pick up anything he sees in the street in case it might be useful. In his pockets you will find implements for his magic that he might use at any moment to entrance an onlooker – a thimble, rubber bands, pieces of string, a penknife and a pack of cards. In his car you will find a compass in case he should ever get lost and by his armchair at home you will find dictionaries testifying to his deep love of words – the eradicable human expressions of life that were never erased in captivity. Fergus is a survivor.

But it took more than his own strength of character to build a future after the war. It took 'his girl', as they used to say, and that was Lucille. She had turned down five marriage proposals while he was holding out in captivity because he had said he would come back. If it were not for her, he might well have remained just glad to be alive on his return home. In his own words, everything good that ever happened to him was because of her. Without her, it is his belief that he would have done nothing and probably been nobody.

The fact is that Lucille, the girl that Fergus instinctively knew would be the girl he would marry from the moment he first set eyes on her, turned out to be exactly the support he needed to pick himself up after the war.

He became a semi-professional magician who was booked and re-booked many times for prestigious venues and for television, leading to him being invited in 1986 to become a Member of the Inner Magic Circle with Gold Star. He also became a full-time teacher and he has given long service in the police Special Constabulary. All of these things, he will tell you, owe much to the stability of the family life that Lucille created. The irony was that the army had told Far East POWs returning from the war that the deprivations they had suffered would almost certainly have rendered them sterile. Fergus and Lucille went on to have two children, Deborah in 1953, and Simon in 1960. Today, Fergus is a proud grandfather of four.

Lucille had shown herself to be unshakeable in her devotedness to Fergus during the war years and determined in her nursing career. These qualities stood her in good stead not only in bringing up the

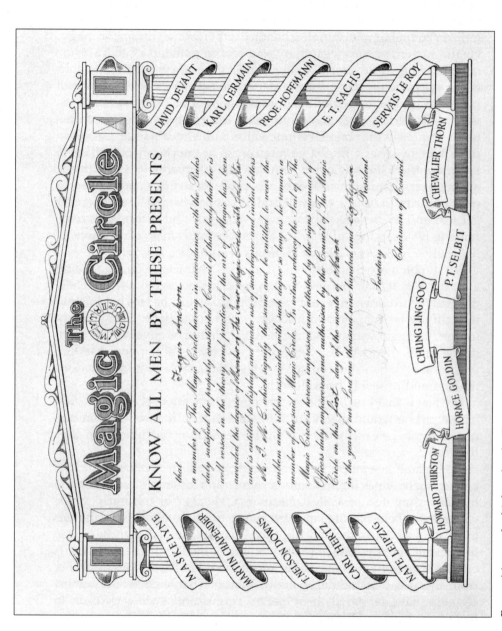

Recognition at the highest levels. Fergus becomes MIMC (Member of the Inner Magic Circle). March 1986.

family but also when she later took up a part-time position teaching at West Kent College while Fergus was also teaching there. They had been looking for someone with nursing qualifications to teach First Aid and the treatment of industrial accidents and diseases. The students were to be mostly young car mechanics with high spirits and colourful language, on day-release courses. Having thought herself probably no good at teaching at all, let alone capable of presenting herself to such challenging youths when she herself was middle-aged, she went ahead and tackled it. Strong inside yet unassuming and modest in attitude, Lucille was deferential, always thinking of herself as no good at anything. Yet she was a first-class nurse and midwife who then became a remarkable teacher who, rather like Fergus in the prison camps, never knew the effect she was having. Acclaim for her teaching skills came in a surprising way, ten years after her early death due to cancer. It was when the Head of Department, Mrs Bond, was retiring. Out of the blue, Fergus received an invitation to her farewell do even though he had himself retired some ten years earlier when Lucille had become ill. After the customary valedictory speeches, the reason why Fergus had been invited became clear. In a forthright manner, Mrs Bond paid tribute to Lucille, remembering that when Lucille entered the staff room the place lit up, and she stated plainly to the audience of accomplished teaching staff that Lucille was one of the best lecturers they'd ever had – the only one she knew of that had been invited to the pub regularly by her students!

To conclude now after only this brief summary of Fergus's life since the war would be insufficient. With Fergus, there is always so much more to say – especially about his magic.

Within a couple of years of his return home, Fergus performed at an International Convention for Magicians in Amsterdam. Besides the prestige of the event, it was notable for the fact that a grand finale was held at one of the big theatres in Amsterdam and at the end of the show, a member of the audience came looking for him. It was Jack Biet, the man who had fashioned the identity bracelet for him to wear in Ubon when it was believed the Japanese guards were preparing to slaughter them all. Jack had attended the show because he had seen the name 'Wizardus' on the publicity bill.

It was not the only big theatre where Wizardus would be billed. At another convention a couple of years later, Fergus performed at the Mogador Théâtre in Paris – a theatre equivalent to our own London Palladium. Back in London he frequently performed at top hotels, the Café Royal and at the Mansion House for the Lord Mayor's Christmas parties.

Through it all, he never thought of himself as anything special. It is typical of Fergus that when someone phoned to speak to him, proclaiming they were from the BBC and asking if he would take part in a regular programme they were making, his reaction was, 'Go on, pull the other one! You're not catching me out with that!' In fact, Fergus went on to perform in two television series, the first being *What Will You Bet?*, in which he demonstrated by magic tricks how he could do the impossible against impossible odds. The second series was called *Things Aren't What They Seem*, in which his spellbinding magic tricks demonstrated how nothing could be taken for granted!

However, some of his most impressive acts were performed on smaller stages and at private parties. One of these involved his doggie, Punch, and another involved his cat. His love of nature and running in the countryside with his dog had translated over the years into a great affinity with animals, and with this gift he developed unique thought-reading acts that he could do with them. His doggie act must have been something to behold. The curtain would go up and the dog would be sitting on his own, centre stage, calmly looking out at the audience. Behind the dog, further back on the stage, there would be a blackboard mounted on an easel. Fergus would then walk on stage holding a white card and he would explain to the audience that written on the card were a number of commands such as 'lie down', 'bark' and 'find slippers', and then he would invite a member of the audience to come up on stage, take the card and write the commands onto the black-board in any order. Then he would ask another member of the audience to come up and put a tick against any one of the commands. The dog would immediately obey each time a tick was made next to a command! Fergus would then challenge the audience, accepting that they would be thinking he had whispered or indicated the command to the dog somehow. He would ask them to tell him where he should stand – with his back to the dog? . . . off the stage? – it made no difference. He would finish the act saying that he was going to leave the stage and go through the audience to the back of the theatre, leaving the dog sitting on the stage. He would tell the audience that once he got to the back, if anyone coughed, the dog would come and join him there, which of course it did, every time, to great applause.

His trick with the cat came about through his practising of a classic card trick in which cards were fanned out, faces down, and a guest would be invited to take any one, look at it and replace it anywhere in the pack, unseen by Fergus. He would then shuffle the pack, invite the guest to shuffle the pack also and then fan the pack out again, face down. Fergus would then immediately pick out the card that the guest had selected. One day while he practiced this, the cat, which had taken to sitting on the table and watching, stretched its paws out and pulled a card from the fanned-out pack. Well, given his rapport with animals, it wasn't long before Fergus had trained the cat to do this on command

238

and it became an act. The guest would select the card, put it back, cards would be shuffled and fanned out and Fergus would then announce that the cat would pick out the guest's card with its paws – which it then did. Fergus performed this act only six times, however, before fate intervened and, as is so often the case with cats, it was unfortunately run over.

This 'thought-reading act' became much talked about at the Magic Circle but no one in the Circle had actually seen it. It wasn't an act he did regularly as it depended on the suitability of the venue. The Circle eventually invited him to come up and give a talk on thought-reading. On the morning before he was due to give the talk, it occurred to Fergus that they would never believe him just talking about it, so he had better do the act as well. However, he had not long had a new doggie, Sam, a black and white Border collie, and he had never done the thought-reading trick with him. Fergus trained him that morning and the act was performed that night, impeccably.

Today, Fergus is the oldest performing member of the Magic Circle, having also been its youngest performing member in 1937. It is as if, after the war, Fergus had 'concert party attitude' ingrained in him as he continued doing his magic shows whilst also holding down a full-time teaching job and carrying out duties in the police Specials.

His career as a police Special is particularly notable bearing in mind that, as a soldier, he had resisted taking on a commission because he feared that he might not have it in him to lead men and that he might turn out to be a coward in battle. Fergus indeed spent the first thirteen years of his service in the Specials as an ordinary constable. But then he was made a sergeant and so it was that in 1963, twenty-four years after he had been called up to become simply Gunner Anckorn in the Artillery, he achieved his first 'rank'. Five years later he was promoted to an inspector and then unexpectedly, a few years after that, straight to deputy commandant. Only two years more and he was made Commandant of the West Kent D Division, thereby reaching the highest pinnacle of command in his area.

His style of policing came out of the experiences he had in the war. So often had he seen officers who were ever full of their status and ever fond of snapping out orders, yet totally unable to show regard for the welfare of men under their command – especially when it was most needed. By contrast, he made a point of always thanking his colleagues for performing their duties and always recognised that their service in the police Specials was voluntary. He would often be out with them even when there was no need except that he wanted to support them and guide their efforts. His war experience had also made him readily combatant too when it came to dealing with troublemakers. Typical of his approach was a situation late one night when he had returned from doing a magic show and was taking his dog out for a late walk before turning in. He was approached by five youths whom he recognised as lads he had turned out of a local pub the week before for rowdy behaviour. He heard one of them saying, 'He's on his own, come on, let's get him!' Fergus stood his ground and faced them saying, 'Alright, you can have a go and I don't doubt you'll put me in hospital. But I promise you this, one of you will be in the hospital bed next to me!' They all cleared off.

In becoming Commandant of West Kent D Division, Fergus was furthering the Anckorn family record of service with the Specials. His father had been Head Special in the Dunton Green area in both the First and Second World Wars and his brother, Gordon, had served as a constable. It was perhaps because of the 'family' record, Fergus believes, that he was awarded the Queen's Silver Jubilee Medal in 1977. The Anckorns had clocked up over seventy-five years of service between them by then.

It was during the early years of being in the Specials that Fergus re-established himself as an athlete again. Some six years after the war ended, he began taking himself out for exercise, 'hobbling' as he puts it, no more than 70 yards to begin with but extending the distance on every outing. Eventually he felt he might enter in the open half-mile race at a local annual sports day in Oxted. He was asked where and when his last race was and when he said that it was the brigade sports day in 1941, they gave him a 25 yard start on the rest of the field. This riled Fergus and challenged his self-respect – boosting his determination to win, as of old! In the race, he allowed the rest of the field to catch up and overtake him at first and then, with the sense of timing he'd learned so well in his army days, he took the lead in the last lengths and won the race by many yards.

Annual police sports became his theatre for athletics after that and in the ten years between 1954 and 1964, he won an array of medals for the 100 yards and half-mile races, making a reputation for himself as unbeatable. His renewed love of running took him out daily with his dog for long distances through his beloved local woods and hills, often doing 70 miles or more a week when time allowed. Later he joined the Blackheath Harriers and ran every Saturday in their cross-country out-ings – always with his dog. He was in good company at the Blackheath Harriers as that was Sydney Woodison's club. He was the leading contender for breaking the world record in the mile race before that honour went to Roger Bannister.

Inevitably, being a witness to the fall of Singapore and a survivor of the infamous Burma Railway that was brought so vividly, albeit in-accurately, to everyone's attention in 1957 by the David Lean film *The Bridge on the River Kwai*, Fergus has been called upon many times by television and radio producers for his views. Notable were his early appearances on the *Blue Peter* programme and on *The Russell Harty Show*. In the *Blue Peter* programme, they dramatised some of the conditions that a POW endured in the camps as informed by Fergus, and in *The Russell Harty Show*, Fergus performed for the first time since 1943 the same 'egg trick' that had almost cost him his life in the Chungkai prison camp. But it was his first appearance in a discussion programme on television about captivity under the Japanese, that set the tone for all his later media appearances on the subject. The BBC had been looking for someone who could meet with a Japanese person on the *Tonight* programme, which was at that time presented by Frank Bough. They wanted an ex-Far East POW who didn't hold a grudge. They had not been able to find anyone in the whole country until someone gave them Fergus's name. The BBC had phoned to speak to him at West Kent College and Fergus was interrupted in the middle of taking a class. Sure enough, he agreed to do it and asked when he would be required. Literally 'tonight!', they said. When he duly arrived at their studios, he found there was to be another ex-POW on the programme – Charles Peall. Charles had been a fellow prisoner with Fergus at the Ubon camp in Thailand. However, Charles did harbour strong feelings about the Japanese and had brought with him a file detailing the atrocities that had been committed. Charles was adamant that he would never forgive and forget and his attitude was therefore diametrically opposed to that of Fergus who, if not forgetting, was at least prepared to forgive, placing blame more on the war itself than on the Japanese.

Before the programme, Fergus, as in so many cases during captivity, brought calm to the situation, pointing out to Charles that they were like brothers in the suffering and starvation they had both endured. Fergus tells how he saw the 'scales fall from his eyes'. They became good friends and as Charles was then Vice President of the Burma Star Association, he invited Fergus to speak at one of their dinners. Fergus was made an honorary member and to this day, he donates monies from any public appearances he makes to that association.

Various associations of Far East POWs were formed after the war and these became, for many, a means to exorcise haunting memories. One such was the Japanese Labour Camp Survivors Association. No one, other than those who had endured the slavery under the Japanese, knew the extent of it and those who had endured it could not find words to describe it to those who hadn't. The world they had been returned to when it was all over simply wanted life to go on and for there to be no pondering over the past. The authorities particularly, seemed to want to bury the episode. What talk there was of the war invariably featured civilian hardships that may well have been significant, but which seemed relatively trivial to ex-Far East POWs.

With no official recognition or description of what had happened to Allied forces captured by the Japanese and no capacity for telling their story themselves, it must have seemed as though it all never happened. But the constant nightmares that survivors suffered would not let them forget that it did happen. The nightmares that Fergus suffered only ended in 2004, when he made his first journey back to Singapore and to the railway with his son, Simon. Until then, the only release for his trapped memories, just like so many other POWs, was the association get-togethers. Just mingling with fellows, tentatively recalling people, places and events, and registering each other's knowing looks and gestures was enough to give just a little comfort.

One of the main associations – FEPOW, the Far East Prisoner of War Association – held a gathering every year at the Festival Hall in London for many years and Fergus was a regular attendee, as was Philip Toosey. However, in what must have seemed like yet another episode of establishment denial, these annual get-togethers were eventually stopped by the Greater London Council.

Fergus nevertheless had another, perhaps more convivial, association to support and to be supported by – the 118th Old Comrades Association. The attendance numbers of members was much less, of course, given that 287 men – more than a third of the regiment – died in the Far East and over the years following the war, more were to die young from their injuries or from ill health caused by their deprivations. When Fergus took his turn as Secretary of the Association, he arranged for a memorial tree to be planted for the regiment in the Garden of Remembrance in Lewisham, where the regiment was formed. Later, Fergus instigated the planting of another memorial tree on behalf of the 118th in the National Memorial Arboretum when it was established at Alrewas, near Burton–on-Trent in Staffordshire. In the planting of that tree, which now thrives amongst so many others today, Fergus had a plaque made and positioned next to the tree reading:

> In memory of
> The many hundreds of the 118th Field Regiment, Royal Artillery,
> who died as slaves of the Japanese.

The many hundreds who died and those that survived must have all asked the question at some time – what were we doing there? – as Fergus has done ever since. Even before their arrival in Singapore, the authorities must have known it was a lost cause. The bitter sense of loss – lost opportunity, lost reputation, lost lives, and biggest of all, loss of empire – was something deeply felt by those who had been in command and lived to reflect upon it. One such expression of this was penned anonymously at the time of a reunion of surviving officers of 18th Infantry Division, shortly after the end of the war.

242

No schoolboy, relishing his country's glory
shall read our victory there.
It has no name,
no statesman cheered the news
or full-page story roused in public bars a toast to fame.
No classic ode commends
or sculpted face
peers from a monument
to those who fell.
Even our movements tactically disgrace
the paper battles soldiers love so well.

Friends avoid, with genuine regret,
mentioning days they'd like us to forget.
Dearer for us to know
as dear to those defeated, sore-afflicted companies
who share no common glory
that from these grievous dishonours
only honour grows.

But not all was lost. Amongst those that suffered and survived there stands much self-respect. Fergus is representative of that. Fact is, he came through it all in his own particular way and remains today – still smiling.

SOURCES AND BIBLIOGRAPHY

Allen, Louis, *Singapore 1941–1942: The Politics and Strategy of the Second World War*, University of Delaware Press, USA, 1977.

Barber, Noel, *A Sinister Twilight: The Fall of Singapore 1942*, Houghton Mifflin Company, Boston, USA, 1968.

Bowden, Tim, *Changi Photographer: George Aspinall's Record of Captivity*, ABC Enterprises and William Collins Pty. Ltd., Sydney, Australia, 2001.

Braddon, Russell, *The Piddingtons*, Werner Laurie, London, 1950.

Charles, H. Robert, *Last Man Out: Surviving the Burma Thailand Death Railway, A Memoir*, Zenith Press, St Paul, USA, 2006.

Chalker, Jack Bridger, *Burma Railway: Images of War*, Mercer Books, Mells, 2007.

Chung, Chit Ong, *Operation Matador*, Times Academic Press, Singapore, 2001.

Churchill, Winston, *The Second World War*, Penguin, London, 1985.

Cruickshank, Charles, *SOE in the Far East*, Oxford University Press, Oxford, 1983.

Davies, Prof. Peter N., *The Man Behind the Bridge: Colonel Toosey and the River Kwai*, Athlone Press, London, 1991.

Dewey, Judy and Stuart, *POW Sketchbook: a story of survival through the diary and drawings of Will Wilder*, Pie Powder Press, Wallingford, 1985.

Dunlop, E.E., *The War Diaries of Weary Dunlop: Java and the Burma-Thailand Railway 1942–45*, Viking Penguin Books Australia Ltd., Camberwell, 1989.

Durnford, John, *Branch Line to Burma*, Macdonald & Co., London, 1958.

Eldredge, Sears, A., *Captive Audiences: Captive Performers*, Macalaster College digital publication, Minnesota, USA, 2010.

Farrell, Brian P., *Defence and Fall of Singapore 1940–1942*, Tempus Publishing Limited, Stroud, 2006.

Farrow, Sgt J.N., *Darkness Before the Dawn: A diary of a Changi POW 1941–1945*, Stamford House Publishing, Peterborough, 2007.

Gibson, Walter, *The Boat*, W.H. Allen, London, 1952.

Gordon, Ernest, *Miracle on the River Kwai*, Wm. Collins Sons & Co. Ltd, Glasgow, 1963.

Horner, Captain R.M., *Singapore Diary*, Spellmount Limited, Tonbridge, 2007.

Hardie, Elspeth, *The Burma-Siam Railway: The Secret Diary of Dr Robert Hardie*, Imperial War Museum, London, 1983.

Jaffe, Sally and Lucy, *Chinthe Women: Women's Auxiliary Service Burma 1942–1946*, privately published, 2001.

Kinvig, Clifford, *Death Railway*, Pan Books Ltd., London, 1973.

Kent Hughes, Colonel W.S., *Slaves of the Samurai*, Oxford University Press, Oxford, 1946.

Lomax, Eric, *The Railway Man*, Jonathan Cape, London, 1995.

MacArthur, Brian, *Surviving the Sword. Prisoners of the Japanese 1942–45*, Time Warner Books, London, 2005.

Moynahan, Brian, *Jungle Soldier: The True Story of Freddie Spencer Chapman*, Quercus Publishing Plc., London, 2009.

Partridge, Jeff, *Alexandra Hospital: From British Military to Civilian Institution 1938–1998*, Alexandra Hospital and Singapore Polytechnic Publication, 1998.

Peek, Ian Denys, *One Fourteenth of an Elephant: A Memoir of Life and Death on the Burma – Thailand Railway*, Doubleday, New York, USA, 2004.

Reed, Bill, *Lost Souls of the River Kwai*, Pen & Sword Military, Barnsley, 2004.

Sebag-Montefiore, Hugh, *Enigma: The Battle for the Code*, Weidenfeld & Nicolson, London, 2000.

Slim, Field Marshal Viscount, *Defeat into Victory*, Pan MacMillan Ltd, London, 2009.

Smith, Colin, *Singapore Burning*, Penguin Books, London, 2006.

Summers, Julie, *The Colonel of Tamarkan: Philip Toosey and the Bridge on the River Kwai*, Simon & Schuster, London, 2005.

Thompson, Peter, *The Battle for Singapore*, Portrait Books, London, 2005.

Webography

www.fepow-community.org.uk – various

www.britain-at-war.org.uk – 'Signalman Wader's Diary'

www.ww2troopships.com – troopship crossings

www.ww2australia.gov – Australia's War 1939–45, 'The Fall of Singapore'

www.ihr.org – Institute for Historical Review, 'The inside story of the Hess flight'

www.spartacus.schoolnet.co.uk – Rudolf Hess

www.burmastarbc.com – Japanese surrender
www.historyplace.com – timeline of the Pacific War
www.hellfirepass.com – various
www.cofepow.org.uk – Convoy 'William Sail'

Imperial War Museum

Collection of Fergus Anckorn.

Collection of Harold Payne.

Collection of Jack Bridger Chalker.

Ross MacArthur diaries.

H.A. & Mrs L. Porter papers.

Convoy William Sail 12X Task Force 14.

Lieutenant Louis Charles Baume: Diaries as a prisoner of war in the Far East, 1942-1945.

Log of Singapore escapees 15 February 1942–10 March 1942, Bombardier C.W.L. Prime.

Letter from Lieutenant M.R. 'Mickey' Burrows to his parents, 18 March 1942.

Building the Burma-Thailand Railway, an epic of World War II, 1942–43, tales by Japanese Army Engineers, created by Kazuo Tamayama, Japan, 2004.

Prisoners of the Japanese in World War II Statistical History, Personal Narratives and memorials concerning POWs in camps and on Hellships, by Van Waterford.

Report of Colonel F.J. Dillon MC – Royal Indian Army Service Corps to the Military Police of the Imperial Japanese Army.

Private papers of Colonel C.H.D. Wild, A report of 'F' Force in Thailand, Documents and Sound Section Ref66/227/1.

National Archives

WO 166/344 CORPS: X11 CORPS: General Staff, Aug 1940–Dec 1941.

WO 166/344 CORPS: X11 CORPS: General Staff, Jun 1940–Dec 1941.

WO 166/1530 Royal Artillery: Field Regiments; 118 Field Regiment, Aug 1939–Sept 1941.

WO 166/464 18th Division: General Staff, Oct 1939–Dec 1940.

WO 166/465 18th Division: General Staff, Jan–Dec 1941.

WO 166/466 18th Division: Adjutant and Quartermaster, Oct 1939–Sept 1940; Dec 1940-Oct 1941.

WO 166/467 18th Division: Commander Royal Artillery, Sept 1939–Aug 1941.

WO 32/17544 Locations and strengths of POW camps and civilian assembly centres in Japan and Japanese occupied territories 1944–1945.

WO 32/17545 Locations and strengths of POW camps and civilian assembly centres in Japan and Japanese occupied territories 1945.

WO 208/3487 Location and composition of POW camps in Japan and Japanese occupied territory July 1945.

WO 208/5151 Japanese POW interrogation reports.

WO 93/48 No. 1 POW Camp, Changi, Malaya: reviews of Courts Martial 1942-1944.

ADM 205/22B Captain Bell's report on the fall of Singapore.

ADM 195/119 Singapore Progress.

ADM 199/12 Operations in the Far East: despatches reports and comments.

ADM 199/19 BN and BS Convoy reports.

BT 26/1212 Port: Liverpool, Oct–Dec 1945.

BT 26/1212/74 SS *Orbita* travelling Rangoon to Liverpool List of passengers disembarking 9 Nov 1945.

WO 106/2579A Fall of Singapore. Request for report by Major General Gordon Bennett.

WO 106/2579B Fall of Singapore. Statements of witnesses, Feb–July 1942.

WO 106/2579D Fall of Singapore. Statement of witnesses, March–June 1942.

WO 106/2582 Defence of Singapore, Jan–May 1942.

WO 106/2550D Singapore. Personal sketches before and after fall.

WO 106/2552 Malaya and Singapore. Chronology of events 8 Dec 1941–15 Feb 1942.

WO 106/2568 Malaya and Singapore. War Council meetings: minutes, Dec 1941–Feb 1942.

WO 106/2529 Singapore and Malaya: maps, 1941–1942.

INDEX

252

White City (London) 20
Wilder, Gunner William, 148, 197
William, Joyce, 25
William Sail, Convoy, 53
Windmill Theatre (Changi), 107
Winston's Special, 52

Wizardus, 34–5, 167, 220, 236
Woodison, Sydney, 240
Woolwich Barracks, 15
Wycherley, Cyril, 34, 114, 116

Yamashita, Lieutenant-General Tomoyuki, 89, 92